E C Tax Law

DAVID W WILLIAMS
Professor of Tax Law
Centre for Commercial Law Studies
Queen Mary and Westfield College
University of London

LONGMAN
LONDON AND NEW YORK

Addison Wesley Longman
Edinburgh Gate
Harlow
Essex CM20 2JE
England
and Associated Companies throughout the world.

*Published in the United States of America
by Addison Wesley Longman Inc., New York.*

© Addison Wesley Longman Limited 1998

First published 1998

ISBN 0 582 30596 9 PPR

British Library Cataloguing-in-Publication Data

A catalogue record of this book is
available from the British Library

Library of Congress Cataloging-in-Publication Data

Williams, David W.
    EC tax law/David W. Williams.
        p. cm. – (European law series)
    Includes bibliographical references and index.
    ISBN 0-582-30596-9
    1. Taxation–Law and legislation–European Union countries.
I. Title.   II. Series.
KJE7105.W55 1998
341.7'5–dc21   97-27073
                                                                CIP

Set by 7 in Sabon
Produced by Longman Singapore Publishers (Pte) Ltd.
Printed in Singapore

To the participants of the Wintercourse

Contents

Preface   ix

General Editor's Preface   xi

Abbreviations   xiii

Table of Cases   xv

Table of Legislation   xviii

Table of Treaties, Conventions and International Agreements   xx

1   Introduction   1

2   Tax in the European Union   22

3   The EU's own taxes   42

4   The EU frontier taxes   53

5   Taxing freely circulating goods   69

6   Taxing the EU's citizens   96

7   Taxing services and service suppliers   119

8   Taxing multinational enterprises   136

9   Taxing cross-border savings and investment   153

10   Tax, competition and tax competition   169

Bibliography   180

Index   184

Preface

This book is an attempt at the skills of my favourite artists – the impressionists. Like them, I do not attempt to catch the detail of the ever-shifting patterns of my subject. Taxation is like the wind: sometimes violent, sometimes murmuring, always harbouring the capacity to bend and to destroy, yet welcome when it brings the rains. You cannot draw it, only its effects. A single work can but hint at its vastness. Hence I must apologise that this is but a study of light and shade. Insofar as there is detail, it is updated to mid-May 1997, after the UK general election, but before the French and Irish ones.

What I have tried to do is to examine taxation and its problems by reference to the basic structure of the EU. I write it as a tax lawyer, not an EU specialist, but I do so with the aim of showing how tax fits – or does not fit – the structures and policies of the EU. I have also attempted to put the study in its contexts: that of the differences between member states, that of the EU structure itself, and that of the wider community. In particular, I have sought to integrate into the study the other means through which EU states cooperate on tax matters. This is because, in my view, some of the tax problems facing the EU cannot be solved by the EU alone. Nor can they be solved by individual states alone. A broader cooperation is necessary. Yet there can be no imposed solutions – they must be acceptable to taxpayers generally. To bring in those issues, I have had to neglect details and adopt a broad approach. I do so in some confidence because of specialist works of others (detailed in the bibliography) to which I can make reference, and whose authors I must thank.

I must also thank many others. I dedicate the book to the Wintercourses with thanks to their participants for teaching me so much: in particular to Guido de Bont, Gaetano Casertano, Cyrille David, Peter Essers, Michael Lang, Geerte Michelse, Albert Radler, Tulio Rosembuj, Franz Vanistendael. I could add many others over the years at the Inland Revenue and Customs and Excise in the UK, the EC, the OECD, the IMF and not least at my own and the other colleges of the University of London. I have learnt much, but not enough, and the opinions – and the mistakes – remain mine. And I must thank Ed, Rick, Tom, and always Lis.

David Williams
CCLS, QMW
May 1997

General Editor's Preface

The Longman European Law Series is the first comprehensive series of topic-based books on EC Law aimed primarily at a student readership, though I have no doubt that they will also be found useful by academic colleagues and interested practitioners. It has become more and more difficult for a single course or a single book to deal comprehensively with all the major topics of Community law, and the intention of this series is to enable students and teachers to 'mix and match' topics which they find to be of interest; it may also be hoped that the publication of this series will encourage the study of areas of Community law which have historically been neglected in degree courses. However, while the series may have a student readership in mind, the authors have been encouraged to take an academic and critical approach, placing each topic in its overall Community context, and also in its socio-economic and political context where relevant.

Despite the apparently limited nature of the express Treaty provisions on the subject, the importance and range of tax issues in the EC can hardly be exaggerated. To give the most obvious examples, as a customs union, the EC has been levying its own duties since 1968, the system of VAT is based on EC legislation, and the question of tax discrimination goes to the heart of the exercise of the basic Treaty freedoms, the movement of goods, persons, services and capital. Professor Williams has brought together this complex material in a cohesive and readable manner in what remains a short book, and raises interesting issues as to the scope of EC tax law.

John A. Usher

Abbreviations

ACT	Advance corporation tax
CAP	Common agricultural policy
COM	EC Commission document
DG	Directorate General (of the EC Commission)
DTC	Double taxation convention
EC	European Communities
EC Treaty	Treaty establishing the European Communities (The Treaty of Rome)
ECJ	European Court of Justice
ECR	European Court Reports
ECSC	European Coal and Steel Community
EEA	European Economic Area
EEC	European Economic Community
EMU	Economic and monetary union
EU	European Union
Euratom	European Atomic Energy Authority
FDI	Foreign direct investment
GATS	General Agreement on Trade in Services
GATT	General Agreement on Tariffs and Trade
GDP	Gross domestic product
GNP	Gross national product
IBFD	International Bureau for Fiscal Documentation
IFA	International Fiscal Association
IFS	Institute for Fiscal Studies
JO	Official Journal of the EC (French version)
OECD	Organisation for Economic Cooperation and Development

ABBREVIATIONS

OECD MTC	OECD Model Tax Convention
OJ	Official Journal of the EC (English version)
STC	Simon's Tax Cases
TARIC	The integrated customs tariff of the EU
TEU	Treaty on European Union (The Maastricht Treaty)
UN	United Nations Organisation
VAT	Value added tax (or value-added tax)
WCO	World Customs Organisation
WTO	World Trade Organisation

Table of European Court of Justice Cases

Aldewereld v Staatsecretaris van Financien, Case 60/93, [1995] ECR I-2991 **113**

Apple and Pear Development Council v Lewis, Case 222/82, [1983] ECR 4083 **74**

Apple and Pear Development Council v Customs and Excise Commissioners, Case 102/86 [1988] STC 221 **74, 88**

Asscher v Staatsecretaris van Financien, Case C-107/94, [1996] STC 1025 **35, 111, 114–18, 122**

Bachmann v Belgium (Case C-204/90) [1994] STC 855, [1992] ECR I-249 **97, 106–9, 129**

Bergandi v Directeur General, Case 252/86, [1991] STC 529 **35**

Biehl v Administration des Contributions du Grand-Duche de Luxembourg (Case C-175/88) [1991] STC 575, [1990] ECR I-1779 **104–6**

Byrne v Conroy, Irish Supreme Court, [1997] 1 CMLR 595 **30**

Co-frutta Case, Case 193/85, [1987] ECR 2085 **62**

Customs and Excise Commissioners v DFDS, Case C-280/95, [1997] STC 384 **135**

Dansk Denkavit v Skaateministeriet, Case C-200/90 [1994] STC 482 **92**

EC Commission v Belgium, Case 325/82, [1984] ECR 777 **84**

EC Commission v Belgium, Case 153/89, [1991] ECR I-3171 **76**

EC Commission v Belgium (Case C-300/90) (see Bachmann v Belgium) **106**

EC Commission v Denmark, Case 171/78, [1980] ECR 447 **75, 76**

EC Commission v Denmark, Case 47/88, [1990] ECR I-4909 **78**

EC Commission v Denmark, Case C-234/91 [1997] STC 721 **92**

EC Commission v France, Case 168/78, [1980] ECR 347 **75**

EC Commission v France, Case 270/83, [1986] ECR 273 **126, 130, 140**

EC Commission v Greece, Case 305/87, [1989] ECR 1461 **104**

EC Commission v Ireland, Case 55/79, [1980] ECR 481 **73, 157**

EC Commission v Italy, Case 7/68, [1968] ECR 423 **60**

EC Commission v Italy, Case 24/68, [1969] ECR 193 **61**

EC Commission v Italy, Case 169/78, [1980] ECR 385 **75**

EC Commission v Italy, Case 340/87, [1989] ECR 1483 **61**

EC Commission v Luxembourg, Case C-151/94, [1995] STC 1047 **106**

TABLE OF CASES

EC Commission v Netherlands, Case 89/76, [1977] ECR 1355 **61**

EC Commission v United Kingdom, Case 170/78 [1983] ECR 2265 **75**

Effem v Hauptzollamt Lüneberg, Case 95/75 [1976] 2 CMLR 86 **47**

Essevi and Salengo Cases, Cases 142–143/80 [1981] ECR 1413 **176**

Feldein v Directeur des Services Fiscaux, Case 43/85 [1987] ECR 3521 **78**

Finanzamt Köln-Alstadt v Schumacker, Case C-279/93 [1995] STC 306 **96, 109–11, 129**

Fink Frucht v Hauptzollamt München Landesbergerstraße, Case 27/67, [1968] ECR 233 **75**

Gaston Schul v Inspecteur der Invoerrechten en Accijzen, Case 15/81, [1982] ECR 1409 **74, 76**

Halliburton Services BV v Staatssecretaris van Financien, Case C-1/93, [1994] STC 655 **130**

Happy Family v Inspecteur der Omzetbelasting, Case 289/86, [1988] ECR 3655 **35**

Hauptzollamt Mainz v Kupfenberg, Case 104/81 [1982] ECR 329 **73**

Humblot v Directeur des Services Fiscaux, Case 112/84, [1985] ECR 1367 **78**

Hurd v Jones, Case 44/84, [1986] STC 127 **51**

ICI v Colmer [1996] STC 352 **139**

Inland Revenue Commissioners v Commerzbank [1990] STC 285 **130**

Italy v EC Commission, Case 173/73, [1974] ECR 709 **176**

Kraus v Land Baden-Württemberg (Case C-19/92) [1993] ECR I-1663 **106**

Lutticke v Hauptzollamt Saarlouis, Case 57/65, [1966] ECR 205 **61, 73**

Mazzalai, Case 111/75, [1976] ECR 657 **84**

Mol v Inspecteur der Invoerrechten en Accijnzen, Case 269/86, [1988] ECR 3627 **35**

Molkerei Zentrale v Hauptzollamt Paderborn, Case 28/67, [1968] ECR 143 **74**

Opinion 1/94, European Court of Justice, 15.11.1994 **127**

Polydor v Harlequin Records, Case 270/80 [1982] ECR 329 **73**

Polysar Investments BV v Inspecteur der Invoerrechten en Accijnzen, Arnhem, Case C-60/90, [1993] STC 222 **89, 141, 157**

R v HM Treasury, ex parte Daily Mail, Case 81/87, [1988] STC 787 **126**

R v Inland Revenue Commissioners, ex parte Commerzbank AG, Case C-330/91, [1993] STC 605 **130**

Rewe v Hauptzollamt Landau-Pfalz, Case 45/75, [1976] ECR 181 **33**

Rewe-Zentral AG v Bundes-monopolverwaltung für Branntwein (Case 120/78) [1979] ECR 649 **109**

Rheinhold & Mahla AUV v Bestuur van der Bedrijfsvereniging voor de Metllnijverheid, Case C-327/92, [1995] ECR I-1223 **113**

Rompelman v Minister van Financien, Case 268/83, [1985] ECR 655 **132**

Ronfeldt v Bundesversicherungsanstalt für Angestellte, [1993] 1 CMLR 73 **113**

Schottle v Finanzamt Freudenstadt, Case 20/76 [1977] ECR 247 **121**

Simmental v Minister of Finance, Case 35/76, [1976] ECR 1861 **121**

Sociaal Fonds voor de Diamentarbeiders v Brachfield, Case 2,3/69, [1969] ECR 211 **60**

Sofitam SA v Ministre charge du Budget, Case C-333/91, reported belatedly at [1997] STC 226 **157**

Sotgiu v Deutsche Bundespost (Case 152/73) [1974] ECR 153 **105**

TABLE OF CASES

Statens Kontrol v Larsen, Case 142/77, [1978] ECR 1554 **74**

Staatsecretaris van Financien v Gaston Schul Douane-Expediteur, Case 47/84, [1985] ECR 1481 **76–7**

Staatssecretaris van Financien v SAFE BV, Case C-320/88 [1991] STC 627 **87**

Tolsma v Inspecteur der Omzetbelasting Leeuwarden, Case C-16/93, [1994] STC 509 **88**

Van Duyn v Home Office (Case 41/74) [1974] ECR 1337 **104**

Van Eycke v ASPA, Case 267/86, [1988] ECR 4769 **157**

Van Poucke v Rijksinstituut voor Sociale Verzekeringen der Selfstandigen, Case C-71/93, [1995] 3 CMLR 346 **113**

Van Tiem v Staatsecretaris van Financien, Case C-186/89, [1993] STC 91 **89**

Werner v Finanzamt Aachen-Innenstadt, Case C-112/91, [1996] STC 961, [1993] ECR I-429 **129**

Wielockx v Inspecteur der Directe Belastingen, Case C-80/94, [1995] STC 876 **129**

Table of Legislation

EU Legislation

Regulations

Community Customs Code (Council Regulation 2913/92/EEC)(1992 OJ L302/1, 19.10.92) **7, 62, 63, 71**

   art 3 **59, 171, 172**

   art 20 **30, 62**

   art 24 **64**

   art 29 **64**

   art 31 **64**

   arts 243–6 **63**

EC Council Regulation 1612/68/EEC (15.10.1968)(1968 OJ Sp Edn II, p 47) **98, 105, 111**

EC Council Regulation 1251/70 **99**

EC Council Regulation 1408/71/EEC (14.6.1971)(reprinted, as substantially amended, at 1983 OJ L 230/6) **99, 112–16**

EC Council Regulation 1111/77 (17.5.1977)[REF] **47**

EC Council Regulation 2137/85/EEC (31.7.1985) (1985 OJ L 199/1) **123**

EC Council Regulation 1553/89/EEC (29.5.1989)(1989 OJ L 159/1) **48**

EC Council Regulation 3284/94/EEC (22.12.1994)(1994 OJ L 349/22) **58**

EC Council Regulation 384/96/EC (22.12.1995)(1996 OJ L56/1) **58**

EC Commission Regulation 574/72 (1972 OJ L74/1, with the official translation at (1972) OJ 159) **112**

EC Commission Regulation (EEC) 2454/93 (2.7.1993)(1993 OJ L 253/1) **62**

Directives

EC Council Directive 67/227/EEC (1967 OJ Sp Edn, 14) **34, 81**

   art 1 **81**

   art 2 **81**

EC Council Directive 67/228/EEC (1967 OJ Sp Edn, 14) **34, 81–2**

EC Council Directive 68/297/EEC (1968 JO L 175) **32**

EC Council Directive 69/335/EEC (17.5.1969)(1969 OJ Special Edn vol II p 412). **159–60**

EC Council Directive 73/79/EEC (18.4.1973)(1973 OJ L 03/13) **159**

EC Council Directive 73/148/EEC (21.5.1973)(1973 OJ L 172/14) **121**

EC Council Directive 77/388/EEC **48, 82–3**

   art 2 **87, 131**

   art 3 **87, 172**

   art 4 **87, 89, 132, 141**

   art 5 **86, 87, 88, 132**

   art 6 **86, 131, 132,**

   art 9 **134, 165**

art 10 **87**

art 11 **87**

art 12 **87**

arts 13–16 **87**

art 13A **133**

art 13B **88, 133, 157–8**

art 13C **88, 158**

art 24 **89, 164**

art 28 **83, 85, 87, 133**

arts 28a–28n **85, 87**

art 33 **92, 158**

EC Council Directive 77/799/EEC (19.12.1977) 1977 OJ L 336/15 **83**

EC Council Directive 79/1072/EEC (6.12.1979) (1979 OJ L 331/11) **83**

EC Council Directive 83/349/EEC (1983 OJ L 193/1) **137**

EC Council Directive 85/303/EEC (15.6.1985)(1985 OJ L 156/23) **159**

EC Council Directive 85/611/EEC (20.12.1985) (1985 OJ L 375/3) **163–4**

EC Council Directive 86/560/EEC (17.11.1986) (1986 OJ L 326/40) **83**

EC Council Directive 88/361/EEC (8.7.1988)(1988 OJ L 178/5) **161**

EC Council Directive 89/465/EEC (18.7.1989) (1989 OJ L 226/21) **83**

EC Council Directive 90/364/EEC (28.6.1990)(1990 OJ L 180/26) **99**

EC Council Directive 90/434/EEC (23.7.1990)(1990 OJ L225/1) **144–6**

EC Council Directive 90/435/EEC (23.7.1990) (1990 OJ L 225/6) **143–4, 146**

EC Council Directive 92/12/EEC (25.2.1992)(1992 OJ L 76/1) **34, 93**

EC Council Directive 92/79/EEC (19.10.1992)(1992 OJ L 316/8) **94**

EC Council Directive 92/80/EEC (19.10.1992)(1992 OJ L 316/10) **94**

EC Council Directive 92/82/EEC (19.10.1992)(1992 OJ L 316/19) **94**

EC Council Directive 92/83/EEC (19.10.1992)(1992 OJ L 316/21) **94**

EC Council Directive 92/84/EEC (19.10.1992)(1992 OJ L 316/29) **94**

EC Council Directive 93/89/EEC(1993 OJ L 279/32) **32**

Decisions

EC Council Decision 70/243 OJ 1970 L94/1 (28.4.1970) **30, 44–50**

EC Council Decision 92/510 (19.10.1992)(1992 OJ L 316/16) **94**

EC Council Decision 94/728 of 31.10.1994 (1994 OJ L 293/9) **45–50, 52**

EC Commission Decision N 684/93 (31.12.1994) 1994 OJ C 390/15 **176**

EC Commission Decision 95/452/EC (12.4.1995) 1995 OJ L 264/30 **177**

Recommendations

EC Commission Recommendation (21.12.1993)(1994 OJ L39) **97**

UK Legislation

Act of Union between England and Scotland in 1701 **53**

Excise Duties (Personal Reliefs) Order 1992, 1992 SI No 3155 **93–4**

Income and Corporation Taxes Act 1988, s 278 **100**

Income and Corporation Taxes Act 1988 ss 468–468I **164**

Travellers' Allowances Order 1994, 1994 SI No 955 **93**

VAT (Isle of Man) Orders 1982, SI 1982 Nos 1067 and 1068 **172**

Table of Treaties, Conventions and International Agreements

EU Treaties

Agreement for partnership and cooperation with Russia **73**

Arbitration Convention (23.7.1990)(1990 OJ C 225/10) **146–8**

EC Treaty **1**

  art 2 **2, 12**
  art 3 **2**
  art 3a **5, 59, 169**
  art 6 **5, 31, 100, 104**
  art 7 **29**
  art 7a **5, 84**
  art 8 **99**
  art 8a **99**
  art 9 **29, 60**
  art 12 **29, 60, 61, 73**
  art 16 **29, 73**
  art 17 **60**
  art 18 **60**
  art 28 **35**
  art 30 **79**
  arts 30–36 **33**
  art 36 **60**
  art 37 **29, 33**
  art 38 **30**
  art 48 **98, 103–8, 110–11, 121–2, 129–30**
  art 51 **35, 97, 98**

  art 52 **115–16, 121–3, 126, 129–30, 139**
  art 58 **123, 130, 139**
  art 59 **107, 121**
  art 60 **119, 123**
  arts 67–73 **153**
  art 67 **106**
  arts 73a–73g **153**
  art 73b **31, 139, 154**
  art 73d **29, 31, 131, 139, 154, 164–5**
  art 75 **32**
  art 91 **32**
  art 92 **33, 175–7 177**
  art 95 **29, 33, 39, 60, 61, 71–9, 121, 127, 176**
  art 96 **33, 75**
  art 97 **33**
  art 98 **33**
  art 99 **8, 32–4, 36, 70, 80**
  art 100 **31, 34, 36**
  art 100a **6, 35**
  art 104c **36**
  art 106 **107**
  art 113 **33, 35, 37, 47**
  art 130f **38**
  art 130r **25, 38, 92**
  art 130s **38, 92**
  art 131 **39**

art 132 **39**
art 133 **39**
art 148 **37**
art 177 **106**
art 189 **31, 32, 112**
art 200 **44**
art 201 **39, 42**
art 201a **40, 42**
art 220 **18, 40, 103**
art 222 **154**
art 227 **171, 172**
art 229 **9**
art 235 **34, 42**
EEC-Cyprus Association Agreement 1973 (1973 OJ L 133/2) **66**
EEC-Switzerland Association Agreement 1973 (1973 OJ L/191) **65, 66**
    art 18 **73**
    art 25 **65**
EEC-Turkey Association Agreement 1973 (1973 OJ C 113/20) **59, 73**
EEC-Turkey Interim Agreement 1973 (1973 OJ L 277) **59**
Euratom Treaty **40**
    art 172 **42**
Europe Agreement with Poland, 1993 (1993 OJ L 348/1) **66**
    art 26 **73**
    art 28 **66**
    art 29 **66**
European Coal and Steel Community Treaty **28**
European Economic Area Agreement **65–6**
    art 8 **65**
    art 26 **65**
    art 29 **113**
European Free Trade Agreement **65**
First Budgetary Treaty 1970 **43**
Protocol on the Privileges and Immunities of the European Communities 1965 **50–1**
Second Budgetary Treaty 1975 **43**

Single European Act **43**
Treaty of European Union **40, 43**
    art F **19**
    art K1 **41**

Other International Agreements
Agreement establishing the WTO **9**
Agreement on Implementation of Article VI of the GATT 1994 **57**
Agreement on Implementation of Article VII of the GATT 1979 **57**
Agreement on Subsidies and Countervailing Measures 1994 **57**
Convention on Diplomatic Relations, Vienna, 1963 **103**
Council of Europe/OECD Convention on Assistance in Tax Matters **21**
European Convention on Human Rights **19–20**
General Agreement on Tariffs and Trade **56–8, 63, 71, 73**
    Art I **56, 71, 127**
    Art III **33, 71–3, 128**
    Art V **58**
    Art VI **57–8**
    Art VII **58, 64**
    Art VIII **58, 60**
    Art IX **58**
    Art XVI **33**
General Agreement on Trade in Services **127**
    Art I **127**
    Art II **127, 128**
    Art XIV **128**
    Art XVII **127, 128**
OECD Convention **11**
OECD Model Tax Convention **12–15, 102**
    arts 1–30 **13–14**
    art 3 **125**
    art 4 **100, 102, 110, 124, 137, 147**
    art 5 **125**
    art 6 **165**
    art 7 **125, 147**

TABLE OF TREATIES

art 9 **138, 147**
art 10 **143, 161**
art 11 **151, 161**
art 12 **151, 166**
art 13 **165**
art 14 **122, 125**
art 15 **102–31, 122**
art 18 **108**

art 19 **103**
art 20 **165**
art 23A **126**
art 23B **126**
art 24 **18, 103, 110, 113**
art 27 **103**
Treaty of Brussels 1952 **56**
Treaty of Marrakech 1994 **56**

CHAPTER ONE

Introduction

Taxation and representation are inseparable ... whatever is a man's own, is absolutely his own; no man hath a right to take it from him without his consent ... whoever does it, commits a robbery; he throws down and destroys the distinction between liberty and slavery. (Lord Camden, House of Lords debate, 7 March 1766)

These thoughts of Lord Camden echoed the famous watchword of James Otis: 'Taxation without representation is tyranny.' This was, of course, the battlecry of those who started the American Revolution and whose efforts led to the foundation of the United States of America. Although more than two centuries later most of us would phrase our thoughts more delicately, this quotation encompasses the central challenge of the development of the European Union.

This book is about taxation by the European Union,[1] and taxation in the European Union. It is about how taxes are raised in the EU, and how those taxes interact with the constitution and principles of the EU. That study – as all studies of taxation – must start with an examination of the constitutional and legal bases for the taxes we examine. We must therefore also reflect on the political

---

1. The European Union, or EU, is used in this book throughout to talk about the composite whole of the EU and its member states as well as the organisation based on the Treaty of (the) EU. This also applies to the taxing powers of the EU itself. Most of the substance of the book is, by contrast, concerned with the limitations on, and coordination between, the taxes imposed by the member states. The source of authority for those actions is the European Community (EC) Treaty, and thus the law concerned is EC law. The proper title of this book should therefore be 'EU and EC Tax Law'. EC law dominates, and hence the title. However, in the book I use EU and EC separately as appropriate. I also use EC or EEC (European Economic Community) where those are the appropriate titles historically.

basis on which those bases are built. We must do so because taxation is an inseparable aspect of government and of the idea of statehood. No social structure of any significant extent can exist without imposing on those in that structure – or others – some cost. That cost is met in most states in most part by taxes. Taxation is, at its heart, the levying of compulsory contributions for the benefit of government for which there is no direct return to the payer.[2]

Throughout history, experience has shown that the cost will not be collected adequately and fairly without compulsion.[3] Lord Camden's point is, quite simply, that in a free society it is for the members of that society to provide the authority to compel the payments. Equally, it is for the members of the society to decide when payments will not be compelled.

To tax or not to tax?

We shall see that there are two opposing aspects to taxation in the EU: the power to tax, and the power to prevent taxation. This may sound trite, but it was fundamental to the initial success of the common market that it could stop its members taxing each other. Much of what we call in this book EC tax law is, in reality, EC law prohibiting taxes. We shall also see that those prohibitions have affected significantly the way that EC policies have developed.

Given that states must raise taxes, the consequence of the EC power to prevent taxes is that other taxes must be raised. They must also be raised within the proscriptions that prohibits those other taxes. From the viewpoint of a member state of the EU, the challenge becomes that of raising taxes that meet those proscriptions. There are, however, several pressures at work within the EU that make such an approach too simplistic.

---

2. This is the working definition of the OECD and IMF. For an expansion of my own views on the definition of taxation as used in this book, see D W Williams, 'Trends in Social Taxation', 1997 Bulletin of the Bureau for International Fiscal Documentation, p. 254.
3. See my argument on that point in 'Trends in Anti-Avoidance' 1996 Bulletin of the Bureau of International Fiscal Documentation, p. 502.

The context of EU taxing powers

One pressure is that of providing funds for the EU itself. As with any governmental authority, the EU institutions must be funded. Those funds must either be levied directly by the authority or be transferred from another authority. If the EU government is to be independent of its constituent members, it must have its own tax revenues. It is, perhaps, the reverse of the position adopted by Lord Camden. A governmental authority without taxing powers has no liberty to act as it chooses. The history of the United States shows that. It also shows that where, as in the USA, the power to tax is divided between different levels of government there will be continuing tensions between those levels.[4]

A second pressure is that of the internal market. Taxes frequently create barriers to free trade. Historically, many taxes were designed specifically for that purpose. A single market requires the removal of these barriers. It must allow goods, services, capital and labour to move freely, and it must do so without distortions to competition. Failure to remove the barriers results in economic inefficiency. It is precisely for this reason that the EC laws against taxes exist. Nevertheless, is this negative approach enough? In practice, any difference in taxation between different parts of the EU creates a distortion of that market, if only because it imposes two sets of compliance costs on the taxpayer rather than one. Viewed from this standpoint, the single market will be achieved only when the EU turns from negative rules to positive ones. It must not only destroy the tax barriers. It must also replace the separate taxes of the member states with harmonised taxes – at least to some extent. Again, the experience of the United States shows that this is so.

A third pressure is that of tax competition. Within a single market, all those in the marketplace find themselves competing. This is intentional. Less obvious at first sight is that this applies as much to tax systems as to any other aspect of the single market. If I am free to move, will I not move to the place where I can optimise my tax burden? The result is that the member states of the EU find themselves competing with each other to attract those wishing to use their freedom of movement.

---

4. For a recent account prepared for European audiences see J E Weiner, 'Tax coordination and competition in the United States of America', Annex 9C to the Ruding Committee Report, p 417.

A fourth pressure is the need to raise government revenues. Each of the three pressures outlined so far force down the taxing abilities of the member states. Yet they have high and growing burdens of public expenditure that they must finance. They are therefore themselves under pressure to raise taxes within the constraints imposed on them. This pressure, as we shall see, is in part unavoidable in any member state. It arises for demographic reasons – an aging population – compounded by the growing incremental cost of health care and other major government expenditures.

A fifth pressure is linked to the battlecry of John Otis. The efficient collection of taxes requires the tolerance or acquiescence of the taxpaying population. Taxes can be collected by compulsion only from a minority in a free society, and in a context where the majority accept the compulsion on the minority. There is still in some parts of the EU the same resistance to taxes as that shown in the former American colonies. Within their memories, people were paying taxes to alien masters, and they therefore learnt to evade those taxes so that they did not support those masters. In times of oppression, many of us will find those sentiments commendable. The problem is that, as the saying goes, old habits die hard.

The need for tolerance goes farther than this, because people have the freedom to avoid taxes and to evade them. If the tax system does not have sufficient respect from the people who must pay the taxes, then they will use their ingenuity to avoid or evade paying. If they do that as a society, the result is civil war. If they do that as individuals, the result may be a more passive form of anarchy but it is also destructive. Governments must therefore ensure, as far as they can, that a balance is struck between freedom and compulsion and between tolerance and avoidance. That balance, in a democratic society, rests with the electorate, but the EU does not have an electorate for this purpose.

The EU power to tax

Somewhere in the constitution of all states there must be provision allocating the power to tax.[5] The provision will often also impose

---

5. In purely constitutional terms, perhaps the nearest analogy to the EU is the Swiss Federation. For an account of its constitutional provisions, see P Thalmann, 'Tax coordination and competition in Switzerland', Annex 9B to the Ruding Committee Report, p 397.

limits on that power – limits that often echo the sentiment with which this chapter started. There is no such power in the constitution of the EU.[6] The need to raise taxes is implicit in the statement of the purposes of the EU set out in article 2 of the EC Treaty, but tax is nowhere mentioned. Nor is there any assertion of a common policy for taxation in the statement of activities in article 3. This only sets out things that the EU will not tax: customs duties are to be eliminated, and obstacles to free movement removed.

Tax policy is implicitly within the scope of the EU because of the needs both of the single internal market and of the economic and monetary union. The former is the reason for the prohibitions, and for more positive action. The latter requires the adoption of an economic policy based on the close coordination of the policies of member states. It also generates the need for sound public finances and a sustainable balance of payments.[7] These impose requirements for taxation to balance the finances.

Tax laws are also subject to both the fundamental principles of the EU and the general principles of EC law. A primary principle is the prohibition against any discrimination on the grounds of nationality.[8] The creation of the internal market 'without internal frontiers in which the free movement of goods, persons, services and capital is ensured'[9] is also of central importance. These are both aspects of 'the principle of an open market economy with free competition'.[10] This book takes these fundamental principles as the framework for its analysis. We examine the interaction of taxation with the four freedoms, as they are often called: goods, persons, services and capital. We also examine the demands imposed on tax systems by the need to ensure nondiscrimination and free competition.

---

6. There is no space in this short book to detail as I would wish the constitutional and legal structure of the EU and EC, but a thorough understanding of that structure and its limitations (both on itself and on others) is necessary for a clear understanding of the way EU and EC tax law operates. There is much good literature on the subject, both in the series of which this is part and more generally. See further the bibliography.

7. EC Treaty, art 3a.

8. EC Treaty, art 6.

9. EC Treaty, art 7a.

10. EC Treaty, art 3a, para 1.

Taxation and representation

The current solution to the challenge is the fiscal veto protected by article 100a of the EC Treaty. No fiscal measure can be adopted by the EU institutions without the unanimous support of all governments. This ensures that no measure is adopted without the support of the democratic representatives of the peoples of each member state of the EU. Unfortunately, this has proved chiefly of negative value for most of the history of the EEC and then EU: no measures are adopted. It is unlikely that the current round of intergovernmental discussions about future developments in Europe will change that rule, even if other areas of veto are relaxed. 'The power to tax is fundamental to the idea of the nation state itself. It provides the money to run the state.' As Camden rightly observed, in a democracy it must be the representatives of the people who decide how that money is raised. At present, there is no obvious European solution to that challenge. I recite it because it is essential to understand this unsolved problem and its consequences for national attitudes when considering the issues addressed in this book.

It is inevitable that the EU must take action in the field of taxation if it is to succeed in its stated objectives. Can the EU have a meaningful approach to taxation if it does not also have a meaningful approach to representation? While the strident language of two centuries ago – when both Europe and America knew the reality of slavery – is far removed from the comitology of Eurodiplomacy, the same issue arises. If the EU cannot answer the challenge positively, it is unlikely to gain tax powers and a coherent tax policy. This is partly because people are unlikely to be enthusiastic about transferring powers to a body suffering a democratic deficit. It is also partly because the governments of all the member states are aware that, without tax powers, there can be no true federal power within the EU. At most, it will be a confederation like its Swiss neighbour. If the EU is left without a coherent tax policy, there will be limits to its present activities and its future development. Those limits will operate on the single market and on the economic and monetary union.

What this book covers

This book, then, is about an area of law of the highest political significance. Of its very essence, it is also a matter of the highest economic significance. That is why, despite the failure to resolve the democratic issues, the EU cannot ignore taxation. Without some tax harmonisation, there could be no common market. Without a considerable degree of tax cooperation, the four freedoms of the EU would be of limited practical use.

What we will see in this book is that the tax policies of the EU have been both an outstanding success and an almost total failure. The Community Customs Code is a remarkable piece of legislation. This is so not only for its content, but for its very existence as a code of law applying directly to the internal and international relationships of eighteen or more sovereign states. At the other extreme, the attempts by the EU to produce a common corporate tax system have failed time and again. It has not even attempted to think about a common social tax system – although it is the most important tax in several member states.

As viewed by some commentators, neither the outstanding success nor the total failure are relevant to a discussion of EC tax law. None of the main works on this subject to date has looked at both these forms of tax, and several mention neither. Why? It is because social taxation is part of social policy, and customs duties are part of trade policy. That it may be so, but this book does not follow that approach. It is written deliberately from the point of view of the taxpayer. Both are, in the view of most taxpayers, taxes. They are fiscal measures that can and do affect free movement within the EU. They are also both measures that raise money for public purposes, and they are both compulsory. For that reason, this book attempts, ambitiously, to touch on all aspects of taxation seen to be of relevance to the taxpayer or advisor. That is ambitious because it adds to a very complex subject the vastness of the range of national taxes.

What this book therefore does not try to do is explain national taxes or tax theory. Anyone studying EC tax law without a sound tax background is strongly urged to look to the national tax system within which he or she is based. This will be the easiest way to get a feel of how a national tax system operates.[11] The temptation

---

11. For an introduction to UK tax law, see G Morse, D Williams and D Salter, *Davies, Principles of Tax Law* (Sweet & Maxwell, 3rd edition, 1996). For an introduction to policy in the UK, see J Kay and M King, *The British Tax System* (Oxford UP, 1991), or D Williams, *Taxation Principles and Policy* (Teach Yourself series, Hodder & Stoughton, 1992).

to give comparative illustrations throughout the book is therefore avoided, both because such details mislead, and because such details date extremely fast.

This book does not try to explain EC law as such. That task is for other books in this series. This book is written on the assumption that the reader understands the general legislative, administrative and judicial structure of the EU. This also applies to the different forms that EU laws may take, the way the European Court of Justice works, the significance of saying that a legislative measure has direct effect, and the ways in which EU law interacts with the national laws of member states. Nor is detail given on the powers of the Commission and of individuals to bring matters of EU law. Also omitted is the resolution of such interactions by the national courts and the European Court. Readers not well versed in those topics are strongly advised to obtain and read both the volumes contributed to the present series by its general editor. These are on the EC institutions and their powers, and on general principles of law.[12]

The structure of discussion in this book is expressly designed to get away from more traditional approaches to the subject. It therefore deliberately does not follow the division of taxes into direct taxes or indirect taxes. This is often derived from article 99 of the EC Treaty, but is increasingly meaningless in both content and context. Nor does it take the tax-by-tax approach common in national accounts of taxation. Nor, as we have noted, does it separate out 'real' taxes from customs duties or 'commercial defence instruments' (as protective duties are called) or hypothecated taxes such as social taxes.

Instead, the book examines all relevant fiscal measures by reference to the EU as an entity, to the freedoms of movement within the EU, and to competition policy. In so doing, we divide the coverage of VAT – somewhat provocatively – into two, dealing with taxation of goods separately from taxation of services. Treatment of the corporate and personal income taxes is divided into several parts. We also confront the distinctions between income taxes and social taxes and between income taxes and the VAT. The reason for this is to concentrate attention on the challenges

12. J A Usher, *General Principles of EC Law* and *EC Institutions and Legislation*, in this series (1997).

currently facing the EU from national tax policies. Conversely, it focuses examination on the challenges facing national tax policies from the existence of the EU and of those freedoms. It is hoped that, as a result, the reader will be able to consider the outstanding successes, the complete failures, and the many stages in between, in a fuller context.

In the rest of this chapter, we continue the examination of the constitutional and legal context of the taxing powers of the EU. We do so by noting the international constraints on the EU and its member states. In Chapter 2 we complete the introduction by noting the wide differences in national approaches to tax within the EU member states. Chapter 3 then reviews the EU's own taxing powers, and the fiscal and financial position regarding the EU's own resources. Chapter 4 looks at the main EU tax, the customs duties applied at the common frontier, and how internal customs duties have been removed.

Chapter 5 starts the analysis of taxation and the freedoms of movement by examining how goods are taxed within the EU. Chapter 6 looks at how tax may affect free movement of persons except for entrepreneurs. These are dealt with as a special case in Chapter 7. In Chapter 8 we complete the review of the freedom of movement of services and the right of establishment by looking at how taxes within the EU affect multinational enterprises. Chapter 9 then examines the fourth of the freedoms, the free movement of capital. Chapter 10 discusses how competition policy conflicts with tax policy, in particular by reference to special tax zones and the rules about state aid. It also seeks to bring together some points of focus from the material covered in the book.

The EU's international tax commitments

The EU's fiscal policies, and those of all the member states, are constrained by the EU's membership of the World Trade Organisation (WTO) and the GATT[13] 1994, with its subsidiary agreements. These are examined in detail in Chapter 4. Those constraints are, however, fundamental to the constitution of the

---

13. The EU's relationship with the GATT is recognised in EC Treaty, art 229, and in the Agreement establishing the WTO.

EU. As a regional trading organisation, it takes its context internationally from being a special grouping within the GATT, and running under rules that must comply with the GATT. The restraints placed on the EU and its members by the GATT are therefore fundamental – a form of basic law to that constitution.[14] Less fundamental, but also important, are the subsidiary agreements on customs duties and related issues formulated within or under the authority of the WTO and GATT. Together, these provide most of the shape for the Community Customs Code.

Besides the GATT, there are few international constraints on the EU as such. This in part reflects the absence of general multilateral treaties on any fiscal subject apart from customs duties. Instead, the tradition is for states to regulate tax matters, if at all, on a bilateral basis.[15] There are several such kinds of bilateral agreement. The most important is that of double tax conventions, dealing with personal and corporate income taxes. A second group covers social taxes as part of the subject matter of a matrix of double social security agreements. Other conventions cover investment and trade issues, with incidental effects on taxation. The interaction between these agreements and EC law is not straightforward.[16] Where relevant, it is considered in more detail in the book.

The role of the OECD[17]

The OECD has established a pivotal role in interstate fiscal relationships through the work of the Committee on Fiscal Affairs and its Fiscal Affairs Department. There are three areas in which it is

14. For a detailed discussion of this theme, and of the relationship between the EU and the WTO and GATT, see D McGoldrick, *International Relations Law of the European Union*, in this series (1997).
15. D W Williams, *Trends in International Taxation* ch 4, 'International tax reform?' (IBFD, 1991).
16. See McGoldrick, op. cit. note 14.
17. The Organisation for Economic Cooperation and Development, based in Paris, was established by the OECD Convention signed at Paris in 1960. It replaced the OEEC (Organisation for European Economic Cooperation). All the member states of the EU and of the EEA are members of the OECD, save for Liechtenstein. The other member states of OECD in 1997 are: Australia, Canada, the Czech Republic, Hungary, Japan, Mexico, New Zealand, Poland, Switzerland, Turkey, and the USA. The EC Commission takes part in the work of the OECD (OECD Convention, art 13).

currently active. The first, and most important, is the production and maintenance of the OECD Model Tax Convention on Income and Capital (OECD MTC), and other model conventions on aspects of taxation. The second is the intergovernmental work on tax policy and practice that takes place through the Committee on Fiscal Affairs and its subcommittee. These produce a series of reports on issues of international taxation for the tax authorities of the member states. Behind these reports are regular ongoing discussions and exchanges of information on a wide range of issues covering all the main direct taxes and, more recently, value added tax (VAT). Outreach is the third relevant area of activity. One policy of the OECD is to contribute to sound economic expansion 'in members as well as nonmember countries in the process of economic development'.[18] This has recently become more prominent in the OECD. It has made major efforts to help the emerging economies of central and eastern Europe and, increasingly, the rest of the world.

The structure of the OECD is fundamentally different from that of the EU. It has no executive powers, and can only work by unanimity and therefore a consensus. Its most formidable power is a recommendation of the OECD Council. That is, in effect, a unanimous recommendation from the member governments to themselves. However, this has made it a more comfortable organisation for some member states than the EU for handling direct tax matters. Because the OECD can inform, but cannot take initiatives, it is regarded as a safe means by which problems of taxation can be discussed and, at times, coordinated. National sovereignty is not threatened in any way, nor can a member state be compelled to give up a particular position. For member states that regard the EU as a threat to sovereignty, working through Paris involves fewer constraints than working through Brussels. It also allows discussions to take place with all the leading economies, not just the European grouping. Some aspects of international tax demand that wider context.

[18.] OECD Convention, art 1. The other policies are to achieve the highest sustainable economic growth consistent with financial stability in the member states and to contribute to the expansion of world trade. There is much common ground between these policies and the tasks of the EU as defined by EC Treaty, art 2.

International tax law and double tax conventions[19]

'International tax law' is the name given to the principles and rules by which states handle the interactions of their national tax systems. Because the national tax systems of states are largely unconstrained by international public law, national tax jurisdictions can and do overlap.[20] States use bilateral agreements – the DTCs – to handle these overlaps. DTCs are now the primary source of rules of international tax law.

The use of DTCs has evolved over the last century. They now provide a set of rules to deal with all aspects of the overlap between two states of their individual and corporate income taxes. A huge network of DTCs has grown up during that time. To impose some sort of structure on the network, efforts have continued since the days of the League of Nations to create a common approach to DTCs. Since 1963, the common approach between the developed states has taken the form of a model DTC. This was revised in 1977, and again in 1992, and is now the OECD MTC.[21] This is a model convention of 30 articles. Between them, they provide a set of rules for determining within which of the two tax jurisdictions any taxpayer is to be taxed on any kind of income. Its contents are summarised in Table 1.1. The model is accompanied by a detailed Commentary. It contains comments about each article, and both observations on the commentary and reservations to each article made by individual states. Taken together these provide a good picture of the consensus view of the OECD in adopting the wording of the article, and the extent of disagreement among members about that consensus.

[19.] These are also known, for reasons of internal law, as double tax treaties (USA) and double tax agreements (UK). The term used is that of the OECD. It is abbreviated to DTC in the rest of the text.

[20.] P Baker, *Double Tax Conventions and International Tax Law* (Sweet & Maxwell, 2nd edition, 1996).

[21.] The 1992 Model has been made ambulatory, and is updated from time to time. It was updated in 1994 and again in 1995. A further update is scheduled for 1997.

Table 1.1   Contents of the OECD Model Tax Convention[22]

Number and title	Content	EC comment
1: Personal scope	DTC applies to all residents	Followed by all EC members
2: Taxes covered	Personal and corporate income and capital taxes	All EC states have relevant taxes
3: General definitions		
4: Resident	Sets rules for allocating dual residents to one state	Important in cross-border cases
5: Permanent establishment	Defines when a PE exists	
6: Taxation of land	Tax to state where land is	EC has no land tax policy
7: Business profits	Tax to state of residence unless PE in other state	Important to right of establishment
8: Shipping, etc ... transport	Tax to state of effective management	
9: Associated enterprises	Primary transfer pricing rule of arm's length	Incorporated in the EC Arbitration Convention
10: Dividends	Source state may impose limited withholding tax	Partly superseded by EC Parent-Subsidiary Directive
11: Interest	Source state may impose limited withholding tax	Proposed Interest Directive would partly supersede
12: Royalties	Tax to state of residence of recipient	Not followed by some states; see proposed directive
13: Capital gains	Unless 5, 6, 8 apply, tax to state of residence of owner	Not all member states have a capital gains tax
14: Independent personal services	Tax to state of residence of professional unless fixed base in other state	Important to free movement of services

22. *Model Tax Convention on Income and on Capital* (1992 with looseleaf updates, OECD, Paris (also available as a condensed version in paperback, 1994)). OECD also has a model tax convention on estate and gifts taxes, which is not within the scope of this book. For detailed analysis see: Baker, op cit note 20; K Vogel, *Double Tax Conventions* (Kluwer, 2nd edition, 1990); M Edwardes-Ker, *International Tax Treaty Service* (In-depth Publishing, updated looseleaf).

15: Dependent personal services	Tax to state of residence unless employee present 183 days in other state	Key rule for free movement of workers
16: Directors' fees	Tax to state of residence of company	See *Asscher* case
17: Artistes and Sportsmen	Overrides 14 and 15. Tax to state of performance	
18: Pensions	Tax to pensioner's state of residence	See *Bachmann* case
19: Government service	Tax to paying state unless business	
20: Students	Exempt in state of studies	
21: Other income	For all other income, tax to state of residence	
22: Capital	Same rules as 13	Few member states tax capital
23: Exists in alternative forms 23A : Exemption Method 23B: Credit Method	States must agree to give relief for tax paid in other state in one of the forms	Practice varies between member states
24: Nondiscrimination	Bars discrimination based on nationality	Compare ECT Treaty art 6
25: Mutual agreement procedure	Machinery for the two parties to discuss problems	Partly superseded by EC Mutual Assistance Directives
26: Exchange of information		Superseded by EC Mutual Assistance Directives
27: Diplomatic Agents	Confirms exemption	Based on separate international agreements applying to all members
28: Territorial extension	Allows parties to extend to dependent territories	May apply beyond EU boundaries
29 and 30: formal	Providing for ratification and termination	

The OECD MTC is but a model. It is not an international agreement[23] – certainly not a multilateral agreement – nor is the commentary therefore legally determinative of the meaning of an actual agreement.[24] Nonetheless, nearly all recent DTCs follow the OECD MTC.[25] The actual agreements now number over 1,300 worldwide. DTCs now govern almost all possible links between member states.[26] The model is therefore an important guide to the rules of international tax law. This is particularly so as there is no international judicial body with competence over tax matters.

Principles of international tax law

Table 1.1 outlines the content of the OECD MTC. The agreed provisions in the MTC are based on a series of agreed principles of international tax law, which in practice have been accepted by all the members of the OECD, and therefore all the EU member states.[27] The main assumption behind the MTC is that the states with taxing rights over any transaction are, with few exceptions, either or both of the state of source of the payment and the state where the taxpayer is resident. In practice, the 'source state' tends to mean not the states where the legal source of a payment is, but the state from which the payment is actually made.[28] This reflects a practical approach taken by taxing authorities in linking formal tax claims to means by which the tax can be collected effectively.

23. The only multilateral agreements of significance in Europe on income taxes are the series of agreements between the states of the Nordic Council: Denmark, Finland, Iceland, Norway, Sweden. They have broadly similar tax systems and have concluded a common multilateral tax convention, supported by multilateral convention on mutual assistance.
24. The precise status of the Commentary is a matter of current discussion. In practice, it is treated as if it were either preparatory works relevant to interpretation or an agreed statement of interpretation. The OECD is expected to report specifically on this issue in the near future: Baker, op cit note 22, ch 3.
25. The OECD Council has recommended formally that its members should negotiate DTCs only on the basis of the model.
26. Netherlands and the UK have concluded DTCs with all other member states: Greece, Ireland and Portugal have only partial networks.
27. There is no consistent worldwide practice. The United Nations published an alternative model in 1980. The chief difference is that the UN Model gives greater rights to the source state.
28. The OECD MTC provides some rules to determine the identity of a source. In other cases it is for the national laws of the relevant states to determine where a payment is sourced.

The primary rule of international tax law is that the state of residence of the taxpayer has the right to tax the worldwide income of the taxpayer.[29] Note that this is *not* defined by reference to nationality. While there is no consistent definition of residence, it is broadly determined by the physical presence and economic and social links of the taxpayer to the state, not by any formal legal provision. In practice, individuals are usually regarded as resident in any state in which they are present for more than 183 days in any year, or in which they have a permanent home. Companies are regarded as resident in any state where they have their seat, or where they are legally registered as companies, or where they are effectively managed.

The existence of alternative tests means that a taxpayer may be a dual resident. In such cases, the DTCs provide rules so that for the purpose of a DTC, a taxpayer has only one residence. That state then has primary taxing rights over that individual. The DTC then lists the situations in which the other state party to the DTC can also tax.

In applying these rules, international tax law recognises the different legal personalities of all persons. A subsidiary company is independent of the parent even though entirely owned by it. This means that relationships between associated persons are treated as relationships between independent persons. International tax law applies the arm's length rule to such relationships. They are to be taxed as if there were no association. This may give rise to a challenge to any transactions between associated persons that are not made at arm's length. That is done by adjusting the accounts of the taxpayers, and sometimes recharacterising them. An adjustment is usually termed a transfer pricing adjustment.

Modern international tax practice also assumes that the state of residence will provide relief for any foreign tax paid by taxpayers on income it is also taxing. For example, a state from which interest is paid to a foreign resident will often require a withholding tax to be deducted on payment. The foreign taxpayer therefore receives only a net payment. If the taxpayer's state of residence reserves the right to tax the receipt of interest, it should provide relief

---

[29.] This right is recognised even where states do not themselves exercise the right. For example, the Netherlands will in some circumstance tax only local source income, and will exempt foreign source income. By contrast, the UK taxes income of residents wherever earned, although it only taxes some foreign income if it is remitted to the United Kingdom.

for the tax already paid. It can do this in two primary ways. Either it can exempt the income on the ground that tax has already been paid, or it can provide credit for the foreign tax against any tax due to it. The OECD MTC provides these as alternative methods, because state practice does not recognise either as the primary method of relief. Within the EU, practice varies between member states, and between kinds of income.

An EC tax convention?

The chief weakness of this structure between EU member states is that 'the solution' is a network of a maximum of 105 bilateral agreements, all of which have some differences from the others. In practice, many differences are minor, but there are important differences in some areas. These inconsistencies add to taxpayer compliance costs, but may equally lend themselves to taxpayer arbitrage.[30] The opportunity for arbitrage means that states have to look to anti-avoidance provisions.

A further weakness of the existing arrangements lies with the interaction of a DTC with national law. In some states, constitutional provisions ensure that the DTC overrides conflicting internal rules.[31] In other states, the DTC only takes effect to the extent that it is incorporated into internal law.[32] That being so, taxpayers cannot determine from the DTC alone precisely what effect it has between the two states parties.

More contentious is the question of interaction between a DTC and EC law. It is now clear that EC law overrides a conflicting provision in a DTC between two member states. It is less clear exactly how far EC law interacts with a DTC between a member state and a third state. There are two facets to this important issue. Can a taxpayer maintain that an EC state must disapply a provision in a DTC if it is conflict with EC law? If so, the assumption

---

30. The practice known as 'treaty shopping' involves exploiting these differences. For example, a payment of a royalty is due from state A to state C. State A imposes a 20 per cent withholding tax on that payment. DTCs provide that a payment to state B is subject only to withholding of 5 per cent, and that there is no withholding on payment from state B to state C. The taxpayer therefore routes the royalty to state C through a subsidiary established in state B. Many DTCs now contain provisions to stop such practices.
31. An example is Italy.
32. An example is the UK.

must be that the EC law overrides the DTC, even though the DTC has itself overridden the national law in question. The reverse of this is the question whether a taxpayer in the other state to a DTC with a non-member state can invoke the DTC to gain equal treatment from the other party to that given to taxpayers elsewhere in the EU.[33] These matters have not yet been addressed at the judicial level.

These and other problems have led many to advocate the formulation of an EC multilateral tax convention, or at least a common approach to conventions so that approximation can occur.[34] The EC Treaty itself is more cautious, only requiring that member states negotiate to deal with double taxation.[35] A multilateral convention was discussed in the context of both the EEC and the EFTA some years ago, but no positive recommendations could be made for lack of agreement among the experts. It may be that an EC Model DTC might be a partial answer to the problem, but this does not exist either.

We shall see that the directives adopted to date in this area have provided some common ground between member states, and the European Court of Justice is, in recent decisions, producing further common ground. The content of member states' DTCs is also the subject of current research to identify common ground more systematically. This will reveal that there are still fundamental differences between states on key issues such as the extent to which foreign income is taxed, the extent to which withholding taxes are used, and the rules used to identify kinds of income and their sources. It is to be hoped that research of the kind indicated may lead to a clear identification of differences so that, at the least, common definitions can be adopted within the EU either by a directive or by agreed model convention clauses. An EC Tax Convention may be desirable, but is most unlikely in the foreseeable future.

Even if there were progress on these points, a model based on

---

33. The argument would be based on the DTC's version of the OECD MTC art 24. This provides a nondiscrimination provision. For example, an agreement between state A and state B will require state A to give B's nationals the same treatment as A's nationals. We shall see that in some cases EC law treats discrimination on residence grounds as if it were discrimination on nationality grounds. Can a taxpayer in a third state couple this principle with art 24? This is of particular significance if the claim is made for a permanent establishment of a foreign company. See further, Baker, commentary on article 24.
34. The Ruding Committee (Report, p 206) urges a common approach.
35. EC Treaty, art 220.

the OECD MTC would apply only to income taxes. The OECD MTC does not apply to VAT, nor does it apply to social taxes and contributions. There are at present no international agreements of any kind outside the EU dealing with double taxation under a VAT. There are a limited series of bilateral agreements dealing with social security contributions and benefits. No attempt has been made to deal with overlaps between different forms of tax – for example, where one state taxes by a social tax what another taxes by income tax and a third by VAT.

This absence of agreement reflects the separate histories that these forms of tax had at international level. It is only in the last few years that any attention at all has been paid to the effective overlaps that exist both legally and economically between these differing taxes. There is therefore no question of foreign tax relief against a claim for income tax for foreign VAT or social taxes. As we shall see, this presents a series of practical problems to tax-payers, but solutions to these problems are some way off.

Human rights and taxation[36]

The quotation with which this chapter was started carries a strong 'rights' flavour. Are the commitments of the EU member states to human rights relevant to the imposition of taxes? All the member states are, of course, members of the Council of Europe and signatories to the European Convention on Human Rights.[37] The Treaty of European Union also commits the EU to those rights.[38] In practice, this poses no restraint on a state imposing general taxes for public purposes, as the European Court of Human Rights has indicated that states must have a wide discretion in deciding public policy on taxation. The Convention could be used in a case where tax procedures fail to respect the fundamental rights of taxpayers. It could also apply were a state to use tax law to invade the property rights of named individual taxpayers in a specific way, or where the taxes would be discriminatory in their effect. We have

---

36. See *Taxation and Human Rights* (IFA Seminar Proceedings, Vol 12, 1988).
37. European Convention for the Protection of Human Rights and Fundamental Freedoms, Rome, 1950. This also forms part of the law of many member states. In 1997 the UK government announced that it would also incorporate the Convention into internal law.
38. TEU, art F para 2.

already seen that DTCs based on the OECD MTC contain measures to combat discrimination based on nationality. The European Convention on Human Rights adds to that a proscription against discrimination on other grounds such as sex, religion and ethnic origin. Happily, European states no longer discriminate on these grounds (save some for discrimination between men and women). Challenges against the formulation of a tax based on human rights issues tend to be politically motivated and with little legal merit, and therefore rarely succeed. Nonetheless, the Convention adds to the legal basis of the argument that taxes should be imposed by general measures, not specific measures, and should not be discriminatory.

Intergovernmental cooperation

The final area of international agreement to be noted relates to intergovernmental cooperation on taxation matters. Traditionally, there was none. Both common law and civil law jurisdictions adopted a non-cooperation approach regarding foreign taxes. States would not allow their courts to enforce tax owed to foreign governments. Similarly, they would not allow the use of court procedures for indirect enforcement of taxation laws, for example in connection with demands for information. This attitude also applied to tax authorities, where the traditional attitude was that there was no exchange of either information or assistance. Another aspect of the mutual non-recognition of foreign tax laws was a refusal to use the criminal processes to support alleged criminal conduct in evading foreign tax. The approach was adopted because tax laws are public laws of the state, and the mutual exclusiveness of national sovereignty means that a state will not enforce the rights of other states as sovereign authorities within its own, sovereign, territory.

This traditional rule is still the primary international rule on enforcement of taxes. It is one of the reasons why tax havens are effective. It is also one of the reasons why a series of international agreements are needed to deal with double taxation.

This mutual non-cooperation is entrenched in state practice, and can therefore only be removed by positive agreement between states. It is for this reason that the OECD MTC contains measures to provide for mutual agreement between parties to a DTC, and

exchange of information between them. In practice, intergovernmental cooperation has gone significantly beyond that in recent
years. This has happened within the EU. It has also happened at
the international level. There are continuing informal links between states to review international tax problems through the
working groups of the OECD Fiscal Affairs Committee. Aside
from that, the 'Group of 4' is an informal group through which
the British, French, German, and United States tax officials
exchange views. The Nordic Council group of Scandinavian
states also have close cooperation, confirmed by a multilateral
agreement.

A more general agreement was formulated by the Council of
Europe in cooperation with the OECD.[39] To date, this has received
limited support, although it is in force between some states.[40]
There are also growing agreements for cooperation on criminal
matters relating to tax and on extradition for tax crimes. The
Council of Europe has also facilitated these. Nonetheless, there is
still some way to go before there is general cooperation between
states in the absence of specific treaties. It is for this reason that
the EC measures are important.

[39.] Convention on Mutual Administrative Assistance in Tax Matters (1988).
[40.] It has been ratified by the Nordic States and Germany and partly by the United
States. The previous government of the UK indicated that it would not ratify the
Convention.

CHAPTER TWO

Tax in the European Union

When the founders first considered establishing the EEC, the tax concerns of the future member states were far removed from those at the time of writing this book. Residents of the time can describe in graphic terms the formidable examination awaiting those[1] who attempted to take themselves or luggage across the frontiers between Belgium and the Netherlands. Rationing was strict. Customs duties and other taxes on goods were high. Movement across borders into other states in western Europe was most difficult, with states – and cities – divided by strict military occupation.

Europe, once a continent of free commerce,[2] was sharply divided. Further, those divisions were themselves the source of much of the revenues of the war-torn states. Fifty years ago, customs duties and excise taxes on goods were their main taxes. Through them, states collected up to 70 per cent of what revenues they could glean from their economies. By contrast, social security systems were being newly established or reestablished, and social contributions had minimal roles to play.

The position at the time of writing this book is sharply different. Customs duties have been removed on all intra-Community trade, and are now almost irrelevant as a source of taxation. Many excise taxes have been swept away. A new tax, value added tax, has replaced those taxes and many other sales taxes. Social security systems, now ripening, are imposing heavy burdens on some national economies. Social contributions, with income taxes, have

---

1. I am indebted in writing this comment to the presentation made by Professor Vanistendael of the Catholic University of Leuven to the EUCOTAX Wintercourse in Leuven in April 1997, on which this account is particularly based.
2. It is worth recalling that there was considerable freedom of movement in Europe at the beginning of the century.

become the dominant method of tax collection in most states. Taxation of labour is therefore now the dominant source of revenues.

The changes over the last 50 years reflect successful solutions to some problems that confronted the founders of the EEC. But as those problems have faded, other forms of tax distortion have become the focus of concern. They may not hinder trade in the obvious ways that happened in those early days, but trade is still hindered. Further, the attempts by member states to solve these problems, each in its own way, have compounded the nature of the problems. If member states had similar tax systems, offering further solutions might be easy. Unfortunately, they do not.

A study of tax in the European Union must start from a recognition that states are still far apart on what they consider to be both the problems and the solutions. A serious student of the subject must accept those differences as the starting point of any attempt to review the nature of the problem. It must also be accepted that those differences are often generated from local democratic responses to major economic and social issues. They cannot therefore be put aside lightly. This chapter outlines the current position.

How EU states raise taxes

Table 2.1 shows the main forms of tax collected by the leading member states of the EU. The table measures two differences between member states. First, it records the shares of taxes categorised into three groups. These groups follow the standard approach adopted in collecting revenue statistics. Direct taxes include general personal and corporate income taxes, wealth and inheritance taxes and other taxes imposed directly on taxpayers. Indirect taxes cover value added tax, excise duties, and other taxes imposed on products or services rather than persons.[3] The figures do not include customs duties. Social contributions include all payments made directly to social funds or payable to government specifically for social funding. In addition, member states also collected other kinds of taxes not listed. For example, the UK collects national business rates on businesses and council tax on

---

3. As noted in ch 1, this is not a tidy distinction. For example, states disagree on the classification of stamp duties. The OECD statistics avoid the categorisation, but it is the traditional approach adopted in the UK.

individuals. Together, these represent about 10 per cent of all tax collected, or a further 5 per cent of gross national product (GNP).

A second difference is the relative level of taxation in the different states. Following usual practice, this is measured as the amount that the tax collected in the year represents as a percentage of the total GNP of that state in that year. GNP is a measure of the total economic output of the state. Therefore, the share of GNP reflects the total share of national output taken in taxation. It will be seen that in Denmark almost half the GNP of the year was taken in tax. If these are taken with all other taxes, the result is that over half the economic effort of Denmark in 1995 was taken by compulsory payments – 51 crowns of every 100 earned.

A third variable is hidden behind this second variable, although it is not made explicit in the table. This is the relative level of the GNPs of the states listed. Across the EU this varies considerably. That is important because, unless this is taken into account, the full amount of money flowing through the tax and social security systems is concealed. In all the states in the table, GNP is high by international standards. For example, the share of GNP taken in taxes in Spain has risen since 1965 from 15 per cent to 34 per cent. This has happened while the GNP per person in Spain has itself risen significantly. In other words, the Spanish economy has gone through a very significant shift from a low-tax funding economy to a pattern not far removed from that in the UK.

Table 2.1   Taxes collected by member states 1995[4]

Member state	Direct tax	Indirect tax	Social contribution
Denmark	31.3	16.7	0.8
France	7.8	12.2	17.2
Germany	11.8	10.9	12.5
Italy	15.2	11.2	9.2
Netherlands	11.6	12.0	15.4
Spain	10.0	9.8	12.4
Sweden	21.6	11.7	13.6
United Kingdom	13.0	12.2	6.0

4.   OECD Revenue Statistics 1965–1995, OECD, Paris 1997.

Differing tax systems

During the birth and growth of the EU, the economies of the states of western Europe have grown significantly, taking the tax systems with them. They have also changed significantly in approach. Furthermore, that change has been a divergent one. In some ways, the overall systems of the member states are now further apart than they were before the EEC was founded. Instead of general reliance in most states on customs duties and indirect taxes, Table 2.1 shows a wide range of approaches to tax.

Taxes on products and services are still a consistent revenue earner for all states. Because of the EC, these taxes are now much closer in form than they were. Note in particular that there are no customs duties in the table at all. Any customs duties collected by the member states are collected as agents for the EU. The duties collected are EU funds, not government funds. Much of the tax in the table is VAT, collected under the common form of tax adopted by all member states. The largest part of the balance is formed by excise on a few products: hydrocarbon oils, alcoholic drinks, and tobacco products. These also have a common EU form.

Beyond this, there is still considerable variety. One new element in that variety is the introduction of taxes aimed at assisting government policies against pollution and environmental degradation. In particular, taxation is now being used to adjust the prices of products to reflect the cost of pollution caused by production of the goods, or on disposal. So far, the EU has been unable to take any concerted action on environmental taxation.[5] Member states have separately adopted measures aimed at curbing pollution.[6]

Consistency is also completely missing from the corporate and personal income taxes. For much of this century, the UK has relied heavily on its income tax. More recently, the separate corporation tax on company profits has also generated revenues. The real burden of the taxes has, however, risen steadily over the last 30 years. That rise is relatively small when compared with the rise of the burden of income tax over the same period in Italy or Denmark. Yet it is far higher than income tax in France, where less than half the population pay any income tax at all. Behind those

---

5. See further the discussion of EC Treaty, art 130r below, p. 38.
6. For a survey, see OECD, *Environmental Taxes in OECD Countries* (1995). The topic is discussed further in ch 5.

general comments, the direct tax systems show a variety of approaches to fundamental issues. For example, there is no common view on whether a family should or should be not recognised as an entity for tax purposes. The same is true of the question whether a 100 per cent subsidiary company should be grouped with its parent company for tax purposes, or whether the link between company and shareholder should be recognised.

The figures also conceal differences in the way the tax bases[7] are defined, both for businesses and for individuals. Corporate profits, as defined for corporate tax purposes, of a German or Austrian company are radically different to those of a British or Irish company with the same commercial earnings. Similarly, states use a wide range of rates and allowances for personal income tax.

That there are such differences is not surprising. It is naive to assume that taxes are only about collecting finance for public use. In reality, there are a wide range of policies influencing a country's choice of taxes.[8] In a democracy, taxes are usually part of a series of measures with specific social aims, or reflecting specific social and political values, accepted by the voters of the state through periodic elections. Politicians do not have the democratic authority to override these choices, although they may work to persuade the voters to change their minds.

Social contributions

The sharpest differences have emerged in the different state practices in imposing and collecting social contributions or taxes. Denmark, until a few years ago, did not have any social taxes. It still has only low levels of contributions on individuals. France, by contrast, collects almost half its total taxes this way. The Netherlands and Germany also have high contribution levels, while the UK's contributions are much less significant in total.

---

7. A tax base is the transaction or other thing on which the tax is levied – for example, net profits of businesses, rents from properties, sales of goods, imports of goods, ownership or use of assets or, in the case of a poll tax, where the taxpayer lives.
8. The point is well put in S Weatherill and P Beaumont, *EC Law* (Penguin, 2nd edition, 1995), at p 422: 'taxation involves politics, not simply economics'. For a general account of the policies behind recent tax reforms, see D Williams, *Trends in International Taxation* (IBFD Publications BV, 1991), chs 2, 3.

Some may object that social contributions are not taxes. This is a controversial view, but in this book it is assumed that compulsory social payments are taxes. This applies if the amounts are imposed by law and are paid to funds from which benefits are only payable by law. To assume otherwise is to ignore the single most significant medium-term pressure on Europe's tax systems, as the European Commission has made clear.[9]

Behind these differences are even greater problems. The stark truth is that Europe's social security funds are going broke. The crisis is now admitted in France, and is worrying Germany. It is also worrying the UK, although the problem is less important there. Why? It is because of the dependency ratio, that is, the ratio between those paying contributions (workers) and those receiving benefits (the retired, unemployed, and sick and disabled). The demographic patterns of the populations of every state in Europe are such that the dependency ratio is rising.

The number of retired people, in particular, is growing steadily higher in comparison with the number of workers. In some states the rise is steady, while in others it is sharp.[10] In the short term, this has forced up the rates of contribution paid by employers and employees in every state that relies on such contributions. A few fund their social benefits through general taxation or compulsory savings schemes not regarded as taxes, but they also have had to make adjustments. For example, in Germany, the total burden has risen over the last 30 years from 8 per cent of GNP to 15 per cent. In Sweden the rise is from 4 per cent to 14 per cent. In Italy it is from 1 per cent to 12 per cent. Only in Denmark has the share not increased significantly. Yet the result of absorbing social costs fully into general taxes in Denmark has been to increase income tax from 12 per cent of GNP to more than 31 per cent, while indirect taxes have also risen.

When the EEC was being established, most of these social security systems were plans. Many followed lead given by the ambitious Beveridge Plan of the UK in attempting to provide for their populations from cradle to grave.[11] Fifty years later, the present position is such that making intelligent comments about harmon-

9. The Commission has repeatedly drawn attention to the shift from other taxes to labour taxes and charges.
10. The subject is reviewed at international level in World Bank, *The Old Age Crisis* (IBRD, 1994).
11. See A Ogus and E Barendt, *The Law of Social Security* (Butterworths, 4th edition, 1995), ch 1, for an account of this report and its consequences.

ising the personal taxation imposed by member states is almost impossible. The starting points are too far apart. This is complicated by a divergence of approach between the EU and its member states. Member states are moving to integrate their contributions and taxes. EC law, by categorising social contributions as part of social policy, and ignoring their role in fiscal policy, forces them apart.[12]

The ECSC and taxes

The first of the European Communities to be established was the European Coal and Steel Community (ECSC) in 1952. Although limited in its scope, it was formidable in its fiscal powers. The ECSC Treaty[13] contains both positive and negative tax provisions. On the negative side, the Treaty required the abolition and prohibition of import and export duties, and of charges having equivalent effect, on relevant products.[14] It also abolished and prohibited any state subsidies, aids or special charges in any form whatever, so preventing internal tax measures as replacements of the duties.[15] The Treaty was drawn up long before current concerns with pollution and the environment, so it is silent on these issues.

On the positive side, the Treaty arranged for what might be regarded as a genuine international tax. The High Authority[16] is given powers under the Treaty to incur expenditure, and to fund that expenditure by a levy on production, if a limited one.[17] As one commentator put it, these 'laconic' provisions mean that the ECSC High Authority 'can authorise revenue because the member states have surrendered to it the sovereign power to raise tax, the levy'.[18]

In the light of the comments at the beginning of this book, it should also be noted that the European Parliament now has a sig-

---

12. See my comment in 'Asscher: the European Court and the power to destroy' (1997) EC Tax Review 4. For a partial response, see P Farmer, (1997) EC Tax Review 56.
13. Treaty establishing the European Coal and Steel Community, Paris, 1951.
14. ECSC Treaty, art 4(a).
15. ECSC Treaty, art 4(c).
16. The executive body for the ECSC.
17. ECSC Treaty, art 49. The levy was limited to 1 per cent by art 50, unless specific approval was given under a set procedure by the ECSC Council.
18. D Strasser, *The Finances of Europe* (European Communities, Luxembourg, 1992) p 24.

nificant role in rate-setting. This has deterred the High Authority from increasing the levy more than once.[19]

The EEC and taxes

The European Economic Community Treaty[20] did not directly follow this supranational lead. While the EEC Treaty contains strong negative rules, its positive powers to tax are less obvious and relate purely to border taxes and adjustments. The lack of specific provisions on internal taxation has come to cause problems within the EU. We therefore need to note in some detail what the EEC Treaty does and does not say. Only one specific relevant provision has been added to the EC Treaty (as it is now called) as it has been amended to date, and that was also negative.[21] The following is an analysis of all relevant provisions in the EC Treaty.

1. Customs duties and related taxes on products

Chapter 4 describes in detail the EC Treaty provisions on customs duties and similar measures. Founded clearly in the principles of the EC, these impose a clear set of negative rules on transfers between member states. They also impose a positive obligation on member states to act in common when levying duties on third states. Both the negative rules and the positive rules are based on the provision in article 9, under the general heading of the Community policy on free movement of goods. The aim is the replacement of the separate customs duty systems of the member states with a common external customs duty. The prohibition against national duties in articles 12 and 16 is supported by a ban on equivalent internal measures in article 95. This is noted below, along with parallel measures to curb misuse of state monopolies contained in article 37.

Since then, the requirement of a single internal market in article 7[22] has removed the means to impose internal customs duties by

19. Strasser, op cit note 18.
20. Signed in Rome, 1957. See also the European Atomic Energy Community Treaty (Euratom) signed at the same time, and using the same provisions where appropriate.
21. EC Treaty, art 73d, discussed in ch 9.
22. Introduced into the EC Treaty by the Single European Act and taking effect from 1993.

removing the frontiers themselves. The Own Resources Decision of 1970[23] completed the internationalisation of the common customs tariff by providing that the duties collected are to form a common resource of the EC, and not part of the resources of the member states. With an EC-wide legal framework now in place in the guise of the Community Customs Code, the creation of a supranational levy is complete. The role of the member states is merely that of collection and enforcement agents.

2. Agricultural products

Agricultural products have been subject to specific EC action. Article 38 imposed on the EC the duty of creating a common agricultural policy (CAP). This has been done. Details of that policy are beyond the scope of this book,[24] save that the fiscal measures forming part of the policy must be noted. The CAP involves imposing tariff barriers against the import of agricultural products from third states. Two sets of levies have been established: a general tariff against external agricultural products, and specific levies on sugar and isoglucose. Since the Own Resources Decision of 1970, these levies have been treated as Community resources like other duties. However, they are seen not as fiscal measures for raising finance, but as measures to protect Community preference policies.

Within the EC, agricultural prices are regulated. These prices are adjusted by monetary compensation amounts. In the broad approach adopted in this book, these are also to be regarded as taxes because there is no option on an agricultural producer required to pay an MCA. Nonetheless, the CAP is a self-contained budget whereby the money collected is used to fund the food support budget. Funds are not therefore collected either for general budgetary purposes or with a view to revenue optimisation. In a recent case, it was held in Ireland that, for general legal purposes, MCAs are not taxes.[25] This decision appears to reflect the prevalent attitude to such payments. Border tax adjustments on foreign agricultural products are nonetheless clearly regarded as part of customs duties,[26] and require no further specific comment. For this reason,

23. See ch 3.
24. See F G Snyder, *The Law of the Common Agricultural Policy* (Sweet & Maxwell, 1985).
25. Byrne v Conroy, Irish High Court, [1997] 1 CMLR 595.
26. Community Customs Code, art 20, para 3(c).

and also because MCAs and agricultural levies are determined by reference only to the policies of the common agricultural policy, these payments are not further discussed save in the context of the EU's own resources.

3. Protecting free movement

The EC Treaty contains no express provisions on income taxation in the articles dealing with the free movement of persons, services and capital. The European Court has therefore to use the general empowering articles for the freedoms of movement to deal with tax questions. These enforce the general principle from article 6 that there shall be no discrimination within the EU on grounds of nationality. We noted in the previous chapter that EU member states do not discriminate in this way for tax purposes. What they actually do is discriminate on grounds of residence. In certain cases, the European Court has been satisfied that this is a disguised form of nationality discrimination. It has also concluded that some of this discrimination is not justified in EC law. As a result, even without express provisions, the Court has found that national tax laws offend EC law.

Under the Treaty of European Union, the member states introduced the first express mention of taxation to this part of the EC Treaty by adding, in article 73d, a proviso to the general freedom of movement of capital confirmed in article 73b. It does so by seeking to protect discrimination in national tax laws based solely on residence. We discuss in chapter 9 the effect of this provision.

Other measures relating to income taxes have been taken only by directives. These are based on the general powers to make directives given by article 100 of the EC Treaty rather than a specific provision.[27] This allows the EC to adopt measures 'binding as to the results to be achieved' but leaving to member states the choice of form and methods.[28] Although directives have been held by the European Court to be directly effective where they are sufficiently unconditional, clear and precise,[29] this still prevents the EC auth-

---

[27] 'The Council shall ... issue directives for the approximation of such laws, regulations or administrative provisions of the member states as directly affect the establishment or functioning of the common market.'

[28] EC Treaty, art 189.

[29] Weatherill and Beaumont, op cit note 8, ch 11.

orities moving towards unification of the law in a way that was possible for customs duties.[30]

4. Transport policy

The EC Treaty is also silent about tax aspects of transport policy. In practice, 'obstacles to the free movement of vehicles registered in one member state and used in another constitute one of the most sensitive problem areas for the movement of individuals within the Community'.[31] The divergent national practices for taxing passenger transport vehicles and heavy goods vehicles have also created obstacles. These can be as detailed as surcharging the fuel in the tank of a motor vehicle intending to drive through a state.[32] They range from the use of road tolls to the taxes charged for the use of vehicles. The arrival of the single market forced decisions to be taken on these matters by directive.[33] This was made partly under the general authority given to the Council to lay down common rules for international transport in article 75.[34]

5. Competition policy

Title V of the EC Treaty includes sections on competition policy, taxation, and approximation of laws. All three of these are important for the operation of taxation in the EU. The competition provisions of the Treaty do not raise tax considerations when dealing with the behaviour of EU business. Nonetheless, they do in respect both of state aid and of dumping and anti-competitive policies by non-member states.

Article 91 authorises the use of anti-dumping duties, but only in

---

30. They are enacted by regulations. A regulation is 'binding in its entirety and directly applicable in all member states': EC Treaty, art 189. The Community Customs Code is a regulation. See generally on EC legislation, Weatherill and Beaumont op cit note 8, ch 5.
31. A J Easson, *Taxation in the European Community* (Athlone Press, 1993), p 168. See also his comments at pp 172–7. See also P Farmer and E Lyal, *EC Tax Law* (OUP, 1994), pp 241–4.
32. Council Directive 68/297 regarding duty-free admission of fuel contained in fuel tanks of commercial vehicles (19 July 1968)(1968 JO L 175).
33. Council Directive 93/89 on the application by member states of taxes on certain vehicles used for the carriage of goods by road and tools and charges for the use of infrastructures (October 1993)(1993 OJ L 279/32).
34. EC Treaty, art 99 was also cited as authority. These are indirect taxes.

the transitional period during which the common customs tariff was being established. Now that the tariff is complete, the authority for anti-dumping duties, and countervailing duties, is granted by article 113, noted below.

Article 92 prohibits 'any aid granted by a member state or through state resources in any form whatsoever which distorts or threatens to distort competition'. This includes taxes, tax-free zones or reduced tax zones, special provisions relating to social taxes and benefits, or any other form of fiscal measure. It is proving to be an important buttress to the curbing of tax competition between states, and is considered in detail in chapter 10. This is, however, a sensitive area and the Community's record in preventing tax havens within the EU is not without blemishes.

The only part of the EC Treaty expressly flagged as dealing with tax provisions is chapter 2 of Title V. This consists of articles 95 to 99. Even then, two of the articles are now of little import. Article 97 is a transitional provision dealing with problems arising before VAT was introduced and is now only of historical interest. Article 98 allows limited action by the Council where there are export or import distortions between member states arising from charges that are not indirect taxes. No proposal has ever been made formally for its use.[35]

By contrast, articles 95 and 96 impose in clear mandatory form two of the fundamental obligations of the GATT.[36] Article 95 prohibits both fiscal discrimination and fiscal protectionism against foreign products. Article 96 prevents tax subsidies on exports to the territory of other member states by the repayment of any internal taxation. These are considered in Chapter 5. These provisions are buttressed by article 37, on commercial monopolies. Article 37 comes from the part of the Treaty dealing with the abolition of quantitative restrictions on the free movement of goods. However, unlike articles 30 to 36, the Court has held that article 37 does apply to fiscal measures.[37]

Article 99 is, at first sight, a most powerful provision. As first agreed in the EEC Treaty, it mandated the Council to 'adopt pro-

---

[35.] For a full analysis of these articles see Farmer and Lyal, op cit note 31, ch 3, 'Articles 95 to 99 of the Treaty'; Easson, op cit note 31, chs 2 and 3.

[36.] See ch 1. The GATT provisions in question are article III and article XVI.

[37.] *Rewe v Hauptzollamt Landau-Pfalz*, Case 45/75, [1976] ECR 181, dealing with a levy imposed on imported spirits to meet a share of the costs of the German monopoly sellers of spirits.

visions for the harmonisation of legislation' concerning all forms of indirect taxation, including specifically turnover taxes and excise duties. By leaving the means of harmonisation silent, the EEC was free to use either regulations or directives to achieve the intended purpose. What was the intended purpose? In the original version of the Treaty, this was determined by reference to the principles set out at the head of the Treaty. This led to much discussion about what harmonisation was needed. The answer, in the recitals to the First VAT Directive[38] in 1967 was:

> such harmonisation of legislation ... as will eliminate, as far as possible, factors that may distort conditions of competition ... and make it possible subsequently to achieve the aim of abolishing the imposition of tax on importation and the remission of tax on exportation in trade between member states.[39]

This statement still stands, but the text of article 99 was itself amended in the Single European Act to specify the purpose of the harmonisation. Harmonisation is now required only to the extent necessary to establish the single market by its launch date.[40] This more restricted approach is reflected in the single market measures, such as the directive on general arrangements for products subject to excise duties.[41] However, the increase in majority voting to ease the passage of single market measures was not applied to article 99 even with this restriction added. Beyond the extent of article 99, the available legislative power is that of article 100, which specifies its objective as approximation. Failing that, the only power available for action within the scope of the EU is the general power granted by article 235 to take 'the appropriate measures'.

---

38. Directive 67/227. The formal title is the First Directive on the Harmonisation of Legislation of Member States concerning Turnover Taxes. The authority for the measure is given as art 99 and art 100.
39. The final recital added that 'it is not possible to foresee at present how and within what period' the further aim would be achieved. As we see in ch 5, that is still true at the time of writing.
40. The launch date having passed, is it possible to argue that art 99 is now spent and that new measures cannot therefore be proposed under this article?
41. Council Directive 92/12/EEC (25 February 1992)(1992 OJ L 76/1), expressed to be made specifically under art 99.

6. Harmonisation, approximation or whatever

The Community Customs Code is presumably a measure for achieving uniformity.[42] VAT, as we have seen, is a measure of harmonisation,[43] as are the measures dealing with excise duties. Various direct tax directives are examples of approximation, while the regulation relating to social security contributions is a coordination measure.[44] This categorisation suggests differences between the processes involved, and in particular between harmonisation and approximation.[45] Neither amount to the same thing as unification or 'uniformisation'[46] but what do they amount to?[47] An attempt at unpicking the meaning might contrast positive harmonisation or approximation with negative harmonisation or approximation. While some measures are actively imposing new rules – presumably with some harmony if not uniformity – others are merely removing differences between national systems but putting nothing in their place. Is the repeal of inconsistent measures a harmonisation measure? This approach to interpretation does not seem to have been adopted.

The terms are widely used elsewhere in EC law, but in the fiscal context it would appear that only limited weight can be placed on any particular nuance of the terms. Thus, in one pair of cases,[48] the European Court referred to the 'harmonisation or approximation' of VAT without discriminating between the terms. Even more loosely, in the *Asscher* case,[49] the Advocate General stated:

---

42. The term used in art 113, which is the legal basis for the Code along with arts 100a and 28.
43. Note, however, that the title to the Sixth VAT Directive includes the phrases 'common system of value added tax: uniform basis of assessment'.
44. Under EC Treaty, art 51.
45. The French terms are, respectively, harmonisation and rapprochement. See D Berlin, *Droit Fiscal Communautaire* (Presses Universitaires de France, 1988), p 221 for a discussion of this terminology.
46. Berlin's French term – which sounds as though it ought to be English (see previous note)! Perhaps it is (see next note)!
47. However, in *Roget's Thesaurus*, at 780.4, uniformise and harmonise are put together as similar terms, along with regularise, equalise, symmetrise, equilibrise, homogenise and standardise.
48. *Mol v Inspecteur der Invoerrechten en Accijnzen*, Case 269/86, [1988] ECR 3627 and *Happy Family v Inspecteur der Omzetbelasting*, Case 289/86, [1988] ECR 3655. These were cited by the Advocate General to this effect in *Bergandi v Directeur General* Case 252/86, [1991] STC 529.
49. *Asscher v Staatsecretaris van Financien* Case C-107/94, [1996] STC 1025, at para 53, p 1033.

Article 99 of the Treaty explicitly gives the Council powers of harmonisation in the field of indirect taxation alone. Laws relating to direct taxation may be harmonised ... under article 100 of the Treaty ...

The precise nuance is further complicated by the federalist sentiments that some see behind the term 'harmonisation' but not behind the term 'approximation'. Others do not sense this aspect of the meaning. Perhaps the debate is best left as expressed by a leading expert in the field at a recent meeting, when referring to 'tax harmonisation, approximation, or whatever'.

In practice, the problem is resolved by another aspect of both article 99 and article 100. Both retain the fiscal veto. Unless all states want action, it will not occur. If they all want action, there is not likely to be any substantive challenge to the precise meaning of the terms in these articles.

7. Economic and monetary policy

The effect of the policy on EMU and moves to a single currency are indirect, but challenge tax policy rather than the details of tax laws. At the centre of the EMU strategy is the obligation on member states to avoid excessive government deficits.[50] Put crudely, this means that taxes have to meet expenditures. It is, of course, not quite so simple as that, but EMU imposes a constraint on all governments to raise taxes or to reduce expenditure, or both. The dynamics of public spending in the member states are, in the long term, driving social expenditure up but driving taxes down.[51] They therefore impose pressure on all states to ensure that they impose and collect taxes efficiently. The dilemma, in the European context, is that most of the successful kinds of tax reform, such as abolishing customs duties and removing withholding taxes on cross-border dividends, result in reduced taxes. The logic of EMU must be that this negative approach is reversed, or member states must take their own initiatives to increase taxes. On this, as we have seen, the EC Treaty is largely silent.

Will the adoption of a single currency make any difference? It will allow member states to scale down the use of the complicated

---

[50.] EC Treaty, art 104c, para 1.
[51.] Because of the increasing number of people on benefit, and not working, for old age reasons. See ch 1.

laws that some of them have to deal with multi-currency accounting for profits. It will also increase tax competition on savings, as tax will be exposed as the only variant[52] on whether an individual saves money in one EU state using the Euro rather than another. From that will follow a difficulty for some states in deciding how their tax jurisdictional rules should be defined in an open and unified monetary economy.

Once a single currency is adopted, an individual will have no problems in having earnings remitted direct to a foreign bank account. He or she could borrow money, arrange a pension, and carry out any other financial transaction outside the tax jurisdiction in which he or she lives.[53] If there is a tax advantage in doing that for either jurisdictional or enforcement reasons, what will stop it happening? We shall see in the closing chapters that the current logic of EC law is that a taxpayer can challenge any adverse effect on him or her caused by discrimination. Governments have no counteracting right under EC law to capture any personal advantage obtained from such a status. Free movers can complain against detriment. Free riders can keep their gains.[54]

8. Common commercial policy

The common commercial policy both builds on, and strengthens, the EU's customs union. Article 113 imposes a requirement that member states adopt a uniform customs tariff and a common approach to dumping and subsidies. In Chapter 4 we see that these common approaches are now fully in place. Further, the power to act under this article is not subject to the fiscal veto.[55] The continued development of the external aspects of the customs union cannot be blocked by a small minority. This is the only aspect of taxation where progress can be made without a complete consensus.

52. Bank charges could also be a variant, but competition is likely to neutralise these. The previous distorting factors were exchange control, charges for the conversion of currency, and the risk of currency depreciation, all of which will have been removed.

53. This has been happening for some time between Belgium and Luxembourg, where there is already a common currency. See ch 9.

54. See D Williams, 'Asscher: the European Court and the power to destroy', (1997) EC Tax Review 4.

55. EC Treaty, art 113, para 4 provides that voting on measures under this article is by a qualified majority. This, in effect, means a two-thirds majority but states have weighted votes: EC Treaty, art 148. Individual anti-dumping measures require only a simple majority.

9. Other policies

Most of the other policies required or facilitated by the EC Treaty have a fiscal element, but the usual reticence on tax matters continues. Express mention of taxation issues appear in two articles. Article 130f sets the objective of strengthening research and development activities. Encouragement is given to the increase of co-operation between undertakings. To that end, the Community 'shall support their efforts to cooperate . . . in particular through . . . the removal of legal and fiscal obstacles to that cooperation'. While this may be commended as an objective, it provides neither directly nor indirectly any specific positive measure to achieve that objective. However, it might be that a discriminatory measure might be attacked more readily because of this statement.

Tax is explicitly mentioned in connection with environmental taxation. The EU sets itself the task of developing a Community policy on the environment in article 130r. That policy is to be based on four principles: the precautionary principle, the principle of taking preventive action rather than remedial action, the principle of rectifying environmental damage at source, 'and that the polluter shall pay'. This is an express recognition of the principle that is driving environmental tax policy. If the market does not impose the price of the environmental damage on the polluter – which it often does not – then taxation may properly be used to impose that cost. This is to ensure that the price of a product includes the cost to the environment of the use of that product.

Power is given to the Council and Commission to act in furtherance of this policy. It will normally do so by qualified majority, but it is specifically provided that where the proposed measure is primarily of a fiscal nature, then the Council must act unanimously.[56] This maintains the fiscal veto over all tax measures that may have internal effect. The result of this provision is that the proposal by the Commission to introduce a carbon tax in furtherance of this policy has not been adopted for want of unanimity.[57]

---

[56]. EC Treaty, art 130s, para 2.
[57]. Amended proposal for a Council Directive introducing a tax on carbon dioxide emissions and energy, COM (95) 172(10 May 1995), made under arts 99 and 130s. See also EC Commission, *A Community strategy to limit carbon dioxide emissions and to improve energy efficiency*, SEC(91)1744 (14 October 1991); M Pearson and S Smith, *The European Carbon Tax: an assessment of the European Commission's proposals* (IFS, 1991).

10. Foreign relations

One of the most interesting aspects of EC and EU laws is the way in which they operate outside the territory of the EU through both international agreements and by example. The EC Treaty makes explicit provision for international agreements that may have fiscal effects. A major mechanism for this is the association agreement, whereby one or more states agree to cooperate with the EU in economic and social relations.[58] In part this follows from the first of the objectives set by the Treaty for such agreements. This requires member states to offer to third states the same terms as they offer other member states.[59] This brings provisions such as article 95 into the context of external trade. This must be reciprocal,[60] thus requiring the other states to adopt the same approach as that used in EC law. The same approach is taken with regard to freedom of movement.

An association agreement is also to be based on the progressive abolition of customs duties on both sides, subject to specific and limited safeguards and to the acceptance of a non-discriminatory tariff.[61] The underlying pattern behind an association agreement is therefore the creation of a free trade area with safeguards against hidden fiscal discrimination or protectionism replacing the customs duties that have been abolished.

Although it is beyond the scope of this book, it may also be noted that EC tax law is imitated by most of the EU's neighbours. Many of them have adopted the EC form of VAT, although there is no express obligation in any agreement to do so. They have also adopted forms of direct taxation based on those in use in the EU. This is to encourage foreign direct investment.

11. Budgetary measures

The primary fiscal obligation on the EU is to provide for its own budget wholly from own resources. The Treaty is, however, silent about the nature of these resources.[62] These are discussed in the

---

[58.] EC Treaty, art 131. See D McGoldrick, *International Relations Law of the EU*, in this series (1997), p 182.

[59.] EC Treaty, art 132, point 1.

[60.] EC Treaty, art 132, point 2.

[61.] EC Treaty, art 133.

[62.] EC Treaty, art 201.

next chapter. Nonetheless, the Commission cannot either propose or amend any activity unless it can show that the activity can be financed out of own resources.[63]

12. General provisions

The final provisions of the Treaty contain the obligation on member states to enter into negotiations with a view of securing for the benefit of their nationals the abolition of double taxation within the Community.[64] This, as we saw in the last chapter, is largely undertaken through the auspices of the OECD. Otherwise, there is nothing of immediate relevance.

The European Atomic Energy Community (Euratom) Treaty[65]

The EC Treaty was parallelled by the Euratom Treaty, for the specific purposes of establishing a regime to handle atomic energy within the EEC. The lead taken by the ECSC in giving direct taxing powers to the executive authorities of the ECSC was not repeated in the Euratom Treaty. It shares the same fiscal mechanism as the EEC (and is now merged with the EEC into the EC). There is therefore no new feature of the Euratom Treaty within the scope of this book save its borrowing powers.

The Treaty of European Union[66]

The amendments made by the TEU to the EEC Treaty (including the renaming of that treaty as the EC Treaty) have been noted in the above analysis. The TEU itself adds little new to the discussion of tax matters. There is nothing of relevance concerning the establishment of a common foreign and security policy. Common justice and home affairs policies are relevant because of the enforcement of taxes. The TEU expressly recognises that customs

---

63. EC Treaty, art 201a.
64. EC Treaty, art 220.
65. Signed at the same time as the EEC Treaty at Rome.
66. Signed at Maastricht, 7 February 1992.

cooperation is a matter of common interest, as is police cooperation with respect to certain aspects of customs cooperation.[67] This is not, however, extended to enforcement of other tax laws. Nonetheless, where a taxpayer breaks the criminal law, this is a matter of common interest.[68]

[67.] TEU, art K1, points 8, 9.
[68.] TEU, art K1, point 7 includes judicial cooperation in criminal matters.

CHAPTER THREE

The EU's own taxes

In 1997 the total annual budget of the European Union institutions reached 90 billion Ecus.[1] The EC Treaty requires that this be financed wholly from own resources.[2] Further, the Commission is prevented from proposing action that cannot be funded from own resources.[3] To meet its expenditure, the EU has borrowing powers in its own right.[4] It also has minor sources of income from charges, fines, dues, and interest payments. In total, these are of limited significance to overall budget revenue requirements. Therefore the main funds of the EU must be derived from alternative fiscal sources. These are the sources known as 'own resources'. This chapter is concerned with identifying these resources. It touches only briefly on the long and fascinating history of a struggle for budgetary control between the member states and the various EU institutions. That history is worth noting, because the argument continues and the fundamental issues about funding the EU are yet to be resolved.

The struggle for budgetary power[5]

When the original six member states set up the ECSC in 1951, they gave the High Authority the power to raise the funds it

1. At the time of writing, 1 Ecu was worth about £0.70, or DM 1.95.
2. EC Treaty, art 201.
3. EC Treaty, art 201a.
4. The Euratom Treaty gives specific borrowing powers: art 172. The EC Treaty contains no express powers, and Council Regulations authorising loans are made under EC Treaty, art 235. See D Strasser, *The Finances of Europe* (European Communities, Luxembourg, 1992), p 100. For an economic analysis, see D Swann, *The Economics of the Common Market* (Penguin, 8th edition, 1995), ch 4, 'The Community budget and borrowing powers'.
5. See ch 2 (under this title) of Strasser, op cit note 4.

needed from levies on the forms of production under its control. They also allowed it to borrow on the market.[6] The levy was, in effect, a (sales) tax of up to 1 per cent (higher if the Council agreed) of the stocks of coal and steel products within the ECSC's jurisdiction. Taken with the borrowing powers that the Treaty also gave to the High Authority, this gave the ECSC fiscal autonomy. The power to exercise that authority was therefore left in the hands of the institutions of the Community. This was a formidable precedent and it still operates.

The member states did not give fiscal autonomy to the EEC and Euratom when they set them up in 1957. Even by then there was less enthusiasm for the supranational approach to budgetary matters that had existed in the immediate aftermath of the Second World War. Articles 99 to 209a of the EC Treaty contain the main rules. They provide for the adoption by the European Council and the European Parliament of an annual budget for each calendar year.

The finances of the EC and EU have traditionally been expenditure-led. In other words, the budget is determined by reference to the proposed expenditure and the resources are then found to meet this expenditure. In the early days of the EEC, this approach arose in part because much of the expenditure of the EEC was compulsory. It was a direct result of the legal instruments establishing the common agricultural policy, and no institution or state had any discretion in it. Reforms of the CAP have reduced the compulsory element of the budget to half the total, and have therefore opened the budget to greater political debate. This debate was, however, curbed by the TEU imposing the requirement that all activities must have available funding. The EU must, in other words, balance its budget. Nonetheless, the process of setting the expenditure budget is still very important.

Procedure for adopting the budget is set out in the original EEC Treaty. It has been controversial, and has been amended by subsequent treaties. The first amendment was in the First Budgetary Treaty of 1970,[7] and several others have followed, notably the TEU.[8] In its current form, the budgetary process is a compromise

---

6. ECSC Treaty (Paris, 1961), art 49.
7. Signed at Luxembourg, 22 April 1970.
8. See also the Second Budgetary Treaty, signed at Brussels, 22 July 1975, and the Single European Act.

between the powers of the Council, representing the states, and Parliament, directly elected by the people. The detail of the compromise, and its workings in practice, are beyond the scope of the present study.[9] They evidence a battle of wills over the levels and purposes of expenditure of the EU.

In the original 1957 EEC Treaty, the matter of raising the funds was expressed in the traditional manner for international organisations: by a differential levy on the individual member states. Article 200 listed two separate proportions of levies, one for the general fund and one for the European Social Fund. The article authorised the alteration of the scale by a unanimous decision of the Council. It was left to the member states to decide how to fund their individual shares of the budget.

Although the EEC Treaty gave the Community borrowing powers, this was clearly an unstable position. It meant that a single state has the power in any year to bring the budgetary arrangements of the EU to a complete halt. This was revealed in the early years of the EEC, when the French adopted their 'empty chair' approach to the Community. This aspect of the budgetary problem was finally solved in 1970 (although not fully implemented until 1980) as part of the Luxembourg Agreements that brought the French back into the EEC. The solution was to replace this flawed annual mechanism with measures to give the EEC its own resources, and thereby some stability.

Creating the EEC's own resources

In 1970, the central budgetary decision facing the EEC was how to finance the common agricultural policy (CAP). There was also a need to meet the other – smaller – aspects of the budget, and a further need to ensure some continuity in the process. The 1970 solution consisted of a series of interlinked agreements and decisions that established a separate financing system for the EEC. This sidestepped the threat of the EEC running out of funds.

The key agreement took the form of Council Decision 70/243.[10]

---

9. See Strasser, op cit note 4; EC Commission, *Community Public Finance* (1991); S Weatherill and P Beaumont, *EC Law* (Penguin, second edition, 1995), ch 4, 'The European Parliament'.
10. Of 28 April 1970 (OJ 1970 L94/1).

This Decision broke away from the caution of the original EEC Treaty text, and gave the EEC its own financial resources. These were to be of three kinds:

(1) the agricultural levies collected by the EEC;
(2) the customs duties collected under the Common Customs Tariff, and
(3) a percentage of the VAT collected by the member states under the First and Second VAT Directives.

This Decision was ratified by the then member states, but was never formalised by an amendment to the Treaties.[11]

The structure of the 1970 Decision has remained as the core of the approach for providing the EU's budgetary resources to date.[12] It proved, however, to be inadequate. It also proved, in the view of the UK, to be unfair to the UK. This was because, from the start of UK membership, the UK's contribution to the budget was, in its view, excessive as compared with the expenditure on the UK.[13] In part, this was because the UK's contribution based on its VAT was higher, while the revenues it derived from the CAP were lower, than a 'fair' share might suggest.

Eventually, in 1984 at the Fontainebleau Council, agreement was reached on a solution to both these problems. The UK was to have a rebate from 1985 in its budgetary contribution, and the EEC was to have its budget expanded. The expansion came in part by increasing the rate of the levy on VAT receipts payable to the EEC by member states. This was also adjusted to provide a rebate to the UK, and a lesser rebate to Germany. The rest of the fiscal deficit was made up by a so-called fourth resource. This was a re-introduction of the levy direct on member states, but in a more dynamic way than that originally provided. Henceforth, the levy was to be apportioned between the member states not by reference to a fixed percentage, but by reference to the size of the economy of the member state, as compared with those of the other members. This

---

11. A Commission proposal for a separate treaty governing the raising of its own resources by the EEC was put forward in 1975, but not accepted by the Council. See Strasser, op cit, note 5, p 32.
12. The 1970 Decision stood until being replaced by a similar Decision in 1985, and a further Decision in 1988. The most recent Decision is Decision 94/728 of 31 October 1994 (1994 OJ L 293/9), taking account of the expanded membership.
13. This point was first made in the accession negotiations in 1970, so was not a surprise to anyone.

compromise was given effect by the Decision of the Council in 1985 amending the 1970 Decision.

The 1985 Decision was a positive political step, but a constitutional retreat. The political step came because it removed (for a time) a major cause for UK grumbling about the EC. The UK was never as ready as some states to accept the argument that a balance between contributions and benefits was not an appropriate approach to take to evaluating the finances of the EEC. It had, throughout its early membership, maintained that approach, under three governments. It chose to agree to resolve the complaint by paying less, rather than receiving more. During the latter stages of agreement, Germany associated itself with that complaint. The result was therefore a cut in EEC activity and an institutionalising of the 'fair shares' approach to the budget.

The constitutional retreat was in the failure of the member states to make good the budget deficit fully by a transfer of new methods of resourcing to the EEC institutions. Instead, the deficit has to be financed by a levy on members. Member states also demanded that the Commission cost all new expenditure, and that there be an indication of any increase in the cost to member states of new policies. This undoubtedly weakened the EEC as an independent entity, although the approach adopted reflected similar changes taking place in the attitude to tax raising and spending at the national level, particularly in Germany and the UK.

Since the 1985 settlement there have been minor adjustments in the approach taken between the then member states, and alterations to reflect the addition of the new members. Behind them, the 1970 settlement, as adjusted in 1985, 1988, and 1994, provides the current methods of raising the EU funds for the EEC and Euratom aspects of the budget.[14] The ECSC self-financing budget remains. We will look in turn briefly at each of the four elements of the current EU revenue resources, as based on the 1994 Own Resources Decision.

1. Agricultural levies

The Commission receives all agricultural levies imposed by the EU as one of its 'traditional' resources.[15] The tradition technically

---

14. The Euratom budget was merged with the EEC Budget in 1970.
15. Own Resources Decision, art 2(1)(a).

dates only to 1970, but it also reflects the self-contained nature of the CAP. Where an agricultural levy is imposed, for example, on the import of food from a third state, then the funds go into the EU budget no matter who collects them. This applies to three kinds of levy, and all related payments:

(a) agricultural levies, premiums and compensatory amounts imposed on trade with nonmember states;[16]
(b) sugar levies paid by sugar companies as part of the sugar market; and
(c) isoglucose levies paid in parallel with the sugar levies.[17]

CAP levies are customs duties on imported (or exported) food. While the rates and incidence are determined by the CAP, the process of imposition is now regulated in entirety by the Community Customs Code. Consequently, we will not discuss these levies separately in this book. The sugar levy is technically separate, because it is a fiscal adjustment to control the market for sugar within the EU. However, it is usually accounted for with the CAP levies, and is also now partly under the Community Customs Code procedures. The isoglucose levies raise an interesting prospect of the EU imposing its own turnover or sales taxes. That it provides a precedent for such a tax does not appear to have been discussed.

Within the EU budget, the levels of agricultural levies fluctuate, as does the level of subsidy. However, reform of the CAP has removed some premiums for EU farmers and others on production in excess of world prices. As a result, the cost of the CAP has dropped with the income from levies. Successful reform of the CAP therefore leads to both sides of the CAP budget declining.

2. Customs duties

Customs duties collected at the common frontiers of the EU on imports are entirely Community own resources.[18] This covers duties levied under article 113 of the EC Treaty and those levied under the ECSC Treaty. Although, for instance, British customs officers collect the duties on goods entering the territory of the EU through

---

16. This is primarily aimed at levies on imports, but also covers levies on exports: Case 95/75 of 9 March 1976 Effem v Hauptzollamt Lüneberg [1976] 2 CMLR 86.
17. These are technically not agricultural products, but are 'like' products. The authority for the levy is Council Regulation 1111/77 (17 May 1977) (1977 OJ L134/7).
18. Own Resources Decision, art 2(1)(b). Export duties would also be Community resources but, aside from agricultural levies, there are none.

the UK, they do so as agents of the EU acting entirely under EU law. Only local aspects of the procedure are British. This was not so at the establishment of the EEC, when customs duties were retained by member states. Until the Own Resources Decisions were taken, only customs duties levied under the ECSC Treaty were a Community own resource. Although the customs duties collected by the UK are still officially listed in the UK annual budget as UK taxes, this is now wrong. The money is remitted to the EU. This also applies to anti-dumping and countervailing duties.

Consequently, no national economy can benefit from any distortion in the operation of the Common Customs Tariff. 'Duty-free' provisions for individuals sold to customers outside the EU may benefit individual travellers, but states will receive no benefit from the customs duty. Conversely, the Commission has a clear incentive to see that customs duties are imposed and collected effectively. There is a competitive, and also a cooperative, reason for individual member states to help the Commission in that aim.

3. Value added tax

The third resource, agreed in 1970, is nominally a levy on the VAT collected by member states. Adoption of this approach to Community resources was a major reason behind the member states adopting the Sixth VAT Directive.[19] As noted above, this was felt not to be 'fair', and led to what has been called politely 'the British problem'.[20] The original plan was to levy the VAT receipts of member states by reference to a set rate (the call-in rate) applied to the VAT receipts of the member states.

Because there was no agreement on the rates of VAT, it was felt to be unfair in 1970 to levy the own resource as a percentage of the VAT actually collected by the member states. Instead, it was levied by applying the agreed percentage call-in rate to the VAT assessment base for the member states.[21] The assessment base is also removed from the actual taxable base for VAT in the member states. Instead, it is an assessment based on the net receipts of member states adjusted by a statistically weighted average.[22] A fur-

---

[19.] See ch 5.
[20.] EC Commission, *Community Public Finance* (1991), p 21, col 1.
[21.] Own Resource Decision, art 2, para 4.
[22.] For the precise definitions see Council Regulation 1553/89 (29 May 1989) (1989 OJ L159/9).

ther problem arose because the assessment base has a different extent in different states because of the differences in their economies. That is complicated for the UK and Ireland. They include a range of supplies within the VAT assessment base but zero-rate them.[23] The response was to cap the size of the assessment base. It was limited to 55 per cent of the GNP of the member state. Following the 1994 settlement of own resources, it was agreed to reduce the extent of this resource. As part of that, the cap is slowly being reduced so that it reaches 50 per cent in 1999. The call-in rate has varied over time, and is also now being reduced from a high point of 1.4 per cent. It will reach 1 per cent in 1999. The two reductions together cut the significance of the VAT resource to a marked extent.

The UK correction requires a calculation of how much it receives from the Community budget in any year as compared with its percentage share of the total budget. Two thirds of this difference is deducted from the UK's share of the VAT third resource by reducing the UK call-in rate. The resultant imbalance between the other states is also adjusted by a secondary adjustment to the payment made by Germany. Consequently, the call-in rate on VAT varies from state to state, as does the VAT assessment base. It is ironic that a tax introduced to be neutral as between taxpayers is therefore not neutral between states. This arrangement, and the solution to the 'British problem' within it, is viewed as temporary and will be reviewed on the expiry of the 1994 Own Resources Decision.

4. The fourth resource

By 1988, the three resources were inadequate for the planned EC budget, and another resource or resources had to be found. The result was an income tax, although it is not called that. The usual name is the 'fourth resource'. It is 'the application of a rate ... to the sum of all the member states' GNP established in accordance with Community rules'.[24] Use of GNP as the base ensured that the richer countries paid more. A cap is placed on total own resources

---

23. The result of the unadjusted formula in the 1970 Decision is therefore to impose an EU levy on items such as food, books, and domestic homes which are zero-rated (and, in effect, subsidised) in the UK. That has the unintended effect of requiring the UK to pay a levy on something on which it does not collect tax.
24. Own Resources Decision, art 2, para 1(d).

to be transferred to the EU by member states.[25] This cap is also expressed as a percentage of GNP, and therefore specifically caps the amount payable under the fourth resource.

The level of this resource is kept in check by the overall reduction planned in the EU budget over the medium term future, with a ceiling planned of 1.335 per cent of GNP. In part, this reflects the reduction in the size of the CAP and the compulsory part of the budget.

5. The ECSC levies

When the institutions of the three European Communities were combined, so were the budgets of the EEC and Euratom. The budget of the ECSC remained distinct. This is partly because the levies that the Commission (taking over from the High Authority) can collect are based on treaty provisions. Those provisions remain in effect, and they constitute a separate fifth resource for the ECSC budget alone.[26]

6. The EU income tax

Besides these resources, the EU introduced its own internal taxes and charges. These reflect the immunity of the EU and its staff from national taxation in the member states. Immunity was granted by the Protocol on the Privileges and Immunities of the European Communities in 1965,[27] and remains. Article 13 provides that:

> Officials and other servants of the Communities shall be liable to a tax for the benefit of the Communities on salaries, wages and emoluments paid to them by the Communities . . .

This requirement is regarded as reciprocal to the immunity that such staff enjoy from national taxes. The tax is a 20 per cent income tax on all earnings.[28]

---

25. Own Resources Decision, art 3.
26. Own Resources Decision, art 2, para 2.
27. Signed at Brussels, 8 April 1965.
28. B Terra and P Wattel observe dryly that 'when this levy was introduced, the salaries were raised by 25 per cent, compensating the new levy' (*European Tax Law* (Kluwer, 1993), p 2). That was, however, a one-off adjustment.

The EU as taxpayer

To complete the picture, we should note the status of the EU itself as a taxpayer. Does it have to make contributions to the member states? No. The EU is exempted from national direct taxes and in-direct taxes, save for incidental taxes and dues.[29] It is also formally exempt from customs duties (although, in practice, there are none).[30] Officers, officials, and servants of the EU are exempt from national taxes on salaries, wages and emoluments paid by the EU,[31] as are members of the Commission,[32] and judges and staff of the European Court.[33] The privileges are, however, those of the EU and its institutions, not of the individuals receiving them. Nor do they extend to those whose employments are related to the EU but are not directly within the scope of the Treaty and Protocol.[34]

Conclusion

Little attention is paid, in most accounts of the EU, to the taxes of the EU itself. They are an interesting range of levies. The EU is en-titled to all trade taxes from imports and exports. It is entitled to industry-based levies on an unlikely set of products: coal, steel, sugar, isoglucose. It also collects income tax from its staff. In other words, there is in place the basis for an EU tax system. It is, how-ever, totally inadequate for the needs of the EU. The balance is made up by the federal technique of revenue sharing applied to VAT, and the standard international technique of contributions based on economic strength.

The question of fiscal federalism – who raises the taxes to pay for the EU budget – is therefore currently solved by a compromise within a compromise. If the EU is to gain anything approaching federal status, it will need to develop its own tax revenues. Those it has are slowly wasting away as the total budget of the EU is

29. Protocol, art 3.
30. Protocol, art 4.
31. Protocol, art 13.
32. Protocol, art 20.
33. Protocol, art 21.
34. *Hurd v Jones*, Case 44/84, [1986] STC 127, concerning a UK national teaching at a European School in the UK. The European Court ruled that he was not within the scope of the immunities granted because the basis for the immunity was not the Treaty.

being increased. This is an unstable position in the longer term, and another budgetary crisis will occur at some time.[35] It will be forced, if for no other reason, by the question of enlargement.[36] Formally, the present decision is to be reconsidered for the end of 1999.[37]

If the EU has a direct call on tax revenues, they cease to be revenues of the member states. This is sensitive for two reasons. First, states are being forced to cut their taxes for both monetary and competitive reasons. Why should they give more to the EU, when they get less? Second, taxes are about taking money from people, as the opening quotation of the book reminded us. Will this be accepted unless there is direct democratic involvement in determining how these taxes are to be levied? Another pressure is that of fiscal coherence between the EU and the member states. There should be some consistency of approach to both EU revenues and national revenues if the policies behind one are not to counteract the policies behind the other.

[35]. Commission President Santer regarded it in 1997 as one of the four main challenges to the EU, along with reforming the Treaties, EMU, and enlargement: *The Economist*, May 10–16 1997, p 40.

[36]. The Commission are to table proposals for reform at the same time as tabling proposals to carry through the enlargement.

[37]. 1994 Own Resources Decision, art 10.

CHAPTER FOUR

The EU frontier taxes

> If you do as you've been told, 'likely there's a chance
> You'll be give a dainty doll, all the way from France,
> With a cap of Valenciennes, and a velvet hood -
> A present from the Gentlemen, along o' being good.
>
> R Kipling, *A Smuggler's Song*

To a modern European traveller, there is nothing spectacular in 'duty free' travel across European frontiers. The customs union that lies at the heart of the economic structure of the EU often seems of little importance. The only distortions that are now of significance to the modern tourist are the continuing differences of tax levels on tobacco and alcoholic drinks. This is because of the success of the European customs union as a central part of the EU itself. It represents a sharp change from the position 50 years ago. Moreover, the position 50 years ago was not far different from that 500 years ago. The customs union represents a break away from the fiscal policies that prevailed through much of Europe's history.

The historic importance of customs duties

For 500 of the last 600 years (and probably more) customs duties were one of the main source of royal/government revenues in England and then the UK.[1] The taxes on the movement of goods into, and from, England were the surest of our taxes. That is, of course,

---

1. While it is beyond the scope of this book to discuss the issue, the Act of Union between England and Scotland in 1701 was, for the large part, concerned with creating a customs union between the two states, harmonising their taxes, and removing other barriers to the creation of a single market between the two states.

reflected in their name: duties of custom. Much of the rest of the Crown's extraordinary revenues (as our taxes used to be called) came from excise duties. Until this century, taxes based on income were fiscally insignificant. By contrast, customs duties are today irrelevant to the British government as a form of taxation.[2] The change over the last century has been profound.

Much the same story appears in the fiscal history of other European states. As noted above,[3] the Europe of the EC's founders had replaced divisions of war by divisions of peace. State frontiers were formidable barriers. The income taxes and social security taxes that now dominate revenue raising activities were created in western European countries only as they emerged from war. In previous centuries, taxation of goods provided most state revenues. In particular, customs duties and tolls charged when goods were moved formed a reliable core of the tax base.

A major reason for the historic dependence on customs duties was a lack of alternatives. In less advanced societies, collecting taxes on intangibles such as services or incomes is difficult. Tax collectors seeking to tax income need records and administration. Taxing tangibles is far easier to enforce. Taxing tangibles on the move is easier still. In a survey of developing states a few years ago, it was found that the most important source of taxes was still customs duties.[4]

There were two sharply different consequences of this form of taxation. The first, at state level, was a need to clamp down on tax evasion. The way to evade customs duties was, of course, smuggling. Smuggling is again in the news in Britain with stories of the van loads of tobacco and beer being bought in mainland Europe and ferried to Britain.[5] Historically, it always was a major problem in frontier areas. The state authorities therefore demanded strong anti-smuggling measures and, in Britain, a tough waterguard force, as the frontier patrols in our island state were called. In other words, the dependence of the state on customs duties led inevitably

---

[2.] Duties amount to about 1 per cent of taxes collected, but these revenues go direct to the EU, and do not form part of British government revenues: see ch 2.

[3.] Ch 2.

[4.] See the survey in 1983 by V Tanzi in N Stern et al, *The Theory of Taxation in Developing Countries*.

[5.] This follows a long and – for some – romantic tradition of the kind portrayed in Faulkner's novel, *Moonfleet*, or in the Kipling poem quoted at the head of the chapter.

to the need to identify, strengthen and guard state frontiers. The revenue needs of the state had the direct effect of requiring the territory of the state to be isolated from other states. Conversely, the abolition of frontier taxes – as has now been achieved within the EU – removes much of the previous significance of frontiers, and of the need to isolate state territories.

The internal effect of high customs tariffs is economic.[6] Businesses within a customs tariff area are protected from outside competition by the size of the customs tariff. High government demands for revenue meant high tariffs, and therefore significant protection for local industries. Economists argue that protected industries are inefficient industries, and that the result of a customs tariff is economic inefficiency.[7] This could – and did – work in two ways. Import duties made foreign goods more expensive compared with domestic equivalents. At the extreme, tariffs of, say, 500 per cent effectively prevented foreign competition and kept outmoded industries from bankruptcy. Export duties had the same effect in reverse. By imposing taxes on exporters, the exports were rendered less competitive in foreign markets, and therefore would encourage sales at home. Tariffs on raw materials were often lower than those on finished goods. A further result was therefore the local manufacture of goods that could have been manufactured more efficiently elsewhere.

A natural consequence of the medieval practice of taxing movements of goods was therefore the strengthening of nation states as entities insulated from each other both geographically and economically. This also had a spillover effect in people's tastes and choices. The rich could – and did – afford the luxury of conspicuously importing and consuming items that bore penal rates of import duty, while the poor bought local goods in the local market without, perhaps, realising that there were better alternatives elsewhere.

6. D Swann, *The Economics of the Common Market* (Penguin, 8th edition, 1995), ch 4, 'Tariff barriers and the customs union', discusses the basic theory of a customs union.
7. But note the reservation that customs unions are not unambiguously beneficial reported by Swann, op cit note 6, p 127, because trade gains are offset by trade diversions.

The worldwide shift from customs duties

During the last half-century, the world's traders worked hard to remove tariff barriers and to create free trade. The first significant attempt to do this was only a partial success. It was planned to establish an International Trade Organisation (ITO) as one of the specialised agencies of the United Nations in the aftermath of the Second World War. States failed to agree on an ITO, but they did agree on the – General Agreement of Tariffs and Trade (GATT).

The GATT facilitated free trade in a number of ways, but in particular it sought to remove the adverse effects of tariff barriers in three ways. First, it required states to apply any tariff barrier on a most-favoured-nation basis.[8] In other words, states could not set discriminatory tariffs on the same goods coming from different exporting states. Second, it provided a mechanism for the overall reduction of the levels of tariffs. Third, it offered a means by which states could standardise the ways in which tariffs were imposed. This aspect was itself of considerable importance. It led to the creation of a Customs Cooperation Council (CCC).[9]

Fifty years on, GATT has now been replaced by GATT 1994.[10] GATT also now has an international body supervising the treaty regime: the World Trade Organisation (WTO). The EU is a member of the WTO in its own right, as are the member states. The EU is also a member of the World Customs Organisation (WCO) that has replaced the CCC. The WCO now supervises an impressive series of agreements about the operation of customs law. Because this law is accepted fully within the EU as the core of its own customs law, we must note the current extent of international agreements on customs law.

Anti-dumping and countervailing duties

The original GATT laid a framework of principles to reduce both the fiscal and protective barriers created by customs laws. One particular problem is the protective use of customs duties. Where a

---

8. GATT, art I.
9. Formally constituted by the Treaty of Brussels in 1952.
10. Formally, GATT 1994 is the original 1948 GATT together with the annexes and other agreements concluded as a result of the Uruguay Round of tariff negotiations accepted in the Treaty of Marrakech with effect from 1994.

state's authorities are of the view that products from another state are being sold as imports at an unfairly low price, customs duties are used as protective duties to counteract the low pricing. GATT therefore contains measures to prevent states using customs duties to target specific foreign products with the aim of protecting specific local products. Article VI of GATT 1994 and the agreements that implement it impose important limits on the protective aspects of customs duties.

Protective duties take two forms: anti-dumping duties and countervailing duties. Anti-dumping duties are permitted to counteract dumping – 'by which products of one country are introduced into the commerce of another country at less than the normal value of the products', if the dumping 'causes or threatens material injury to an established industry ... or materially retards the establishment of a domestic injury'.[11] Countervailing duties cancel out any export subsidy from the exporting state. Countervailing duties are permitted only to the extent that they are 'of an amount equal to the estimated bounty or subsidy determined to have been granted, directly or indirectly, on the manufacture, production or export of such product in the country of origin or exportation, including any special subsidy to the transportation of a particular subsidy',[12] for example by an excessive tax rebate, by a counteracting import duty. Both forms of protective duty can therefore be used to defend the economy against imports, but they were also capable of misuse to protect against imports being sold on fully commercial terms by the exporter if the importing state chose to identify dumping or subsidies.

To stop the misuse of these duties, article VI imposed a set of standards upon the practice. Disputed use of a protective duty could be made subject to the GATT disputes procedures, including arbitration by an independent panel. GATT 1994 now takes this process of regulation much further. Article VI is now supplemented by two supplementary agreements: the Agreement on Implementation of article VI of the GATT 1994, and the Agreement on Subsidies and Countervailing Measures. Both provide detailed procedures for applying the principles of article VI and for resolving disputed applications.[13]

---

11. GATT, art VI, para 1.
12. GATT, art VI, para 3.
13. The texts of art VI and the agreements are set out as appendices to C Stanbrook and P Bentley, *Dumping and Subsidies* (Kluwer, 3rd edition, 1996).

The two agreements are binding on the EU, as is article VI. Article VI and the anti-dumping code is implemented through Council Regulation 384/96.[14] The measures dealing with countervailing duties are implemented through Council Regulation 3284/94.[15] The Regulations also fill gaps left in the GATT regime to give the EU a complete set of rules for using what the EU terms 'commercial defence instruments'. Detailed study of these provisions is beyond the scope of this introduction.[16] However, we must note that the effect of these measures is that they cannot be used by the EU for purely fiscal purposes, and that they preclude action by the individual member states.

International customs laws

GATT 1994 and the creation of the World Customs Organisation have taken further the advancing process of securing detailed agreement to an international set of standards for applying fiscal customs duties. The GATT started this process by protecting freedom of goods in transit from duties,[17] by setting out common principles of customs valuation,[18] by seeking to limit the fees and formalities associated with customs duties,[19] and by setting rules for marking the origin of goods.[20] GATT 1994 adds or incorporates separate supplementary agreements on valuation,[21] inspections and rules of origin.

The WCO and its predecessor, the CCC, have additionally agreed a harmonised commodity description and coding system. This provides a common set of descriptors for all forms of goods.

---

14. Regulation 384/96 of 22 December 1995 on protection against dumped imports from countries not members of the EC (1996 OJ L56/1).
15. Regulation 3284/94 of 22 December 1994 on protection against subsidised imports from countries not members of the EC (1994 OJ L349/22).
16. Anti-dumping duties are regularly used by the EC, although countervailing duties are less common. There is, in consequence, a growing case law on challenges to the legality of anti-dumping duties before the European Court of Justice. For a comprehensive discussion of the subject see Standbrook and Bentley, op cit note 13.
17. Art V. 18. Art VII.
19. Art VIII. 20. Art IX.
21. The Agreement on Customs Valuation, perhaps the most important of the agreements, dates from 1979, and replaced separate and inconsistent approaches to customs valuation in different states on a notional basis with a common rule relying primarily on the actual transaction value.

The members of the CCC also concluded sixteen other international agreements dealing with more limited aspects of customs
duty application and administration. Again, the EU is a party to all
these agreements. Its customs law is therefore to a significant extent the regional application of international standards. However,
reflecting the multi-state membership of the EU, there are two aspects to EU customs law. The first is the set of internal rules preventing members states applying customs duties to each other. The
second is the external customs law applying to goods imported
into the EU from third countries.

EC internal customs law

There are no customs duties of any kind levied within the EU customs territory. The territory is not co-extensive with the territories
of the fifteen member states. There are minor exclusions from the
national territory in Europe of the member states (for example, the
Faeroe islands are excluded) but there are also major additions.
The Channel Isles and the Isle of Man form part of the territory, as
do Monaco and San Marino.[22] More significantly, Turkey became
part of the customs union in 1996. This major extension of the
customs union was initially agreed 22 years before in the EC-Turkey
Association Agreement.[23] This was the only agreement of its kind
that the EC has entered into. Agreements with other European
states seeking eventual EU membership include only free trade
arrangements.[24]

The law imposing the internal law of the customs union is the
first area of substantive law detailed in the EC Treaty.[25] Provision

---

22. The territory is defined by Customs Code, art 3, as amended to include Austria,
Finland and Sweden.
23. The commitment to form a customs union involving Turkey was made by the
EEC in the Agreement establishing an Association between the EEC and Turkey
signed at Ankara 12 September 1963, arts 2–5 (reprinted at 1973 OJ C 113/2,
24 December 1973). The details were agreed in an additional protocol signed at
Brussels in 1970 (1973 OJ C 113/20, 24 December 1973). These started to have
effect with the signing of the Interim Agreement between the EEC and Turkey
signed on 30 June 1973 (1973 OJ L 277).
24. See p 65 below.
25. It is thus the first of the policies in Part III of the EC Treaty. This is also
reflected by the statement that the elimination of customs duties is the first of
the activities of the Community: EC Treaty, art 3(a).

is made in articles 9 to 29 of the EC Treaty for the customs union, but much of this is concerned with phasing in the reduction of tariffs and is now spent for the established member states. The principles are set out in articles 9 and 18, but the core internal obligation is contained in article 12:

> Member States shall refrain from introducing between themselves any new customs duties on imports or exports or any charges having equivalent effect . . .

Article 17.1 states that this also applies to customs duties of a fiscal nature. Article 17.3 provides the fiscal alternative by reserving the right for member states to introduce internal taxes as a replacement for duties, provided that the forms of tax comply with article 95.

In practice, no problem has arisen with the ban on customs duties as such. However, some states have sought to impose border charges that have been justified as being for some other purpose than a customs duty. In other cases, states have attempted to disguise customs duties as internal measures, so sidestepping article 12. The European Court has made it clear that any kind of border charge, direct or indirect, is prohibited by article 12, save only charges for services provided that are proportional to those services. For example, the Italian government imposed a tax on art exports as a deterrent against such exports. This was found by the Court in an early decision[26] to be a violation of article 12. The charge was an export duty in its effect, and the purpose behind the charge did not justify that effect.[27] Another early decision of the Court affirmed this approach also applied to a charge applied for social purposes.[28]

The question of charges is a more sensitive one. However, the extension of the prohibition is to charges 'of equivalent effect'. This recognises the GATT prohibition on all fees and charges of whatever character beyond the approximate cost of services rendered.[29] Again, the Court took a strict stand on the issue, limiting

---

26. *EC Commission v Italy*, Case 7/68, [1968] ECR 423.
27. Italy also failed in its attempt to justify the levy by reference to EC Treaty, art 36. The Court ruled that art 36 was not relevant to a fiscal measure under art 12.
28. *Sociaal Fonds voor de Diamentarbeiders v Brachfield* Case 2,3/69, [1969] ECR 211. A small contribution was being levied by Belgium on the value of imported diamonds to pay towards the Belgian diamond workers' social fund.
29. GATT 1994, art VIII.1.

states only if and to the extent that a charge is proportionate to the benefit supplied for the charge. Further, a charge cannot be made for standard customs or similar procedures – there must be an agreement to provide some extra service.[30] The removal of frontier posts within the single market has rendered any occasion to impose customs duties as such now irrelevant, but any other requirements (perhaps within or related to a supposed internal tax) will still be caught by article 12. The only other permitted payment in connection with goods crossing an internal frontier of the EU is one imposed by Community law or international obligation. For example, if a fee were demanded for registering a cow as clear of disease before its movement were allowed, then this would not constitute a customs duty if the fee is levied 'by reason of Community obligation or international requirement.[31]

States tried to maintain their customs duties after explicit abolition by disguising them as internal taxes. We shall examine later how limits are applied to those taxes to prevent this happening. However, there is a prior question to be determined. Can an internal tax be regarded as a customs duty? In other words, will the proscription of article 12 follow the fiscal charges from the borders into internal taxation? The significance of the answer lies in the fact that under article 12 a customs duty must fail totally, while the equivalent internal provision (article 95) does not impose an absolute ban. The Court has determined that the provisions proscribing customs duties and those regulating internal taxes cannot apply to the same case: a charge is either a customs duty or an internal tax.[32] The Court took an early opportunity to define the separate scope of these measures in an Italian case concerning the imposition of a statistical levy on imports.[33] If a charge is occasioned by goods crossing frontiers, then, regardless of its size, name or mode of application or of whether it has any fiscal intent or discriminatory effect, it falls to be reviewed under article 12. A measure can only be considered as an internal measure if it is part of general internal taxation or a parafiscal measure and does not discriminate against imported products.

---

30. For example, in *Commission v Italy* Case 340/87, [1989] ECR 1483, the Court rejected an attempt to levy charge for customs services based on the long opening hours of Italian frontier posts.
31. See, for example, *Commission v Netherlands* Case 89/76, [1977] ECR 1355.
32. *Lutticke v Hauptzollamt Saarlouis* Case 57/65, [1966] ECR 205.
33. *EC Commission v Italy* Case 24/68, [1969] ECR 193.

The ban against customs duties of imports does not stop a tax charge being occasioned by the import of goods if the tax meets these requirements. This applies also in the case where a tax is applied to imported goods where there are no equivalent domestic goods.[34] This is particularly important in smaller states. More generally, as we shall see, VAT operates to a significant extent in some states as a neutral, inland economic substitute for customs duties. It is not, however, regarded as a legal equivalent.

EU external customs law

EU external customs law is laid down in two impressive documents. The primary document is the Community Customs Code. This is a Council Regulation[35] applying directly throughout the customs territory of the EU. It is supplemented by a massive Commission Regulation[36] – also directly applicable – making provision for implementing the Customs Code. The Council Regulation consolidates and updates 25 regulations and directives, and is an impressive piece of legislative codification in its own right. It stands within the EU as a shining example of the advantages of codified laws. The Commission Regulation is best described as daunting. These must be read together with the separate Community Customs Tariff.[37] The tariff contains the political decisions about the precise level of customs duty. The Customs Code does not of itself indicate the amount of duty payable on any particular import.

This vast body of law is, however, not self-contained and needs further supplementation at national level. In particular, the prin-

---

34. The Co-*frutta Case* Case 193/85, [1987] ECR 2085.
35. Regulation (EEC) 2913/92 of 12 October 1992 establishing the Community Customs Code (1992 ON L302/1, 19 October 1992).
36. Regulation (EEC) 2454/93 of 2 July 1993 laying down provisions for the implementation of Council Regulation (EEC) 2913/92 establishing the Community Customs Code (1993 OJ L 253/1, 11 October 1993). The term 'massive' may seem an understatement – the regulation has a nominal 915 articles and 113 annexes. With amendments and corrections, there are already 125 annexes, and the document has every sign that it will further expand. No attempt is made even to outline this enormous wealth of detail.
37. This consists of all the measures laid down or agreed by the EU that determine the amount of customs duty imposed on goods being imported or exported: Customs Code, art 20. The tariffs are collected into a single register known as the TARIC (integrated Community tariff). The introduction to the TARIC is published as 1993 OJ C 143/1, 24 May 1993.

ciple of subsidiarity, linked with the lack of EC powers to handle criminal law matters, means that the criminal sanctions needed to underpin the effective operation of the law are a matter for national decision. So are many of the minor matters of procedure and enforcement powers. They must, nonetheless, be operated in the context of the EC law. The Customs Code is comprehensive in areas of Community competence. It also ensures full compliance by member states with GATT 1994 and all relevant subsidiary agreements. The Code is now fully into effect. It finally came into effect in 1995, when the UK accepted the obligation[38] to provide a means of appeal against a customs ruling.

One further important aspect of the common basis of the EU customs duties is that the moneys collected belong to the EU and not to the member states.[39] As a result, individual member states have nothing directly to gain or to lose by the way in which the customs duties are applied. This means that the customs regime removes any incentives for a member state to encourage, or discourage, use of its ports, airports or frontiers as points of access to the EU.

The customs duty on an import, or export, is determined by reference to:

- the tariff classification of the goods;
- the origin of the goods;
- the quantity;
- the customs valuation of the goods;
- the tariff rate.

Tariff classification is determined by reference to a standard combined nomenclature. Typically, this is a code of up to eight digits. For example, 0407 10 11 is for eggs for hatching turkeys or other poultry, while at the other extreme of flight, 8411 12 90 is for aircraft turbojet engines.

The question of origin is important in deciding not only from where something is imported, but what is imported. For example, if I import all the parts of a motor car, and then assemble them within the EU, have I imported the car, or its parts? This may affect significantly the duty payable on the imports both by reference

---

38. Articles 243–246 of the Customs Code.
39. This is discussed in detail at p 47.

to the identity of the goods imported, and the customs value on import. The key rule of origin in such a case is:

> Goods whose production involved more than one country shall be deemed to originate in the country where they underwent their last, substantial, economically justified processing or working in an undertaking equipped for that purpose and resulting in the manufacture of a new product or representing an important stage of manufacture.[40]

The rule of origin gives scope for dispute, for example, where most of the parts of a car are manufactured outside the Community and assembled within the Community. If the resulting car is regarded as originating in the Community, it is in free circulation without any hindrance. Duty will be payable only on the parts. However, if the car is regarded as being an imported car, it will need to be cleared for customs duty purposes before it can be sold within the EU. The use of what has been termed 'screwdriver assembly' of imported parts in attempts to reduce customs duty or bypass customs controls has led to a number of disputes with the Commission and member states.

In the past, the question of customs valuation was also a matter for regular disputes, both with individual customs authorities and between states. The general principles only of valuation were set out in article VII of the GATT. In 1980 a common set of rules for customs valuation were adopted by the GATT member states.[41] These rules were reaffirmed in GATT 1994, and form the basis for the Customs Code rules. The main rule is that the customs value is the transaction value, ie the price actually paid or payable for the goods.[42] The Code lays down the assumptions on which the transaction is assumed to be based, as well as rules for cases where the main rule does not apply. It is interesting to note that if the Code rules fail to provide an answer, the value is to be determined by reference to the principles of GATT and the implementing agreement.[43]

---

40. Customs Code, art 24. The Commission implementing regulation contains detailed rules for applying this general rule to specific kinds of product.
41. The Brussels Agreement of 1979 on implementation of art VII of the GATT.
42. Customs Code, art 29(1).
43. Customs Code, art 31.1.

Preferential customs treatment

Imports from third states do not all enter the EU customs under the same conditions or subject to the same tariffs. The EU, like most customs areas, has preferential agreements with some states giving them preferred status against the general tariff. In the case of the EU, there are three levels of treatment to third states: states with free trade agreements with the EU; states with preferential status; and other states.

The core of the EU's trading relationships is the free trade area agreed under the European Economic Area Agreement (EEA Agreement).[44] A free trade area is based on a more limited agreement than that of a customs union. As the European Court has emphasised, a customs union is a single entity, while a free trade area is based on an agreement between independent sovereign states. Further, a free trade area is normally an agreement for free movement of goods originating in the signatory states, and is often limited to certain kinds of product only. This is true of the EEA Agreement, which applies to most kinds of industrial products, but with important exclusions.[45] However, it also applies to agricultural products.

Within the EEA, the prohibition on customs duties is similar in terms to that within the EU itself, as are the supporting provisions. However, the further detail is filled by the GATT and its implementing agreements rather than the Community Customs Code. A separate provision bars the signatories from using anti-dumping and countervailing duties against each other, save in specified circumstances.[46] The effective cooperation within the free trade area is strengthened by a series of more minor agreements. For example, a recent agreement between the EU and Norway empowers the Norwegian customs authority to act as agent for the

---

44. The Agreement has taken effect with Norway, Iceland and Liechtenstein, all members of the European Free Trade Area (EFTA). Switzerland is also a member of EFTA but not of the EEA Agreement. The EU has separate agreements with Switzerland that also create a free trade area (and, as a member of EFTA, Switzerland has a free trade agreement with the other members of the EEA Agreement). The EU-Switzerland Agreement dates from 1973 (see 1973 OJ L /191). It is in similar terms to the EFTA, and like the EFTA is limited to industrial products.

45. EEA Agreement, art 8. Protocol 2 also lists specific exclusions.

46. EEA Agreement, art 26. By contrast, the agreement with Switzerland reserves the right for either party to use, subject to additional limits, the measures allowed under art VI of the GATT (Switzerland Agreement, art 25).

EU on imports from outside the EEA.[47] Effectively, therefore, the customs area is moved outwards to cover Norway.

The Europe Agreements concluded with central and eastern European states[48] will in due course add to the free trade area. The agreements provide for the establishment of a free trade area between the EU and each state over a ten-year period.[49] This is subject to limited rights of derogation by the state,[50] and is subject to the reservation of limited rights to use anti-dumping duties or countervailing duties.[51] In the transitional stage of the agreements, provision is made for phasing out all existing customs duties and for preventing any new duties being established. The long-term intention is, of course, to extend the membership of the EU to include all these states. Similar agreements exist with Cyprus[52] and Malta.[53]

Beyond Europe, other special agreements exist. The EU has recently been concluding a series of Euro-Med agreements with favourable trade terms. However, these agreements provide for preferential tariffs for agreed classes of import between the EU and the other state parties. Special relationships also exist with the former dependent territories of member states, and in particular with the overseas territories and remaining dependent territories of, for example, the UK and France. Beyond that, there are general preferential agreements with the sub-Saharan African states.

The EU's preferential agreements, like its general approach to customs duties, complies fully with the GATT and WTO requirements. As part of this, tariffs are still being reduced. For example, in 1997 the EU indicated its agreement to further tariff reductions and eventual abolition of tariffs on information technology products and on certain alcoholic drinks (spirits) in the Singapore discussions held by the WTO.[54]

---

47. Bulletin of the European Communities, vol 10/96, p 71.
48. Agreements have been concluded in very similar terms with Bulgaria, the Czech Republic, Hungary, Poland, Romania, Slovakia, Slovenia, and the three Baltic republics.
49. For example, Europe Agreement with Poland, 13 December 1993 (1993 OJ L 348/1), art 6.
50. Poland Agreement, art 28.
51. Poland Agreement, art 29. The terms are similar to those in the Switzerland Agreement, note 44 above.
52. Association Agreement 1973 (1973 L 133/2, 21 May 1973).
53. The agreement is currently being reconsidered at the request of the Maltese government.
54. Com(97) 96, the Commission's formal proposal to the Council for ratification of the agreements.

Customs administration

Although the EU's customs duties are now based on a common Customs Code and common tariffs, and the revenues are EU revenues, there is no unified customs administration. The only EU personnel involved are the customs policy staff of the Commission.[55] All other customs staff are employees of the member states. The customs administrations of the member states are still part of their own national administrations, acting as agents for the EU. The size of the customs staff of several of the member states has been much reduced since the advent of the single market, and in some states the staff are now integrated into a national tax administration.[56]

The functions of the customs administrations of member states have changed significantly in recent decades, particularly since the single market was created. It is still their task to collect the duties that are payable, but they are also now much more concerned with dealing with illicit trade, such as drugs, counterfeit goods, or imports prohibited on health, safety, public policy or environmental grounds. States no longer try to discourage these products – as once they did – by penal rates of import duty. Rather, they are banned in total. As such, these prohibited products cannot be subject to duties or taxes. The proceeds of illegal trade, such as funds being laundered, are also monitored.

Customs administrations work closely together, both in their revenue functions and in their policing functions. In common with Community policies elsewhere, there is a programme of common training. Staff also work with the Commission policy staff to shape common approaches to their common task.[57]

Conclusion

It will be some time before general tariffs cease to be meaningful fiscal measures in world trade. They have, however, ceased to be

[55.] The staff are part of DG XXI.
[56.] For example, Denmark has a fully integrated tax and customs service. The UK, by contrast, still maintains a separate Customs and Excise department and Inland Revenue department.
[57.] A plan for common action was published as Customs 2000 by DG XXI of the Commission in 1993. For an account see R Condon, (1995/96) EC Tax Journal, 1.

of any significance at all between the member states, both in theory and in practice. The customs union now extends beyond the EU, and blends into multilateral free trade areas around the EU customs area. Beyond that, wider free trade areas are developing, and there are many states with preferential access to EU markets. Even where the full tariffs apply, their real significance is steadily declining, and they operate in a non-discriminatory manner as between third countries. This is a far cry from the position when the EEC was first being considered.

Only protective duties remain as a deliberate hindrance to imports to the EU. Here, however, a strict framework exists to ensure proper use of these instruments. As a result, they are valid trade measures which have only an incidental fiscal element. They may raise money, but they are not primarily designed to collect money.

CHAPTER FIVE

Taxing freely circulating goods

Goods or products originating in the EU customs area[1] may be circulated freely around the area without customs duties or similar charges payable when they are moved from one country to another. Similarly, goods originating outside the customs area can be circulated freely without any further customs duties or border taxes, provided that any relevant duty is paid on entering the customs area and the goods have been released for free circulation.

Preventing internalised customs duties

The removal of customs duty at the frontier is no protection against tax barriers being erected against foreign products in the internal tax systems of the member states. Ensuring that goods circulate freely without any fiscal impediment or discrimination also requires that the internal tax systems of all member states are free of any distortion or discrimination between local products and foreign products. Discrimination can operate in several ways. First, the local tax system can impose heavier or different taxes on foreign products than on those that originate within the state. Second, subsidies can be provided from within the tax system for local products, but not their foreign equivalents. Third, formalities or charges can impose administrative barriers. Fourth, if the requirements of the local tax system of the state to which the products are sent do not fit with the requirements of the system of the state from which the products are sent, a barrier may be created. Finally, there may be double taxation of products moving between

---

[1]. For the rule identifying the origin of products, see ch 4, p 64.

states. This can happen if the state of production and the state of consumption both impose local taxes on the same product, even if each tax individually does not discriminate.

The easiest way to remove all these barriers is to have one form of goods taxation working evenly throughout the EU. That was the assumption on which the EC Treaty was first agreed, as is recorded in the original version of article 99 of the Treaty. This imposed an obligation on the EC Council to harmonise the legislation relating to 'turnover taxes, excise duties and other forms of indirect taxation'.

This has not happened. It has now been realised that it does not need to happen. The United States of America operates quite successfully as a customs union although indirect taxation has never been harmonised. Nor is the USA ever likely to harmonise its local taxes fully. The US Constitution gives no express power to the US federal government to establish a common set of indirect taxes. Individual states are not likely to cede the power to Congress or the President to impose federal goods taxation because they would thereby lose a major source of local revenue to the federal powers. The transfer to the centre of similar powers in other federations, for example Canada, has also proved problematic. This was even true in Switzerland, which only adopted a common form of general indirect tax[2] after four plebiscites.

The need for a more limited rationalisation of internal taxes, rather than full harmonisation, was accepted in the revised version of article 99 adopted in the Maastricht Treaty.[3] The article now imposes an obligation to harmonise 'to the extent that such harmonisation is necessary to ensure the establishment and the operation of the single market'. In other words, it is now accepted that there is no need for a single set of EU-wide indirect taxes. Provided that the problems listed above are solved sufficiently, it is now agreed that no further action need be taken. Even this goes further than the USA, where there are inter-state distortions in trade (such as the extensive practice of buying mail order goods from states with no local sales taxes). However, the EU has yet to realise the targets it has set itself. In this chapter, we examine how far the EU has achieved the requirements of article 99 in its modified form, and the other protections against intra-Community barriers of this sort.

[2.] The tax was a value added tax based on the French form of the EC tax.
[3.] Treaty of European Union, taking effect in 1992.

Removing discriminatory treatment

The first, and most important, task of EC law in this area was to prevent member states internalising their customs duties when they removed them from the frontiers. This could have been done if the duties were replaced by internal taxes to the same discriminatory effect. For example, if an internal sales tax was 15 per cent higher on imported goods than on locally produced goods, the effect would have been the same as a customs duty. This obvious side-stepping of the removal of tariffs is also tackled in the GATT.

Article III of the GATT prohibits GATT member states from disguising their customs duties as internal taxes. It does so by requiring that imported products receive the same treatment as national products (the national treatment provision):

> The products[4] of ... any ... party imported into ... any other ... party shall not be subject, directly or indirectly, to internal taxes or other internal charges of any kind in excess of those applied to like domestic products.[5]

Further, this article is expressly linked to article I of the GATT.[6] This is the article that imposes most favoured nation (MFN) treatment on all member states for all other member states. Reading article I and article III together, a GATT member therefore cannot use its internal indirect taxes to discriminate between any two foreign states. Further, it must accord all foreign products national treatment, that is, it must treat all foreign products, regardless of origin, in the same way as it treats its own products.

The EU is a member of the GATT. It is therefore the duty of the EU to ensure that all member states comply with the GATT requirement. Unlike the provisions of the Customs Code, this has been left in part to the member states. The obligation on them to comply with the EU's international obligations is separate from, and independent of, any duty imposed on the member states as a result of the creation of the single market.[7]

The whole thrust of trade policy under GATT 1994 is to create free trade by turning non-fiscal measures against products into fis-

---

4. The extent to which 'products' includes services is examined in ch 7.
5. GATT 1994, art III, para 2.
6. GATT 1994, art I, para 1.
7. This is separate from art 95, which only applies specifically to products moving between member states.

cal measures, then making those fiscal measures transparent, and finally phasing out the fiscal measures. This the EU needs to do exhaustively if we are to have a genuine single market. The measures discussed in this chapter are therefore of fundamental importance.

Article 95

The primary legal authority designed to ensure that member states do not discriminate against non-domestic products is article 95 of the EC Treaty. This provision is both more specific and wider than GATT, article III. As interpreted by the ECJ, it has become a formidable weapon in establishing and maintaining the single market in products. It has been termed 'the most important of the Treaty provisions relating to taxation'.[8] More recently, that importance has waned. This is partly because the creation of the single market now removes many of the opportunities for discrimination that previously existed. Attempts by states to discriminate against other EU goods can now be defeated by ordinary consumers cross-border shopping and by mail orders of goods. The current reduction in use of article 95 is because of the aggressive and successful use in previous years by the Commission supported, in the result, by the European Court.

Article 95 provides that:

> No member state shall impose, directly or indirectly, on the products of other member states any internal taxation of any kind in excess of that imposed directly or indirectly on similar domestic products

and:

> ... no member state shall impose on the products of other member states any internal taxation of such a nature as to afford indirect protection to other products.

The wording common to article 95 and article III is clear, but the overall effect of the language of the EU obligation is stronger. Article 95 does not, as such, impose the obligations placed on member states as members of the GATT. Rather, the obligations are limited to actions taken against other member states. But

---

[8]. A J Easson, *Taxation in the European Community* (Athlone Press, 1993), p 21.

behind the text lies the GATT article III obligations for non-member states.

The full effect of the relevant international obligations includes not only GATT 1994 but also similar provisions in all relevant EU agreements with third states. These include the European Economic Area Agreement (EEA Agreement) which contains an obligation almost identical in wording to article 95.[9] They also include the Europe Agreements and other bilateral trade agreements. Several of these contain provisions that, at the least, reaffirm the GATT obligations and are sometimes in a form that echoes article 95.[10] The European Court has recognised that similar wording to article 95 in an association agreement does not necessarily set the same strict standard as in article 95 itself.[11] Nonetheless, the obligations in such agreements, even if not identical to article 95, will be given effect by the Court. Taken together, article 95, the EU's specific obligations to many third states, and the EU's membership of the WTO and GATT 1994 impose stiff requirements on member states not to use internal taxes to discriminate in any way by reason of the origin of products to which any taxes or charges apply.

The specific obligations of article 95 have been ruled by the ECJ to be directly effective, and therefore enforceable against member states.[12] We noted in the previous chapter that article 95 takes effect when articles 12 and 16 cease to operate (that is, when a tax

---

9. EEA Agreement, art 14. Art 44 of the Agreement with Turkey takes a similar approach. The identity of wording does not indicate an identity of interpretation. See *Polydor v Harlequin Records*, Case 270/80 [1982] ECR 329.

10. The Europe Agreement with Poland proscribes 'any measures or practice of an internal fiscal nature establishing, whether directly or indirectly, discrimination between the products of one party and like products originating in the territory of the other party' (art 26, para 1). This wording is almost identical to that in the Agreement with Switzerland (art 18), and reflects the EFTA provisions. The Agreement of Partnership and Cooperation with Russia, by contrast, echoes the GATT provision (art 11, para 1), as do agreements with other eastern European states. This, in some cases, establishes a GATT standard of conduct with those states before they have become members of the WTO and therefore directly subject to GATT 1994.

11. See, for example, *Hauptzollamt Mainz v Kupfenberg* Case 104/81, [1982] ECR 329. The Court takes the point that an agreement of this nature is an agreement between sovereign states, not an internal agreement to a customs union.

12. *Lutticke v Hauptzollamt Saarlouis* Case 57/65, [1966] ECR 205. The direct effect applied to the original member states from 1962. Direct effect does not depend on prior harmonisation under art 99: *Commission v Ireland*, Case 55/79, [1980] ECR 481.

has been internalised and can no longer be regarded as a customs duty).[13] Together, however, the two sets of principles provide a regime applicable on one or other basis to all forms of taxation or charge on goods. They therefore cover all fiscal measures applying to products as such that can cause discrimination. They also operate alongside the Treaty provisions dealing with non-fiscal measures to complete the range of measures[14] designed to create and maintain a genuine single market for products.

The taxes covered

Although it is clear that article 95 applies to 'internal taxation' and not to customs duties. Does this mean all internal taxation? Paragraph 1 refers to 'any internal tax of any kind', although this is not repeated in paragraph 2. The text avoids the reference to indirect taxation found in article 99. Nonetheless, the article has the same focus, as it applies to taxes 'on ... products'.[15] It applies to VAT,[16] and all specific taxes on products provided that they are internal taxes.[17] It also covers any other compulsory charge, whether or not it is called a tax.[18] The reference to taxes imposed 'directly or indirectly' on domestic products includes taxes of any kind applied on the raw materials or earlier stages of production of any product.[19] As the article is restricted to products, it does not apply to taxes on services or financial transactions.[20]

---

13. See p 60. In practice, there are considerable problems in drawing the line between the operation of art 12 on 'charges of equivalent effect' and the meaning of 'tax' in art 95. See Easson, op cit note 8, p 22; P Farmer and R Lyal, *EC Tax Law* (OUP, 1994), p 38.
14. The main provision is art 30. For a discussion about the possible interaction between art 95 and art 30 see Farmer and Lyal op cit note 13, p 43.
15. *Molkerei Zentrale v Hauptzollamt Paderborn* Case 28/67, [1968] ECR 143.
16. *Gaston Schul v Inspecteur der Invoerrechten en Accijzen* Case 15/81, [1982] ECR 1409. In practice, problems of the kind caught in that case have now been dealt with by specific EC legislation.
17. *Statens Kontrol v Larsen* Case 142/77, [1978] ECR 1554. In that case art 95 was applied to a tax that applies to imports, exports and internal handling of precious metal, because all transactions were included 'according to the same criteria and without any distinction as to origin or destination' (para 14).
18. See, for example, the levy on growers in *Apple and Pear Development Council v Lewis* Case 222/82, [1983] ECR 4083. This levy was later analysed in connection with VAT and found not to be a payment for a supply: see p 88.
19. See the *Molkerei Zentrale* case, note 15 above.
20. This is discussed in chs 7 and 9, as this chapter focuses on goods alone.

Prohibiting fiscal discrimination[21]

The main thrust of GATT, article III and article 95, paragraph 1 is the prohibition of fiscal discrimination between domestic products and 'similar' foreign products. The European Court has developed a considerable jurisprudence in interpreting this broad test. In particular, it has been concerned to identify when products are similar. Naturally, a foreign producer who sees the market, in its view, skewed in favour of local products, is concerned to protect its own, foreign, products, and will be keen to use article 95 to help if possible. Such a producer will take a broad view of what is 'similar'. Having identified the similar goods, discrimination against the foreign products must be shown. Again, the temptation will be to look for any difference at all between treatment of local products and treatment of other products. By contrast, the local system may have been 'skewed' for policy reasons that have nothing to do with the location of production.

How has the Court balanced these two pressures? It has undoubtedly given article 95, paragraph 1 an extensive meaning. In particular, it has adopted a broad approach to identifying what is 'similar'. Initially, it was tempted to take the customs approach,[22] but it has since backed away from this. The technical approach was replaced by a broader consumer-orientated approach. This reached its furthest limit in a series of cases about alcoholic drinks. In these cases the European Court found itself confronted with the question: is whiskey (or whisky) the same thing as brandy?[23] Any

---

21. In his pioneering *Droit fiscal communautaire*, Dominque Berlin divided this topic into three: interdiction of fiscal discrimination (art 95, para 1) (ch 1); interdiction of defensive fiscal protectionism (art 95, para 2) (ch 2, part I), and interdiction of offensive fiscal protectionism (art 96) (ch 2, part II). This is the broad approach adopted, with acknowledgement, in this chapter. See also Easson op cit note 8 ch 2; Farmer and Lyal, op cit note 13, ch 3; B Terra and P Wattel, *European Tax Law* (Kluwer, 1993), ch 2; S Weatherill and P Beaumont, *EC Law* (Penguin, 2nd edition, 1995), ch 14.

22. The approach was to see if the products had common customs tariff numbering: *Fink Frucht v Hauptzollamt München Landesbergerstraße* Case 27/67, [1968] ECR 233.

23. See *EC Commission v France* Case 168/78, [1980] ECR 347. See the similar case of *EC Commission v Italy* for the added complication of whether either of them are like rum: Case 169/78, [1980] ECR 385. Having sorted that out, move on to whether the Danish are right to see a distinction in aquavit and schnapps: *EC Commission v Denmark* Case 171/78, [1980] ECR 447. Then test whether you are right by looking at *EC Commission v United Kingdom* Case 170/78, [1983] ECR 2265 (similar case, but decided on different grounds).

self-respecting drinker would unhesitatingly say no – but why? The Commission's view was that these are all similar products because they have similar characteristics and meet similar consumer needs. In the view of the Commission this had to be viewed by consumers over the Community as a whole. It also took the view that consumer habits varied in time and space, as did the appraisal of a particular product. The member states – needless to say – found a whole series of reasons for differentiating between the drinks.[24] The European Court agreed with the broad approach. But it then did a splendid example of dodging the question, deciding that 'Article 95, taken as a whole, may apply without distinction to all the products concerned'.[25] Nonetheless, member states lost most of these cases, and the effect in removing discriminatory taxes on various kinds of alcoholic drink has been significant.

Once products are found to be similar, how is discrimination established? This was easy in connection with drinks: the tax on similar quantities was clearly different. More often, the allegation is that there is indirect discrimination. A good example is one of the beer cases: *EC Commission v Belgium*.[26] The Belgians had taken the view that there was a lower wastage on brewing Belgian beer than on foreign beer,[27] and therefore imposed an excise duty that worked out higher on imported beer. The Court found this to be a breach of article 95. Other forms of discrimination include the formalities required in connection with the tax or the time the tax is paid.

More problematic are the cases where a tax is applied without any discrimination with regard to origin on domestic and foreign products alike, but some other element interacts with the tax to unbalance the overall effect of the levy. This problem is illustrated by the two *Gaston Schul* cases.[28] The taxpayer bought a second-

---

24. Though none of them dealt with the matter as succinctly as Robert Burns: 'Freedom and Whisky gang thegither!' (*The Author's Earnest Cry and Prayer*). The Court's sympathies lay, rather, with President Jefferson's view in 1818 that 'No nation is drunken when wine is cheap; and none sober when the dearness of wine substitutes ardent spirits as the common beverage. It is, in truth, the only antidote to the bane of whiskey' – which is, in effect, a sharp example of the point behind art 95, para 2.
25. See *EC Commission v Denmark* (note 23 above), judgment at para 12.
26. Case 153/89, [1991] ECR I-3171. The temptation to make remarks about Belgian beer is resisted.
27. See note 26 above.
28. *Gaston Schul v Inspecteur der Invoerrechten en Accijzen*, Case 15/81, [1982] ECR 1409 and, because the national court did not understand that judgment, *Staatssecretaris van Financien v Gaston Schul Douane-Expediteur*, Case 47/84, [1985] ECR 1481.

hand boat in one state and took it across the frontier to another state. In the second state he was charged VAT on the import value, in accordance with the VAT laws of that state (and the EC rules). The taxpayer objected that he had been taxed twice. This was because there was VAT in the price he had paid in the first country and for which he could not seek a rebate (because the boat was sold as a private sale). In this case, there was nothing wrong at all with the VAT laws of the second state. They were not discriminatory, and complied with the EC rules. For this reason, the Commission took the view that the discrimination could only be avoided by further legislation. The Court disagreed, and found that the second state had to make allowances for the VAT in the import value that had been paid in the first state. This decision has been criticised strongly as 'an open invitation to tax evasion'.[29] It has since ceased as a problem because of the creation of the single market.

The opposite variant of the *Schul* cases is where the adjustment takes place after the tax, for example by taxing every product of a certain kind with a nondiscriminatory tax and then rebating the tax in a selective way. If this is done specifically with the proceeds of a tax, it can amount to a disguised customs duty. Where it is part of the system of taxation generally, article 95 may be breached. If the adjustment favours the foreign products against the domestic products, article 95 is not offended, although article 92 may be.[30]

Prohibiting fiscal protectionism[31]

Paragraph 2 of article 95 poses a much broader test: are the products to be compared in competition with each other, so that the domestic producers may be the beneficiaries of protection? Identifying the protection for paragraph 2 poses the same issues as paragraph 1, but when are products in competition?

---

29. Easson op cit note 8, p 41. For a more neutral view, see N Green, T C Hartley and J A Usher, *The Legal Foundations of the Single European Market* (OUP, 1991), p 46.
30. See ch 10.
31. See D Berlin, *Droit Fiscal Communautaire* (Presses Universitaires de France, 1988), p 155; Easson, op cit note 8, p 49; Farmer and Lyal, op cit note 13, p 65; Weatherill and Beaumont, op cit note 21, p 409.

Two continuing series of disputes illustrate the importance of this rule clearly, but also show its difficulties. The cases concern, respectively, differing alcoholic drinks and different cars. Consider the following two questions: Is beer in competition with table wine? Is a (smaller) Renault car in competition with a (larger) Mercedes car?

The troubling concept that beer and wine are similar caused even the European Court to pause awhile in Case 170/78.[32] After a period of reflection, the Court dealt with the matter not as one of similarity, but as one of competition, or product substitution. Undoubtedly, the case touched on a sensitive point, for the UK had long imposed higher taxes on wines than beers.[33] After full economic argument, the Court found in favour of the Commission's challenge against the British excise duty rates. This has started a long-term downward drift in the rates of taxation of wine in the UK, which may or may not help explain a steady growth in the sales of wine in the UK. More recently, the effect of cross-border shopping has exposed more sharply the differences between tax levels, and has allowed consumers to decide for themselves what are distortions to competition in this area.

The erratic history of the taxation of cars in the EU is a much more obvious example of protection – though some of it is environmental protection rather than product protection. The Humblot case[34] from France first drew attention to these issues. The taxpayer was annoyed that his Mercedes car was subject to a special tax because it had a very large engine capacity. The French tax system imposed a tax on cars proportionate to engine size, but with a surcharge on the larger engines which, the evidence showed, were found only in imported cars. This the Court found discriminatory.[35] This could not be true of a similar tax in Denmark[36] because the Danes do not build cars. Consequently, a challenge against their heavy taxes on larger cars did not discriminate in

---

32. Note 23 above.
33. The reverse was true elsewhere in the Community, for instance Germany, which has refused to impose an excise duty on wine because, inter alia, of the difficulty of collecting it. That was not a problem in the UK.
34. *Humblot v Directeur des Services Fiscaux* Case 112/84, [1985] ECR 1367.
35. The French therefore adjusted the system, but it still hit cars hardest above the largest engine size of French cars. The European Court was not impressed: *Feldain v Directeur des Services Fiscaux* Case 433/85, [1987] ECR 3521.
36. *EC Commission v Denmark* Case 47/88, [1990] ECR I-4909.

favour of, or protect, locally made cars, because there were none.[37] This was outside the scope of article 95.[38]

As the few examples in this account have shown, the two paragraphs of article 95 have together occupied much of the time of the Commission and Court. It is noticeable that complaints about infringements of this article have faded since the start of the single internal market. Perhaps this is because genuine competition is now dealing with the problem behind paragraph 2. Open frontiers have certainly dealt with many of the problems behind paragraph 1. Although we have not concentrated on the issue in this chapter, it has also dealt with discrimination against goods from third states. These are not subject to article 95 protection. However, discrimination in one state can be avoided by the simple approach of importing to another state and then exercising the freedom of circulation of those goods once imported.

Value added tax

During the last 50 years, huge changes have taken place in the way states tax goods and services. In the EU, as we have just seen, this is in part because member states now derive nothing from internal frontier duties. Instead, with few exceptions,[39] states have adopted a general form of taxation known as value-added tax.[40] The adoption of VAT in over 100 countries in all parts of the world derives in large part from decisions first taken by the six original member states of the EEC. This chapter outlines how the EEC came to adopt VAT, and why it was then adopted by so many other states.

---

37. But what of local second-hand cars, as against imported second-hand cars?
38. The Court did hint that art 30 might be involved, though this seems wrong in principle and may no longer be the Court's view: Farmer and Lyal, op cit note 13, p 43; Weatherill and Beaumont, op cit note 21, p 419.
39. In 1997, the only major states that did not have some form of VAT operating at national level were Australia and the USA.
40. The hyphenation is deliberate. It is the form used in international discussion and is also used in Ireland and other states. The UK, in using the name without the hyphen, has adopted a name which does not make grammatical sense as the noun precedes the adjective. The excuse is, perhaps, that the French name, from which the English is taken, is *taxe sur la valeur ajoutee*.

The need to harmonise

The member states recognised, when negotiating the EEC Treaty, that they would need to harmonise their taxation of goods and services. This was because a common market requires common forms of indirect taxation – that is, taxation of products and transactions. When the EEC was established, each of the six states had a different way of imposing these taxes. Many of them had multi-level taxes; imposing taxes on items as they were manufactured, mined or grown, and then at each stage until they were sold. This led to multiple taxation as a new tax was added at each level of production and distribution. Multi-level taxes then caused 'cascading', the process of tax-on-tax as the tax on each level of production came to form part of the tax base for the next level of tax. A direct consequence of this was vertical integration of the economy. It made considerable sense to cut down the number of levels of production and distribution, because this produced a direct reduction in the amount of tax to be paid, and abated the cascading. Furthermore, if some of the stages of production and distribution took place in one member state, and the rest in another state, both states would be adding their (differing) taxes to the price of the goods or services. The fact that states had differing systems of itself also imposed a barrier against intra-Community trading. This was accentuated by the need to continue frontier controls over goods for internal tax purposes even though the customs barriers had been removed.

The French government had reformed this multi-level system in 1954 by introducing the tax we now call VAT. This had solved the cascade problem in France, although it did not solve the international problems caused by different systems. The other states had not made any similar reform. They gave themselves the task of doing so in article 99 of the EEC Treaty, on a proposal from the Commission. The Commission set about fulfilling its duty under article 99 by asking two expert sets of committees to look at the problem and recommend a way forward. These committees[41] were given the task of looking not only at the problems of the different

---

[41.] The first committee was a working group of Commission officials and national officials that produced what came to be called the ABC Report, as it broke into three subgroups (A, B, and C) which each produced separate reports. The other was a committee of fiscal and financial experts known, after its chairman, as the Neumark Committee. An English translation of the reports, *The EEC Reports on Tax Harmonisation*, was published by the IBFD in 1963.

tax systems in obstructing free movement, but also the effects of these differences on competition.

In 1962, the Neumark Committee made sweeping recommendations for reform in its report. Taking a lead from the ABC reports,[42] it recommended the harmonisation of sales taxes into a form of VAT. This represented something of a victory for the French, as it amounted to an endorsement of their 1954 reforms. The Commission took the initiative and tabled a draft directive[43] that year for a partial VAT. In particular, the Commission was proposing a common form of tax only for business-to-business transactions. It also exercised caution in suggested that the new tax be introduced in several stages over a number of years. This proved too hesitant an approach, and the Commission produced more comprehensive proposals in 1965.[44] These were adopted early in 1967, and became the First and Second VAT Directives.[45]

The First and Second VAT Directives

The First VAT Directive is fundamental to the EC VAT system. It sets out in its recitals and first two articles the principles on which the system is designed. The recitals record the necessity of a common form of turnover tax to avoid both distortions of competition and hindrances to the free movement of goods and services.[46] They also record that the aim of establishing the highest degree of simplicity and neutrality is best achieved when the tax is as general as possible, but that this aim may not be achieved immediately.[47]

Article 1 of the First Directive simply requires member states to replace their current turnover taxes with the common form of VAT. Article 2 defines this common form by reference to the principle of a tax applying to goods and services 'on consumption exactly proportional to the price of the goods and services, whatever the number of transactions which take place in the production and distribution process before the stage at which the tax is charged'. The other articles provide the machinery for further implementing these provisions.

---

42. See note 41.
43. 1964 OJ 2512.
44. 1966 OJ 561.
45. Directives 67/227/EEC and 67/228/EEC, 1967 OJ Sp Edn, 14.
46. Directive 67/277/EEC, recital 2.
47. Ibid, recitals 5, 6.

The detail of the common VAT was left to the Second Directive. This set out the necessary details to the extent that member states had agreed them. However, the Second Directive answered only some of the issues necessary to establish a truly common form of VAT in the Community. It also allowed member states to retain significant derogations from the common form of VAT in a number of sensitive areas. The differences left the common market incomplete. The result was only a partial removal of the distortions to competition and the hindrances to free movement. The regime as a whole was to come into effect in 1970 – later postponed for some of the states. The common system finally entered into effect in all six states in 1973, when Italy adopted it.

The two first VAT directives left work incomplete. The most important area of inconsistency left by the Second Directive was that it was for member states to decide which goods and services were within the charge to tax and which were to be exempted from it. An exempt supply, as we shall see, creates significant distortions at any stage of economic activity. This was therefore a fundamental deficiency in the 1967 VAT framework. Other deficiencies included national differences in identifying who should be subject to VAT, and how VAT was applied to both imported goods and cross-border supplies of services. In other words, the VAT adopted in each member state might have common principles, but it was far short of being a common tax.

Nonetheless, the pressure for further harmonisation for the tax base of VAT came not from concerns about competition and free movement but from the 1970 Decision introducing the Community's own resources. Once the EEC had decided to use VAT as a source of revenues, the freedom of a state to choose its own exemptions became nonsustainable. This was because exemptions could be used to cut that state's contribution to the common resources of the EEC unilaterally. The 1970 Decision was scheduled to come into effect by 1975.

The Sixth VAT Directive

Work therefore started to replace the Second VAT Directive with a more detailed provision consistent with the principle of the First VAT Directive. Though this process was complicated by the expansion of the EEC to nine states during work on the draft, the Sixth VAT Directive was adopted to replace the Second Directive in 1977. It was scheduled to come into effect in 1978. It did so in some states, but only came fully into effect in 1987, when Greece adopted the required legislation.

The Sixth Directive was significantly more comprehensive than the Second Directive. It provided a common set of rules for most of the key questions: taxable persons subject to the tax; territory covered by the tax; common definition of taxable transactions; common rules for identifying where and when a taxable transaction occurs; common valuation rules; common procedures; and, most significant for the 1970 Decision, a common list of exemptions.

After 1987, when the Sixth Directive was in effect throughout the EC, it could be said that there was a common form of VAT. But it still fell far short of being the same tax in each state. The 1977 measure still left some important gaps, and also allowed states to derogate from the common form of tax. The most important gaps were: no common rates of tax; no common way of handling small undertakings; no common treatment of agriculture; no common form of treatment for goods such as antiques and second-hand cars. Besides these gaps, states were allowed to retain existing derogations and special treatments in several areas.[48] The immediate problems created by the 1970 Decision had been solved, but the more elusive aims of the removal of distortions and hindrances had only been partly achieved.

Abolishing fiscal frontiers

By 1990, the common form of VAT was becoming a reality. Besides the framework directives, several others had been adopted. These included an agreement for mutual assistance of tax authorities,[49] measures allowing traders from other states and from outside the EC to claim VAT refunds in appropriate cases,[50] and some moves towards reduction of the various national derogations.[51]

---

48. Article 28 of the Sixth Directive preserves the right to continue existing derogations from the Second Directive.
49. Directive 77/799/EEC of 19 December 1977, 1977 OJ L 336/15.
50. The Eighth VAT Directive (79/1072/EEC) of 6 December 1979 (1979 OJ L 331/11), dealing with traders in other EC states and the Thirteenth VAT Directive (86/560/EEC) of 17 November 1986 (1986 OJ L 326/40), dealing with traders in third states.
51. The Eighteenth VAT Directive (89/465/EEC) of 18 July 1989 (1989 OJ L 226/21) abolishing some of the derogations permitted by art 28(3) of the Sixth Directive.

The European Court had also become active in this area prompted by both the Commission and by taxpayers. The first substantive VAT case had not come before the European Court until 1976,[52] and the first case alleging specific infraction under the VAT Directives against a member state was not heard until 1984.[53] By 1990, however, the case law was becoming an important aspect of the development of the tax. In particular, two cases from the UK did much to set the tone for development of the tax in this country.

Despite all this legislative and judicial activity, VAT was still a tax requiring border controls. This was because, in the way that VAT was organised, each exporting state removed any VAT from exported products by refunding it to the exporter. The importing state then intercepted the imported goods in the same way as for customs duty, and imposed a VAT charge on the value of the goods at import. In effect, much of the VAT on goods was collected in exactly the same way as if VAT on imports was a customs duty. This approach could not be maintained in a single market without internal frontiers. The next major reform of VAT therefore had to be a redesign to remove the need for frontier controls on imports.

The reason why border controls were needed was because VAT was imposed as a destination-based tax. In the view of the Commission, and various committees, VAT could avoid the problems of border controls only if it became an origin-based tax, or at least an origin-collected tax.[54] To achieve this change in the VAT, the Commission needed to persuade all member states of its desirability. It failed to do so. Indeed, for some considerable time it was completely unclear how member states were going to change the system in time for the start of the single internal market.[55]

---

52. *Mazzalai* Case 111/75, [1976] ECR 657.
53. *EC Commission v Belgium* Case 325/82, [1984] ECR 777.
54. An origin-based VAT is one where liability is imposed in, and the revenue is retained by, the state of export. An origin-collected tax is one where liability is imposed in the state of export on behalf of the state of import. The export state must therefore account in some way to the import state for the VAT on any export between the states. In effect, VAT is collected as a sort of withholding tax in this case. An origin-collected tax therefore requires some kind of clearing system at Community or national level between the member states.
55. The formal start of the single internal market on 1 January 1993 was guaranteed by art 7a of the EC Treaty (as amended by the Single European Act).

Eventually, an untidy compromise was adopted.[56] Under the agreed approach, the origin basis of VAT was adopted (without any clearance procedure) for mail order goods, excise goods and new means of transport. In all other cases, the existing system was to remain. In order to make a VAT charge on imports work without customs controls, a series of inward processing controls were used instead, requiring accounts from the person to whom goods bought by a cross-border acquisition[57] were delivered. A high degree of information exchange was also set in place between the member states, much of it in terms of electronic data exchange.[58] The compromise was said to be transition, and to await the adoption of a permanent system. At the time of writing, the Commission is still working on this system, which is meant to be put in place when the third stage of economic and monetary union takes effect.[59] It is not clear that unanimous political will exists to adopt any such change of system at the present time. Until it is, and several other areas of national difference are removed, the VAT will remain incomplete and faulty, even as judged by the target set in the First and Sixth VAT Directives. As we shall see, these Directives themselves contain major problems, and the tax is far from perfect.

The charges to VAT

The main charging provision of the Sixth VAT Directive is article 2. This imposes a three-fold charge to VAT:

- on supplies of goods or services effected for consideration within the territory of a member state by a taxable person acting as such;
- on cross-border acquisitions of goods from other member states; and
- on imports of goods from outside the customs territory of the EU.

The charge on imports of goods takes place in exactly the same way as customs duties are, or could be, imposed on those goods.

---

56. It is to be found in art 28 and following articles in the Sixth VAT Directive.
57. After 1 January 1993, goods could not by definition be imported or exported between member states; the new phraseology therefore has to be used.
58. The details are technical and not explored here.
59. Originally this was to be 1997. At the time of writing it is intended as 1999.

This therefore requires no further discussion in this chapter.[60] The charge on cross-border acquisitions of goods takes place by means of an accounting procedure imposed on the person to whom the goods are supplied on import. In other words, it is a tax on the business customer of the goods. As it only applies to businesses registered for VAT, it is in effect a bookkeeping exercise by these businesses, and is not further discussed here.[61] We will therefore focus only on the internal supplies.

In the English version, VAT appears to be a single tax applying without differential to supplies of goods and supplies of services. This is misleading. The French – and most other language – version of the Sixth VAT Directive differentiates more clearly between supplies of goods and supplies of services. Indeed, there is no equivalent of the word 'supply' in those other languages. Instead, we read of 'les livraisons de biens et les prestations de services'.[62] Further, the Directive offers no common definition of 'supply'. Rather, it offers separate definitions of the phrases 'supply of goods'[63] and 'supply of services'.[64] While many of the VAT rules apply in the same way to supplies of goods as to supplies of services (in particular the identity of taxable persons), key provisions such as that of the location of a supply vary. In this book we are deliberately[65] presenting the treatment of supplies of goods separately from that of supplies of services, and only deal with the former here.

[60.] See the discussion in ch 4.

[61.] In many cases the person receiving the goods will account for VAT on the value of the goods as received in its accounts. This will not actually be paid as VAT to the tax authorities on the specific items in most cases. Nor is it paid to the person supplying the goods. Instead, it forms part of the general accounting for VAT by the business for the VAT it receives on its own sales to its customers.

[62.] In German, 'Lieferungen von Gegenstanden und Dienstleistungen'. In the Second VAT Directive in the English version the text also reads 'the supply of goods and the provision of services'.

[63.] Sixth VAT Directive, art 5, para 1: 'supply of goods' shall mean the transfer of the right to dispose of tangible property as owner. Art 5 also allows optional extensions of the scope of the phrase to include, for example, hire of goods.

[64.] Sixth VAT Directive, art 6, para 1: 'supply of services' shall mean any transaction [Fr: operation] which does not constitute a supply of goods within the meaning of art 5.

[65.] The two are usually presented together. Nonetheless, it is not only the rules of location and timing that vary between goods and services, but also the policy behind, and the comprehensiveness of, the tax as a whole. Crucially, in the EU, the tax on supplies of services is usually at the same rate as that on the supplies of goods, but this conceals rather than removes the underlying differences.

VAT on goods

There is a supply of goods for VAT purposes whenever there is a transaction by which the right to dispose of the goods is transferred from one person to another.[66] VAT must be imposed on the supply of goods within the territory of a member state[67] if the following conditions apply:

(a) the supply of goods is subject to VAT[68] and not exempt;[69]
(b) the supply is made by a taxable person;[70]
(c) the supply is made as part of the economic activity of that person; [71]
(d) the supply is made, or deemed to be made, for consideration.[72]

If VAT applies to a supply of goods, then the taxable person making the supply must collect from the customer the amount of VAT chargeable on the supply. The amount of VAT is the appropriate rate applied to the taxable amount of the supply.[73] The rate is determined according to national legislation, but must be either a standard rate not lower than 15 per cent, or a lower rate of not less than 5 per cent.[74] The taxable amount is, in most cases, 'everything which constitutes the consideration which has been or is to be obtained by the supplier from the purchaser, the customer or a third party for such supplies including subsidies directly linked to the price of such supplies'.[75] Consideration is therefore important in determining both whether a supply is within the scope of the

---

66. Sixth VAT Directive, art 5, as interpreted in *Staatsecretaris van Financien v SAFE BV* Case C-320/88 [1991] STC 627, where the Court stressed the need to have a test that applied throughout the EC independently of the commercial laws of individual jurisdictions.

67. The territorial extent is partially defined by Sixth VAT Directive, art 3. It is not coterminous with the customs territory of the EU (see p 59), which is a potential source of problems.

68. A supply of goods within the scope of VAT but not exempt is referred to as a taxable supply.

69. All supplies of goods (within the scope of the phrase as defined) are taxable unless they are expressly exempt under arts 13–16 or 28–28n.

70. Sixth VAT Directive, arts 2, 4.

71. Sixth VAT Directive, arts 2, 4.

72. Sixth VAT Directive, arts 2, 11.

73. Sixth VAT Directive, arts 10, 11.

74. Sixth VAT Directive, art 12.

75. Sixth VAT Directive, art 11, para 1(a). If there is no consideration, or it cannot be valued, or in certain cases the consideration may not be at market value, then the open market value of the goods supplied may be used instead. However, the primary rule is the actual price paid for the supply. This is the same basic principle as now applies to customs duties, although the detailed determination of the price (for example, by reference to any other taxes or duties charged) is not the same.

tax, and also the taxable amount of the resulting charge to VAT. The European Court has interpreted the term 'consideration' to give it a meaning independent of national contract laws. Reflecting wording in the Sixth Directive, the Court has ruled that for a payment to be regarded as consideration for a supply, there must be a direct link between the two.[76]

Subject to the definition of the divide between supplies of goods and supplies of services,[77] the assumption of the Sixth Directive is that all supplies of goods are within the scope of the tax subject to express exemption in the national law. Because national differences in the way goods are defined as exempt can cause major distortions between states[78] the drafters attempted to limit the range of goods that may be exempted from VAT. The Directive also provides that exemptions are mandatory, subject only to a limited range of discretions left to member states. The main categories of exempt goods relate to supplies as part of health, education, cultural and welfare services.

There is also an important exemption relating to supplies of land and buildings. A sale, or long lease, of land or a building may be treated as a supply of goods for VAT purposes in order to bring it potentially within the scope of the tax.[79] Subject to important discretions left to member states,[80] if land and buildings are within the scope of the tax, then most sales of undeveloped land, and sales of buildings, are to be exempt.[81]

Taxable persons

The other key concepts in identifying the scope of VAT are those of 'taxable persons acting as such'. The operation of this provision is again a mixture of EC provisions and national law. A person is a 'taxable person' if registered or required to be registered under the

---

76. *Apple and Pear Development Council v Customs and Excise Commissioners* Case 102/86 [1988] STC 221; *Tolsma v Inspecteur der Omzetbelasting Leeuwarden* Case C-16/93, [1994] STC 509.
77. Discussed in ch 7.
78. And also because the Sixth VAT Directive was motivated in part by the Own Resources decisions, and therefore needed a common VAT base in the member states.
79. The 'may' is deliberate: see Sixth VAT Directive, art 5, para 2.
80. Who may themselves pass the discretion to individual taxable persons: Sixth VAT Directive, art 13C.
81. Sixth VAT Directive, art 13B (b), (g), and (h).

VAT law of a member state. It is for the member state to determine precisely how and when the registration duty arises and is fulfilled. The Sixth Directive provides only a framework within which this duty arises.[82] The Directive also gives member states a discretion to exempt taxable persons from the duty to collect the tax below a nationally determined threshold.[83] As a result, in some states anyone who is engaged in a business is regarded as a taxable person, while some other states have used the provision to exempt many small businesses.[84]

Once a person is registered, or required to be registered, by the national legislation, all taxable supplies of goods are to be subject to VAT if the supplies are made as part of any economic activity of the taxable person making them. 'Economic activity' is regarded as a wide concept. This is stressed by the Directive emphasising that the purposes or results of such activities are irrelevant.[85] The European Court has emphasised in its cases on this provision that it has a very wide scope, and that the width of the scope is necessary because of the principle that the common form of VAT should be neutral as between different kinds of transaction or activity,[86] provided only that the person is engaged in activities that can be regarded as economic.[87] In practical terms, this brings all the business activities of a person whatever their nature within the scope of the tax. Only purely passive arrangements,[88] or the non-business activities of individuals,[89] would fall outside this.

[82.] See art 4.

[83.] Art 24.

[84.] In Italy all companies and most individuals in business are required to register, regardless of how much business each conducts. In the UK, by contrast, a person (company or individual) is only required to register if that person's total turnover of taxable supplies of goods and services exceeds £48,000 in a year (this sum is reviewed annually).

[85.] Art 4, para 2.

[86.] See *van Tiem v Staatsecretaris van Financien* Case C-186/89, [1993] STC 91, and cases cited there.

[87.] In *Polysar Investments BV v Inspecteur der Invoerrechten en Accijnzen, Arnhem* Case C-60/90, [1993] STC 222, the Court ruled that a holding company that did nothing but act as the passive owner of shares in other companies was not a taxable person. The Court referred to the *van Tiem* case (see note 86), and stressed that the principle of neutrality meant that the system of VAT applied to all transactions whatever their legal form, by which it is sought to obtain income from the goods in question on a continuing basis. The holding company in the case did not do this.

[88.] These will be taxable as investment activities. See ch 9.

[89.] An individual who sells, for example, furniture owned as part of her or his own private possessions, is not 'acting as such' in the sale, even though a taxable person, unless the sale takes place through or by reason of that person's business activities.

Why a value-added tax?

The tax described so far might be a straightforward, if wide, sales tax, consumption tax, or turnover tax on goods. Why is the EC tax a value-added tax? At the technical level, it might be objected that the EC form of VAT is not really a VAT at all – it is a consumption tax or possibly a consumer tax. Nonetheless, the aim behind the tax is that of isolating out and taxing the value added to products by each economic operator in the process of producing and distributing those products. The best way of describing how this is done is by a short example.

An example of VAT

C makes small souvenirs out of sea-shells collected from the sea shore. Because C is successful at making these models, and employs a few people to help, C is registered for VAT. C sells most of the souvenirs to a series of local shops, and the shops sell the souvenirs to tourists. Most of the shops are also registered for VAT. Let us say that C can make a sea-shell souvenir for almost no cost at all (there will be a small amount for glue, but not much). C can sell each souvenir to a local shop for $4 (including any VAT), and the local shop can sell the souvenir to a visitor for $8 (including any VAT). The rate of VAT is 10 per cent.

C sells a sea-shell for $4 including VAT, or $3.64 plus VAT of $0.36, to S, a local shop. C has no expenses apart from payments to (non-registered) local staff and her own time and (rent-free) use of a store room. The whole of the $3.64 is value added by C.

S sells the sea-shell to a tourist for $8 including VAT, or $7.27 plus VAT of $0.73. It cost S $3.64 plus $0.36 to buy the shell. Let us assume that S has no other costs in selling this shell (an unlikely assumption in the real world). On that basis, S has added value to the shell to the extent of the difference between S's buying price and S's selling price: in other words $7.27 less $3.64, or $3.63. On this basis, the tax on the value added by S ought to be the tax on $3.63, while the tax on the value added by C should be the tax on $3.64, and the tourist should pay both of these to reflect tax on the total value added in taking the sea-shell from the sea shore and turning it into an item of goods for sale to the tourist. Under the EC VAT, this is exactly what happens.

C must account to the tax authorities for the VAT on the $3.64, which C receives from S. S receives VAT on $7.27 from the tourist, but is allowed to recover the VAT on the $3.64 paid out to C from this tax. S must then account for the difference between the VAT received from the tourist, and the VAT paid out to C, to the tax authorities. The tax paid out by S – just to confuse you – is known as the input tax. The tax collected in by S is known as the output tax.[90] A registered person is required to account to the tax authorities only for the difference between the output tax collected and the input tax paid.[91]

Permissible national taxes

EU member states are required to impose VAT. Does this prevent them levying other taxes on goods? Article 33 of the Sixth VAT Directive provides the answer. Member states may maintain or introduce 'taxes on insurance contracts, taxes on betting and gambling, excise duties, stamp duties and, more generally, any taxes duties or charges which cannot be characterised as turnover taxes, provided however that those taxes, duties or charges do not ... give rise to formalities connected with the crossing of frontiers'.

The European Court has interpreted this provision as prohibiting a state from adopting a wide-based turnover tax that could rival VAT. In particular, it prohibited the Danish government from introducing a levy, known as the labour market contribution, on enterprises. In the case of an enterprise registered for VAT, the levy was based on the same turnover figures as for VAT. It also applied to enterprises not subject to VAT. The aim of the levy was to finance social expenditure that the Danish government had agreed to take from employees. In other words, it was designed to shift some of the tax burden from employers to consumers.

90. Because it is the tax on the input (the sea-shell). In VAT, the focus is on the goods, not the money paid for those goods.
91. The thoughtful will want to know what happens when the input tax exceeds the output tax in a period. The answer is, in principle, that the tax authorities must refund the difference to the taxable person. However, for what should be obvious reasons, this will be subject to anti-evasion and anti-avoidance safeguards.

The Court ruled that this was a turnover tax of a kind prohibited by article 33.[92] After noting similarities and differences between the levy and VAT, the Court commented: 'it is not necessary for it to resemble VAT in every respect; it is sufficient for it to exhibit the essential characteristics of VAT.' In the Court's view, the levy did so, and was therefore adopted in breach of article 33. Several other governments have also been prevented from introducing wide-based taxes by this provision.[93]

Member states have maintained excise duties and stamp duties throughout the (short) history of VAT. Many abolished a wide range of individual sales taxes when they introduced VAT. In recent years, the specific taxes have been returning. A range of reasons, or justifications, are given for these taxes. They are undoubtedly driven by the continuing need to find new forms of revenue, given that article 33 has effectively prevented states having more than one widely based turnover tax.

There are several justifications offered for continuing or introducing specific taxes. One is that there is now no higher rate of VAT. If states wish to impose a luxury rate of tax on a product, this is done by a combination of a specific tax and VAT. This is a primary justification for continuing the excise duties that have long been levied on specific goods throughout the EU. Another justification is the growth of environmental taxes, such as taxes on plastic bags or disposable razors. The aim of these taxes is to apply to specific products the 'polluter pays' principle.[94] A third reason, more relevant in practice to services than goods, is the use of specific taxes to tax supplies exempt from VAT. There can also be an overlap with income and social taxes, for example where those impose tax liabilities on supplies by employers to employees.[95]

---

[92] *Dansk Denkavit v Skaateministeriet* Case C-200/90, [1994] STC 482. The Court subsequently confirmed this decision in an infraction action concerning the same levy: *EC Commission v Denmark* Case C-234/91, [1997] STC 721. That report confirmed that the Danish government had repealed the levy, and adjusted the VAT.

[93] See the cases cited in the *Dansk Denkavit* case, note 92.

[94] This is approved at EU level by art 130r of the EC Treaty, but does not apply to taxes at EU level without unanimous agreement: art 130s. To date, there has been no such agreement, and individual states have taken their own initiatives in doing this. The EC Commission has recently encouraged these initiatives: COM (97)9, *Environmental Taxes and Charges in the Single Market*. For an analysis of measures that might be taken, see S Tindale and G Holtham, *Green Tax Reform* (Institute for Public Policy Research, London, 1997).

[95] For example, on supplies of goods by employers to employees.

Excise duties

The excise duties or taxes levied by all member states are a modern version of ancient taxes.[96] Currently, they are applied throughout the EU to three groups of products: tobacco products, alcoholic drinks, and mineral oils. Most states also have other forms of excisable goods and services.[97]

Much effort has been expended within the EU and its predecessors in trying to harmonise the excise duties under article 99. That they distort trading patterns can be seen by the problems experienced in southern Britain since the UK joined the EC. British excise duties on alcoholic drinks and on tobacco products are traditionally high, and in particular are significantly higher than those in France and Belgium respectively.

This has led to two developments in trading patterns between Britain and its neighbours. The first was the growth of 'duty-free shops' at most British ports and airports.[98] This allowed individuals to buy limited amounts of products[99] free of excise duty and VAT when leaving one EC state to travel to another. The state to which the traveller was going also exempted the products on arrival. This practice, particularly popular with British travellers, was intended to be discontinued when the single market was established, but was maintained for a transitional period.

---

96. The *Oxford English Dictionary* suggests the term is a modification of the Dutch term, now *accijnzen*, and traces it back with its present meaning to 1409, thence to the Latin *adcensare*.

97. Many states also have other excise duties, but there is no universal fourth group. Cars, or their use, are a common target. Originally, excises duties were levied only on products. They are now increasingly levied on the use of goods or other services. In the absence of specific EU measures, such as the prohibition on discrimination or the use of an excise duty as a disguised state aid, there is no issue relevant to free movement of goods in the imposition of most of these forms of excise, and they are not further discussed.

98. More properly called tax-free shops (because there is no longer any customs duty), these are permitted within the EU until 30 June 1999 by Council Directive 92/12/EEC (the horizontal excise directive: see note 106), art 28.

99. Typically, 1 litre of spirits or more of less strong drinks, and 200 cigarettes or equivalent in other tobacco products. The same reliefs also apply to reliefs from both internal taxes and customs duties for travellers to and from third states. The current authority in the UK is the Travellers' Allowances Order 1994, 1994 SI No 955. See also the Excise Duties (Personal Reliefs) Order 1992, 1992 SI No 3155, which is the authority under which UK customs officers currently act in connection with alcoholic drinks and tobacco purchased in France and Belgium.

The second practice is the widespread cross-border shopping by British residents in France and Belgium, including cross-channel shopping excursions, for excise products. The UK government has repeatedly seized excessive[100] quantities of goods brought back to Britain, and has repeatedly indicated that it is losing large sums of revenue for this reason. It has also reduced the real value of some of the excises in question.

The solution to the cross-border shopping problem would be the harmonisation of both the rates and incidences of the excises, so as to remove the differentials. The Commission has attempted to secure this on a number of occasions since 1967, with limited success.[101] The arrival of the single market forced the adoption of two directives on the excise duties on alcoholic drinks, imposing common definitions and minimum rates of duty.[102] Even these appear to offer more than they actually achieve. Faced with a German refusal to impose any form of excise on wine, the minimum rate eventually agreed was zero. There was slightly more success with the proposals to harmonise the levy of excises on tobacco, but not much. As a result of a combination of measures, a minimum tax levy on cigarettes of the most popular kind was set at 57 per cent of the retail price.[103] This is a combination of excise duties levied in both of two ways and VAT. The equivalent measure dealing with mineral oils was left as a patchwork, with only partial setting of rates, and with all member states benefiting from at least one derogation.[104]

The Commission's efforts at proposing legislation had greater success with its proposals to harmonise the methods for handling excise goods. For an excise duty to work, a framework is necessary to keep goods out of the market until the excise is paid. Within the single market, this required measures to allow goods to be trans-

---

100. Because the amount is in excess of the amount that the carrier has obtained for his own use in the course of cross-border shopping and which he has transported': Excise Duties (Personal Reliefs) Order 1992, reg 3 (see note 99).

101. For a history, see Easson op cit note 8, ch 4; Farmer and Lyal, op cit note 13, ch 10; Terra and Wattel, op cit note 21, ch 7.

102. Council Directives 92/83 and 92/84 (19 October 1992)(1992 OJ L 316/21 and 316/29).

103. Council Directive 92/79 (19 October 1992)(1992 OJ L 316/8). A parallel directive, 92/80 of the same date (1992 OJ L 316/10) applies to other tobacco products.

104. See Council Directive 92/82 (19 October 1992)(1992 OJ L 316/19), and Council Decision 92/510 (19 October 1992)(1992 OJ L 316/16).

ferred between states, and held in states, while in bond.[105] What has been termed the horizontal excise duty directive achieved this in 1992.[106] By this means, free movement of excisable goods is ensured while the national excise revenues are protected.[107]

---

105. This is, until the duty had been paid, and the goods released for sale by the excise tax authorities. Goods may be handled until that time under the general provisions of a bond to the authorities for any duty payable.

106. Council Directive 92/12/EEC on the General Arrangements for Products subject to Excise Duty and on the Holding, Movement and Monitoring of such Products (25 February 1992)(1992 OJ L 76/1). This applies to excises on mineral oils, alcohol and alcoholic beverages, and manufactured tobacco (art 3) but not to other products.

107. Details of the regime are beyond the scope of this book. See the works cited at note 101 for further details.

CHAPTER SIX

Taxing the EU's citizens

The way that a state taxes its citizens varies widely within the EU. So do arrangements for social security. While all member states have some form of social security, they range from schemes that are highly centralised and state-run to others that rely on making membership of semi-private schemes compulsory. The variations also apply to the generosity of the schemes and therefore the total levels of taxes and social contribution. There is further variation in the way the cost of the schemes are spread among those who must pay. For example, some schemes focus on families, while others treat each individual separately.[1] Some schemes expect the rich to pay far more than the poor, and impose strongly progressive tax systems,[2] while other have more neutral systems.[3]

Fundamental policy decisions therefore lie behind the patterns of individual taxation in the EU states. These decisions express, at least indirectly, what the societies regard as 'fair'.[4] The states of northern Europe have strongly egalitarian systems which absorb perhaps half the nation's wealth,[5] while other systems leave more to the individual or family and provide only a 'safety net' for the

[1.] See the 'splitting rule' illustrated in the Schumacker case, note 62.
[2.] A progressive tax system is one where the richer pay proportionately more than the poorer, for example because of increasing rates of tax on higher income.
[3.] For a full discussion, see D W Williams 'Trends in Social Taxation' (1997), Bulletin of the International Bureau for Fiscal Documentation, p 254.
[4.] There is considerable literature on fairness in taxation, starting with the still definitive statements of Adam Smith (sometimes called the father of income tax) in his *Wealth of Nations*. See for an introductory account, 'Good and bad taxes' in D Williams, *Taxation Principles and Policy* (Teach Yourself series, Hodder & Stoughton, 1992).
[5.] For a recent discussion see R Brunn (ed), *Comparative Welfare Benefits* (Macmillan 1996).

poor.[6] Further, these systems are deeply entrenched in the democratic structures of those states. Reform of personal taxes requires a political consensus. If it is absent, the attempt to change the methods of taxing individuals may prove impossible. This is because, as all tax authorities know, an effective tax may take the form of a compulsory levy, but it depends in large part in its acceptance by most of those who must pay it.[7]

Harmonising personal taxes?

Awareness of these variations and constraints no doubt contributed to the reluctance of the EEC founders to interfere with these systems. The EC Treaty is almost silent on the subject of individual taxation. It also requires only the coordination of social security systems, not their harmonisation.[8] Action in the field of social security has accordingly provided for coordination, but no more. There has been no action at all at the legislative level concerning individual direct taxes.

There were early ambitions within the EEC to harmonise the individual income tax,[9] but these were abandoned several Commissions ago,[10] and are most unlikely to be revived. The only legislative initiative taken by the Commission in the field of personal direct tax have concerned frontier workers (those who live on one side of a national frontier and work on the other, or who cross national frontiers regularly as part of their work), but there has been no formal progress on the proposal.[11] Similarly, although

6. For a recent review, see C A de Kam, 'Who pays the taxes? The distribution of effective tax burdens in four EU countries', 1996 EC Tax Review, p 175.
7. The clearest example – but not the only one – of a tax that taxpayers would not pay is the so-called poll tax, or community charge, imposed in the UK in 1990. See 'The poll tax disaster', in Williams, op cit note 4, ch 1.
8. EC Treaty, art 51.
9. The Neumark Committee proposed this in 1963, and the Commission went as far as proposing a programme of partial harmonisation in 1967. See S Cnossen, Tax Coordination in the EC, (Kluwer, 1987), p 41.
10. In 1979 Commissioner Burke stated that it 'is not our ambition to harmonise the personal income tax in general': R Burke, 'Harmonisation of Taxation in Europe', 1979 Intertax 46.
11. In recent years, the Commission has confined itself to a recommendation of 21 December 1993 on taxation of non-residents (10 February 1994) (1994 OJ L39) seeking the avoidance of double taxation. This has, however, encouraged Advocates General to argue for similar solutions before the Court. See, for example, the arguments in Bachmann v Belgium Case C-204/90, [1994] STC at 859.

the EEC adopted a detailed scheme for coordinating social security schemes in 1971, and has extended it since, there has been no formal action on the harmonisation of schemes. Again, there were early ambitions in this area, but they made no progress.[12]

The absence of any formal attempt at harmonisation after the early days of the EEC is a reflection of the political intractability of action in this area. It also reflects a general view that the creation of the European Union did not require a common form of income tax or a common social security system. The initial plans were overambitious, and were not necessary for a free Europe. The focus should, instead, be only on impediments to the freedoms of movement or of competition.

Free movement of citizens

The EC Treaty, in article 48, provided unequivocally for the freedom for those seeking work as employees to move between the member states of the EU to find and take up jobs. 'Freedom of movement of workers shall be secured . . . '.[13] That freedom 'shall entail the abolition of any discrimination based on nationality . . . as regards employment, remuneration and other conditions of work and employment'.[14] Further, the European Council is under a duty to 'adopt such measures in the field of social security as are necessary to provide freedom of movement of workers'.[15] These provisions are designed to ensure that the proscription against discrimination on grounds of nationality[16] actually works in the most important areas of economic effort for most people, their jobs and pensions.

Early effect was given to these general statements by a series of subordinate measures. Two are of particular importance for tax purposes. Regulation 1612/68[17] provides that a worker who is a national of one member state working in another member state

---

12. For a detailed background note, see Cnossen, op cit note 9, p 42.
13. EC Treaty, art 48, para 1.
14. EC Treaty, art 48, para 2.
15. EC Treaty, art 51.
16. In EC Treaty, art 6.
17. Regulation 1612/68 of the Council on freedom of movement for workers within the Community (15 October 1968)(1968 OJ Sp Edn II, p 47).

'shall enjoy the same social and tax advantages as national workers'.[18] While there is no other express mention of taxation, a detailed measure, Regulation 1408/71,[19] aims at ensuring that a worker is always within one, but only one, social security system as he or she moves around the EU.

The rights originally given to workers have been expanded substantially not only to the self-employed but, subject to limits,[20] to all European citizens.[21] These extensions are made without mention of the tax position, save only that a charge for a residence permit cannot be used to impose a separate concealed tax.[22]

It may be surmised that when the EEC was first established, tax was not seen as a significant element in the barriers against the mobility of labour. The tax barriers against employees moving from one state to another were limited as compared with barriers of employment law, immigration and direct discrimination. It is also observable that relatively few people have chosen to exercise their right of free movement. Since those early days, the explicit barriers have fallen away. As a result, the tax barriers are becoming more important. Changes in tax systems in most member states over the last 50 years have also contributed to making the barriers higher, thereby accentuating the problem.

Tax barriers to freedom of movement

What are those barriers? Potentially, there are several. One occurs when income tax in a state is imposed on migrant workers more heavily than on local workers. This usually happens because the local worker is entitled to deductions or allowances not available to the migrant. A second is where the migrant worker is faced with two charges to income tax: one levy by the state of employment, and the other by the state of residence.

[18.] Regulation 1612/68, art 7, para 2.

[19.] Regulation 1408/71 of the Council on the application of social security schemes to employed persons, to self-employed persons and to members of their families moving within the Community (14 June 1971)(reprinted, as substantially amended, at 1983 OJ L 230/6).

[20.] See in particular the conditions in Council Directive 90/364/EEC on the right of residence (28 June 1990)(1990 OJ L 180/26).

[21.] As defined in EC Treaty, art 8. The right of movement of citizens is in art 8a.

[22.] See Council Regulation 1251/70, art 6.

Other problems occur because employees and their employers find themselves paying contributions to two systems at the same time, while only being entitled to one set of benefits. The interaction of different levels of tax and social security contribution rates add a further layer of problem. For example, income tax rates in one state may be lower than in another, but the social contribution rates higher. A migrant worker may find that he or she is caught by the higher income tax rates and the higher social contribution rates.

These issues have been exacerbated in recent years because underlying shifts in the patterns of taxation have been adding both to income tax and to social contributions. This is in part because of a shift from taxation on capital income to taxation on earnings. The shift is driven, in part, by the growing costs of social security benefits. In addition, because capital is more mobile than labour, it has proved more difficult to tax it. Overall, therefore, taxation and social contributions payable by and for labour have risen.[23]

To see how these barriers operate and the measures taken to remove them, we examine how national systems handle migrant workers first for income tax and then for social security systems. We then discuss how far EC law requires those barriers to be removed, and how successful it has been in achieving this.

Taxing foreign workers

An individual who has been living and working in one state, and who moves to work in another state, may be confronted with several tax problems. It is encouraging to note that nationality is rarely one of those problems. None of the member states of the EU base their claims to levy personal income tax on the grounds of nationality.[24] The proscription in article 6 of the EC Treaty is therefore rarely directly in issue.[25]

23. This has been identified as an issue of concern by the Commission: Commission Discussion Paper SEC(96)487.
24. This approach to income tax is used by the USA, Mexico and the Philippines, but not by any other major state.
25. Some minor measures have been based on nationality. For example, personal allowances to the UK income tax were traditionally available to all residents, and to all Commonwealth citizens and citizens of the Republic of Ireland (Income and Corporation Taxes Act 1988, s 278). Following criticism, this was amended in 1996 to refer to EEA nationals and not just nationals of Ireland.

Instead, the consistent European practice is to tax individuals who are resident within the tax jurisdiction of the state. It is accepted practice that an individual who is resident may be taxed on his or her worldwide income earned while a resident.[26] Some states tax only locally earned income, and exempt foreign income from tax, but they usually do so by what is termed 'exemption with progression'. This means that they calculate the total worldwide income of the individual, but only tax the locally sourced proportion of it.

Residence is variously defined among the member states but the predominant element in the test is that of presence. An individual who is present in a country for 183 days or more in any year (whether continuously or during several visits) is usually regarded as resident there.[27] Those who visit for shorter periods but over a period of years may also be regarded as resident.[28] So may those who maintain a home in the country, even though it is not visited at all during a year. It follows that a taxpayer can be a resident for income tax purposes of two or more countries at the same time.

National systems often discriminate deliberately between residents and non-residents. For example, personal allowances or credits may not be granted to non-residents. Other discrimination against non-residents may be less obvious. One common problem is that of contributions to private pension schemes. A contribution to a pension scheme often attracts tax relief for the contributor. However, the tax relief is usually available only for schemes that meet strict national conditions. Typically, one of the conditions is that the pension scheme is established in the country. If it is not, then tax relief is refused. This poses a problem for the migrant worker who is contributing to a pension scheme in the previous state of residence. The state of residence will refuse an allowance for the contribution. But the contributor also loses out if he or she has no income in the state where the pension scheme is established, and so gets no tax relief there either. A similar problem also occurs over gifts to charities. Again, states frequently allow a deduction for a contribution to a charity against tax, but only if the charity is

---

26. This is the basis on which the income tax has been levied in the UK since 1803.
27. For a full account of the UK approach, see the Inland Revenue leaflet IR20, *Residence and ordinary residence in the UK*.
28. For example, the UK has an alternative test of ordinary residence. An individual can become ordinarily resident following visits of 90 days or more for four or more years: see note 21.

recognised by the tax authority. In practice, that means the charity must be established in the country where the deduction is claimed.

Double tax conventions

The tax problems of the migrant worker are traditionally tackled not by national legislation but through the use of double tax conventions. The OECD Model Convention provides several relevant answers to the position of the employee who has moved jobs from one country to another. The answers, or variants of them,[29] apply to almost all migrant workers within the EU.

The most important answer is that a migrant worker will be regarded as resident in one state only – usually the state in which the worker has a permanent home.[30] This avoids the risk of the employee being taxed on worldwide income in two states at the same time. Further, where the employee is resident in one state,[31] and works in another, the employee can be taxed in the state of employment only if the '183 day rule', as it is called, is met. An employee resident in one state but exercising the employment in another, can be taxed by the other state only if:

(a) the employee is present in the state for 183 days or more in any year;
  or
(b) the employee is paid by or on behalf of an employer resident in the state;
  or
(c) the cost of the pay is borne by a branch or permanent establishment of the employer based in the state.[32]

The effect of the 183 day rule is to prevent an employee being taxed in another state by reason only of short visits to that other state on behalf of an employer not based in the other state. There

---

29. As discussed in ch 3, the account here is based on the OECD Model, although individual double taxation conventions contain some variations from these rules.
30. OECD Model DTC, art 4, para 2.
31. Including cases where that residence is decided by art 4.
32. OECD Model DTC, art 15.

are exceptions to this general rule for special cases such as transport workers,[33] those in government service,[34] and diplomats.[35]

Migrant workers are also protected to some extent by the non-discrimination provision usually contained in a DTC. This is designed to bar tax discrimination against a foreign national simply because of nationality. It is, however, a limited protection. In particular, the OECD Model form of the provision applies only to individuals 'in the same circumstances, in particular with respect to residence'.[36] Further, there is a specific reservation against the provision being used as a basis for a non-resident claiming personal allowances or reliefs based on civil status or family responsibilities.[37]

The EU position

The conclusion of double tax conventions between member states satisfies the only express requirement of the EC Treaty relevant to the taxation of migrant workers.[38] Does it, however, ensure full respect for the freedom protected by article 48 and the subordinate legislation? We have seen elsewhere that it is not a sufficient defence to a claim of discrimination that a member state can show a double tax convention has been agreed. This is because the convention is itself also subject to EU law. Nonetheless, in practical terms the rules about single residence and the 183 day rule solve many problems. Do they solve enough?

Tackling hidden discrimination

The European Court of Justice, in a series of cases, has upheld challenges to the system just described as insufficient fully to ensure the absence of discrimination. It has done so by drawing on

33. Art 15, para 3.
34. OECD Model DTC, art 19.
35. OECD Model DTC, art 27, reflecting the separate immunity given to diplomats by the Vienna Convention on Diplomatic Relations 1963. This, and similar conventions on consular officers and international organisations, are accepted by all EU member states.
36. OECD Model DTC, art 24, para 1.
37. OECD Model DTC, art 24, para 3.
38. EC Treaty, art 220.

EC law established in non-tax cases but applied by the Court to what it saw to be similar problems in tax law. In so doing, the Court has encountered significant criticism.

The first case dealing specifically with the tax problems of a migrant worker was that of *Biehl*.[39] Biehl was a German national who worked in Luxembourg for ten years before changing jobs to one in Germany. Income tax and solidarity tax were both withheld from his Luxembourg pay by his employer in accordance with usual practice. In the year in which he left, the amount deducted was higher than his final tax liability in Luxembourg. His application for the refund of the excess was, however, refused, on the basis of a legal provision turning the withholding tax on those who were resident in Luxembourg for only part of the year into a final withholding tax.[40] Biehl challenged this as indirect discrimination, but the tax administration resisted his claim on the ground that the provision was designed to stop taxpayers gaining undue advantages by becoming non-resident. The matter was taken to the Conseil d'Etat du Luxembourg. That court referred the matter to the European Court to decide if article 6 of the EC Treaty, article 48, or any other provision of EC law were relevant to the question before it.

Before the European Court, the Luxembourg authorities defended their action on grounds both of law and of fairness. The Commission supported the taxpayer, as did Advocate General Darmon. The Advocate General took the opportunity to spell out some guidelines for the Court. He recognised that 'in the present state of Community law, the sphere of direct taxation is outside the ambit of the EEC Treaty' and that it was for member states alone to decide how to legislate for these taxes. However, the obligations imposed by article 48 were directly opposable to such national legislation[41] if there were discrimination involved.[42] In his view, there was discrimination on the facts if the effect of any dif-

---

39. *Biehl v Administration des Contributions du Grand-Duche de Luxembourg* Case C-175/88, [1991] STC 575, [1990] ECR I-1779.

40. A final withholding tax, more commonly used on income from capital, is not open to review in the context of the total income of the recipient (for example, over a year as a whole).

41. The direct effect of art 48 was established in *Van Duyn v Home Office* Case 41/74, [1974] ECR 1337.

42. The Advocate General reminded the Court that art 6 (then 7) was not itself of direct effect, as it was implemented through more specific provisions, such as art 48: *EC Commission v Greece* Case 305/87, [1989] ECR 1461.

ferences in the treatment of different groups of people could amount to covert nationality discrimination. For this proposition, he relied on the *Sotgiu* case [43] as establishing that a discrimination expressed to be on the basis of the residence of individuals could be a disguised discrimination on rounds of nationality. In the Advocate General's view, this was so on the facts of the *Biehl* case. He also recommended that the non-contentious appeal procedure that could have been made available to the taxpayer was not an appropriate remedy for any discrimination because it could not always remedy the insecurity caused by the tax provision. In that basis, the Advocate General found that the Luxembourg law offended against article 48, paragraphs 1 and 2, and Regulation 1612/68.

The Court reached the conclusion that the law was discriminatory, although it rested its decision on article 48, paragraph 2 alone. It found there was discrimination in the law because 'it will work in particular against taxpayers who are nationals of other member states. It is often such persons who will in the course of the year leave the country or take up residence there'.[44] The rights in article 48 are expressly made subject to 'limitations justified on grounds of public policy, public security or public health'.[45] Although no express reference was made to this provision, the Luxembourg authority had argued the policy justification for its rule as being to protect the progressive nature of the income tax.[46] The Court rejected this approach to justification by reference to examples it considered discriminatory. In so doing, the Court adopted an absolute approach of regarding the provision as discriminatory because in some circumstances it could be discriminatory, rather than by deciding that there was discrimination.

---

43. *Sotgiu v Deutsche Bundespost* Case 152/73, [1974] ECR 153.
44. There is nothing in the record of the case to show the factual basis for this assertion. While it may be accurate, it does not follow that it is. However, there is a dilemma for a state that does not base its taxes on nationality grounds because it will not have any statistics available either to confirm or refute this assumption. The converse to this is that it may also not be possible to show the validity of the Luxembourg administration's assumption on grounds of fairness.
45. Art 48, para 3.
46. No mention appears to have been made of the relevance of any double tax convention. Under the usual rules discussed above these might have operated to have Biehl treated as a resident in the year in question. Alternatively, there may have been other remedies against any double taxation.

This approach is no doubt a reflection of the limited role of the European Court in cases such as this – it can interpret but not apply.[47] However, it leads to a greater confrontation between EC law and national law than may be necessary. This is because this absolutist approach to the interaction of article 48 and national law means that article 48 overrides national law when there might be discrimination leading to a barrier against free movement rather than when there actually is such discrimination. This means that a taxpayer can also take advantage of the interaction to pay less tax than a resident taxpayer as well as to avoid paying more. It was the latter that occurred in Biehl's case because of excessive protection by Luxembourg against the danger of the former.[48]

Protecting national tax systems

The Court had dealt lightly in the Biehl case with the concerns of the national tax authority. However, in the Bachmann[49] case which followed it, these objections were taken more seriously.[50] The Bachmann case raised one of the central fiscal problems of personal income taxes in Europe: how to deal with pensions. Most states provide by one means or another generous tax reliefs to encourage employers and employees together to provide pensions for the employees after their employment has ended for age or health reasons. A common approach is to regard pensions as deferred

---

47. EC Treaty, art 177. See generally, S Weatherill and P Beaumont, *EC Law* (Penguin, 2nd edition, 1995) ch 9.

48. It may be concerns of this nature that led the Luxembourg authorities to take only limited action following this decision. They also felt that the Biehl case had not given sufficient weight to the alternative remedies available to someone in Biehl's position. Consequently, they declined to change the substantive rule in question. This prompted the Commission to refer the matter back to the European Court under art 169 of the EC Treaty. The court heard this reference in *EC Commission v Luxembourg* Case C-151/94, [1995] STC 1047. The Court upheld the Commission objection to the Luxembourg failure to act. In failing to amend the substantive legislation, it had failed to fulfill its treaty obligations.

49. *Bachmann v Belgium* Case C-204/90, [1994] STC 855, [1992] ECR I-249.

50. The case was parallelled by a separate case brought against Belgium by the Commission, essentially on the same grounds: *EC Commission v Belgium* Case C-300/90. It was followed in *Kraus v Land Baden-Wurttemberg* Case C-19/92, [1993] ECR I-1663, a case concerning formalities relating to the use of post-graduate degrees.

remuneration. A tax allowance or deduction is granted so that the employee is not taxed on any sums paid into a pension scheme or reserve for the employee either directly or from the employer. Frequently, the pension scheme income is also exempt from tax. Instead, the pension is taxed when it is paid from the pension fund or reserve to the employee. This approach often applies to voluntary schemes and those that are, in effect, mandatory by reason of a particular employment.

The cost of the tax foregone by reference to pensions can be considerable, and consequently states are alert to restrict benefits. A common form of restriction is to allow tax relief only if the pension scheme is approved within the state. Such approval can usually be obtained only by schemes established within the jurisdiction of the state.

This was the problem that faced Bachmann. He was a German national employed in Belgium. He was a member of a voluntary German pension scheme that he had joined before moving to Belgium. In making his tax returns in Belgium, Bachmann claimed a deduction for the premiums paid to the German scheme. These were rejected by the Belgian tax authorities. Bachmann then challenged the rejection before the courts, invoking articles 48, 59,[51] 67[52] and 106 of the EEC Treaty in his support.

The Court resisted Bachmann's claims. While finding that the Belgian legislation was discriminatory under article 48,[53] the Court found that the discrimination was justified 'by the need to preserve the cohesion of the applicable tax system'.[54] In finding that there was discrimination, the Court showed little sympathy for the argument that the taxpayer should have taken out a new policy in Belgium, or the argument that the Belgian authorities would not have taxed the pension if they had not allowed a deduction for the pre-

---

51. The focus on art 59 was on the other side of the payment at issue, namely the provision of pension and insurance services. The argument was that this forced the insurer to be established in Belgium. The court accepted this argument. The issues are explored in ch 7.

52. This was a reference to the aspect of the case involving freedom of movement of capital. Art 67 has now been repealed: see ch 9.

53. And art 59.

54. [1994] STC at 880, formal ruling of the court. Several commentators have drawn attention to a translation error in the English language versions of the judgment (which was originally in French). The word 'cohesion' should have been 'coherence'. As 'cohesion' does not make sense in this context, the word 'coherence' is used throughout this account.

miums.[55] That argument was rejected because the non-national, on returning home, would probably be taxed on the pension, and would therefore not enjoy the Belgian tax exemption. In particular, the Court recorded the view that the absence of harmonisation in this area could not constitute a condition precedent for the application of article 48.

The court faced stronger arguments over policy justifications of the Belgian approach. Although this had been challenged directly by the Commission, as well as by the Commission's support for Bachmann, the Belgian case was supported by the German, Dutch and Danish governments. This is the first mark of a concern growing among member states about the potential effects of the Court's possible actions in this area. The key argument presented by the governments was that of the fiscal purpose of the Belgian law. The loss of revenue of the tax exemption of contributions was, over the lifetime of a taxpayer, to be offset by the tax paid on the pension. This would not happen if the tax exemption were given to Bachmann, as it would be the German government that would receive the offset for the Belgian government's exemption.

The Court noted that a solution could be found to the issue by reference to a double tax convention. No such solution was in issue here.[56] Nor were there any EC coordination or harmonisation measures. It followed that the Belgian government was entitled to take measures to protect the loss. As no measures less restrictive than those actually used were available to the government, its actions were necessary to protect the public interest.

The Court's judgment therefore supported the main case made by the governments involved. It went against the opinion of Advocate General Mischo. The Advocate General had supported the argument that there was a breach of article 48 for which there was no justification. He recognised that the fundamental question was whether the Belgian approach could be justified by the need for effective fiscal control, and noted the Court's observation to that

---

55. This is a common policy alternative to the approach outlined above. There is a need either to exempt the contribution, or to exempt the benefit. To tax both would be excessive taxation. To tax neither would amount to a subsidy of the arrangement.

56. The OECD Model DTC contains no provision dealing directly with these problems. Art 18 provides that the usual rule is that pensions are taxed where the pensioner is resident. The Commentary to the DTC suggests wording to deal with the tax treatment of contributions or premiums on a reciprocal basis, but was not in issue here (Commentary, art 18, para 11).

effect in the *Cassis de Dijon* case.[57] The Advocate General's view was that Belgium could have adopted some lesser measure than the complete rejection of Bachmann's claim. He was, in particular, attracted to the solution offered by the Commission in its 1980 draft proposal.[58] He also noted that the Belgian government had concluded agreements with France, Luxembourg and the Netherlands to deal with the situation that arose here by administrative machinery that helped prevent any tax evasion.[59] These various alternatives meant that the approach taken by the Belgian government was not the only way of solving the problem.[60]

The Court was next challenged by a case raising the reverse problem to *Bachmann*, namely the refusal of the German tax authorities to grant full personal allowances to a Belgian national,[61] Schumacker, employed in Germany and earning most of his income there.[62]

The *Schumacker* case started as a challenge by the taxpayer to adverse treatment, as he saw it, in the way his income was reviewed by the German tax authorities at the end of a year. It was rapidly elevated into a conflict between the Commission and the taxpayer on the one hand, and national governments on the other. This was evidenced by the submission of written observations by not only Germany, but also Greece, France, the Netherlands, and the UK, with the Danish government also adding comments at the oral stage.

The core of the dispute in *Schumacker* was the differential treatment given by the German income tax law to habitual residents of Germany as compared with those with no such habitual residence. In accordance with common practice, Germany taxed non-

---

57. *Rewe-Zentral AG v Bundesmonpolverwaltung für Branntwien* Case 120/78, [1979] ECR 649 at 662 : 'Obstacles to movement . . . must be accepted . . . as necessary in order to satisfy mandatory requirements relating in particular to the effectiveness of fiscal supervision . . . '
58. See note 54 at p. 878.
59. The term used was 'evasion' but 'avoidance' was probably intended.
60. The criticism that this decision received, together with the hint about double tax conventions, made another case in the series predictable: the *Wielockx* case. See ch 7.
61. The series of cases involving Belgian, Dutch and German nationals reflects the tortuous but open physical nature of the border between these three states, and the vagaries of the boundaries between different zones of linguistic dominance in the area. In particular there are enclaves of Belgian territory completely surrounded by Dutch territory in the area of Baarle-Hertog.
62. *Finanzamt Koln-Alstadt v Schumacker* Case C-279/93, [1995] STC 306.

residents only on income arising in Germany, while residents were taxed on total income. Again, based on usual practice, the German authorities assumed that the non-resident would be taxed elsewhere, and therefore withheld from non-residents certain personal allowances.[63] Non-residents were also subject to a final withholding of tax on earnings without year end adjustment similar to that applied by the Luxembourg authorities.[64] Schumacker and his family lived in Belgium, but he worked in Germany and his wife was unemployed. However, the right to tax his income in Germany arose under article 15 of the relevant double tax convention.[65] The particular feature of the case was that virtually all the taxpayer's income was earned in Germany despite the long term residence in Belgium.

Advocate General Leger reflected the nature of the challenge to national tax systems in his opinion. He noted that, unlike VAT, 'direct tax is at a purely embryonic stage of harmonisation' and that therefore the member states had exclusive powers in the area of law under consideration. 'They are nevertheless required to adopt, in those areas, rules which respect the great freedoms laid down by Community law.' In particular, article 48, paragraph 2 must be respected. Nor could the exercise of rights under that article be conditional. Observance could not depend on the contents of a double tax treaty. At the same time, the Advocate General cited a caution against taking the principle of nondiscrimination too far.[66]

After careful consideration of the principles involved, and also the terms of the usual non-discrimination provision in a double tax convention,[67] the Advocate General followed the lead given by that article and concluded that a person subject to unlimited taxation in Germany by reason of residence was not in a comparable position to a person subject to limited taxation by reason of non-residence. However, the special feature in Schumacker's case was that almost all his income was from his German work, and he was

63. These included family allowances, and the right to split incomes between husband and wife, reducing the effect of the progressive tax rates where the income of one of the couple was higher than that of the other.
64. See note 39.
65. See note 32. It would seem on the facts that he was clearly resident in Belgium under the usual DTC rules (art 4), but was caught by the 183 day rule.
66. F Vanistendael in 'The Limits to the New Community Tax Order', (1994) CMLRev at p 293.
67. Art 24. See note 36.

not therefore taxed in Belgium. His was the classic case of the frontier worker. This was well known to the tax authorities, who had adopted rules to deal with the case[68] where the frontier workers came from the Netherlands. This recognition of the inadequacy of the distinction between resident and non-resident in such a case was, however, an indication of the discrimination that might otherwise arise. In this case, the national solution did not apply, and discrimination did arise. Further, the tax authorities could not plead the coherence of their system in their defence if they were able elsewhere to deal with the problem. In effect, what would then emerge would be discrimination in Germany between Dutch and Belgian resident frontier workers. Any limitation on tax benefits in this way must be nondiscriminatory.[69]

The Court also accepted that there was discrimination in this case. There was no doubt that article 48 was relevant to the case, as was Regulation 1612/68. It accepted that residents and non-residents were not in the same situation. However, this was a special case because the taxpayer receives no significant income in his place of residence, but receives the major part of it in the state of employment. This did give rise to discrimination. Further, the argument of coherence of the tax system was not a defence here. This is because there could be no reconsideration of the taxpayer's situation in the state of residence. The state of employment was therefore required to treat the taxpayer as a resident. Although the Court did not express its decision in those terms, the effect was to extend to the Belgian taxpayer the treatment he would have received under the bilateral agreement had he been a Dutch resident working in Germany. Put on that basis, this was a narrow exception to the *Bachmann* approach. How narrow fell to be reviewed in a later case in the series, *Asscher*.[70] That case, however, also involved social security issues and we must therefore review these rules before analysing that decision.

---

68. Both Germany and the Netherlands treat someone who receives 90 per cent more of his or her taxable income in that country, while being resident in the other country, as a resident for tax purposes. This was agreed as a protocol to the double tax convention operating between the two states in 1980.

69. The Advocate General notes that this point had already been made in the German courts in a judgment of 20 April 1989 (I R 219/82, BstBl 1990, vol II p 701), because it offended against the Basic Law of Germany.

70. *Asscher v Staatssecretaris van Financien* Case C-107/94, [1996] STC 1025.

Coordinating social security systems[71]

As previously noted, it is not the task of the EU to set a common social security system for all. Instead, it has the more limited, but not easy, task of coordinating social security systems of the member states. The chief instrument of coordination has been Regulation 1408/71, as amended and extended several times since first adoption.[72] Even though the rules are limited only to coordination, a formidable set of rules have been generated, along with considerable case law.

Most of the rules, and much of the case law, relate to social security benefits. These are beyond the scope of this book. There is also an important set of provisions dealing with contribution liability. In several member states this is significantly greater than liability to income tax for most employees, at least when account is taken of contributions paid by employers. Further, the process of collecting income tax and social contributions is increasingly being integrated. This is true of the rules under which the tax and contributions are imposed, of the way they are collected, and of the ways in which the uses of the two forms of fund are seen as part of a greater whole. As a consequence, the divisions between tax liability and social security contribution liability – regarded as fundamental by some – is increasingly hard to maintain from either a policy viewpoint or from practical considerations.[73]

The rules about contribution coordination are set out in Title II of Regulation 1408/71.[74] Of this the European Court has observed:

71. See generally P Watson, *Social Security Law in the EEC* (Croom Helm, 1979); D Wyatt and A Dashwood, *The Law of the European Communities* (Sweet & Maxwell, 1993), ch 14.

72. It is also supplemented at the practical level by Commission Regulation 574/72 (1972 JO L74/1, with the official translation at 1972 OJ 159).

73. As is noted below, integration is most advanced in the Netherlands. There has been significant work done in Britain on integrating income tax on employees with NI contributions. At the other extreme, it is being accepted in France that there should be more alignment. Failing such alignment, general taxes are being used to keep social security schemes properly funded as contributions fail to do so. Hence the policy convergence even where there has been limited practical or legal convergence.

74. As they are laid down in a regulation, these provisions are of course directly binding in their entirety on the member states: EC Treaty, art 189. They supersede not only the national laws of the member states, but also the series of bilateral agreements concluded between the member states before membership. This makes an interesting contrast with the analogous position for income tax, where there are no express coordination rules.

the provisions of Title II of the Regulation ... constitute a complete and uniform system of conflict rules the aim of which it to ensure that workers moving within the Community shall be subject to the social security schemes of only one state, in order to prevent more than one legislative system from being applicable and to avoid the complications which may result from that situation.[75]

Provided that there is a direct and sufficient link between the contributions in question, and one of the rules of EC law that it is sought to invoke,[76] the Community rules can be applied if they work to the contributor's benefit.[77] They also apply within the European Economic Area,[78] and may apply to EU national employees working in third states[79] if two or more member states are involved.

The general principle applied in all these cases is that the employee is liable to pay contributions in the state where he or she is employed.[80] This is the reverse of the general income tax law,[81] and applies notwithstanding that difference or that the employer is based in another state. However, if the employee normally works in two or more states (as with a cross-frontier worker such as a truck driver), then the same rule as for income tax will be used: habitual residence.[82] The effect of the rule is to prevent the second state requiring contributions from the employee.[83]

Specific rules deal with a number of special cases. The most important are those of the true frontier worker and the migrant worker temporarily in another state. A frontier worker is made

---

75. *Van Poucke v Rijksinstituut voor Sociale Verzekeringen der Selfstandigen* Case C-71/93, [1995] 3 CMLR 346.

76. In *Rheinhold & Mahla AUV v Bestuur van der Bedrijfsvereniging voor de Metllnijverheid* Case C-327/92, [1995] ECR I-1223, the Court found there was no direct and sufficient link between contributions due of an employer and the basis for invoking EC law. The payment in question was not a contribution but a liability to make good lost revenue. The Regulation did not therefore apply.

77. The rules cannot be invoked to leave a worker worse off than would otherwise be the case: *Ronfeldt v Bundesversicherungsanstalt für Angestellte* [1993] 1 CMLR 73.

78. By reason of the EEA Agreement, art 29 and annex VI.

79. See *Aldewereld v Staatsecretaris van Financien* Case 60/93, [1995] ECR I-2991.

80. Reg 1408/71, art 13, para 2.

81. See note 26. The primary taxing power is that of the state of residence, which is normally where the taxpayer lives: OECD Model DTC, art 4.

82. Reg 1408/71, art 14, para 2.

83. This emphasises the mismatch in the *Bachmann* case between the country of liability and the country in which Bachmann chose to make his arrangements for insurance. Had he stayed in Belgium a sufficient time, any liability to contribute would have arisen under Belgian law, not German law.

liable for contributions in the state where the employer is based.[84] A worker working temporarily in a state but who remains employed by an employer from another state remains liable to the social security system of that other state for up to twelve months – a period which may be extended.[85] The wide differences in levels of social security contributions lead employers to use the temporary rule as much as possible when transferring employees from a low contribution state to a high contribution state. The rule may be contrasted with the 183 day rule that applies for income tax purposes, which suggests different approaches to avoidance.[86]

It will be seen from this brief summary of the social security contribution position that there will be a variety of cases where the primary income tax liability of a migrant worker is in one state, while the primary social security contribution liability is in another state. This is an unavoidable consequence of the different policy approaches taken by different EU states. In the view of the Commission, which is undoubtedly correct, this can lead to excess compulsory liability being imposed on some employees. This will happen where the employee's work is in a state with high contributions, while his or her residence is in a state with high income tax rates. Conversely, an employee who arranges affairs so that the contributions and income tax are both lower is in a sheltered position compared with most employees.

The *Asscher* case

The most recent of the series of migrant worker cases is also the most intriguing, for it brings together most of the issues discussed in this chapter, and in particular looks at the interaction between tax and social security. The central character in the *Asscher* case[87] was a Dutch national who worked in the Netherlands as the director of a company of which he was sole shareholder. As such he was

---

84. Reg 1408/71, art 14, para 3.
85. Reg 1408/71, art 14, para 1, as interpreted with Recommendation 16 of the Administrative Commission of the EC of Social Security for Migrant Workers (see Williams, *The National Insurance Contributions Handbook* (FT Law & Tax, updated looseleaf), para D 1.28).
86. It is common for income tax purposes to find people who might be caught by the 183 day rule being given two jobs, one of which is in the 'new' state, and one of which is elsewhere, perhaps in a third, low tax state. This reduces the amount of income caught by the 'new' state.
87. See note 70.

treated in the Netherlands in the same way as an employee. He had moved some years before to Belgium, and had become a Belgian resident. He also worked in Belgium. Because of the Belgian job, Asscher received less than 90 per cent of his earnings from the Netherlands, and was therefore not treated as a resident under the migrant worker rules applying between the Netherlands and Belgium.

Under the relevant tax laws and bilateral convention, Asscher therefore paid tax solely in the Netherlands on the Dutch director-ship, but was liable to tax in Belgium on other income. Under Regulation 1408/71, he paid Belgian social security contributions and therefore was excluded from the Netherlands scheme. Because the Netherlands income tax and social security contribution schemes are closely integrated, this meant that Asscher was not liable to pay the 30 per cent combined rate of tax and contributions to which most Netherlands employees were liable. Of this, 13 per cent was income tax. To stop avoidance of tax in this position, Asscher was required to pay income tax at a special rate of 25 per cent because he was not liable to the social security contribution.

Asscher challenged his tax liability on the ground that he should only pay tax at 13 per cent. Otherwise, he argued, he was discriminated against under article 48. His challenge, when it was referred to the European Court, attracted even more national interest than its predecessors, with the Belgian, Dutch, French, German and UK governments all commenting on the case.

The Court, in its judgment, found that the application of the higher income tax rate to Asscher was discrimination. To reach this conclusion the Court had to take several successive decisions, some of which have been criticised strongly. The first step was to treat Asscher as self-employed rather than an employee. This raises the vexed question of the borderline between employment and self-employment, and therefore between article 48 and article 52. The Court found, without any sustained reasoning, that Asscher was to be treated as self-employed not employed.[88] It was therefore article

---

88. He ... 'is the director of a company of which he is the sole shareholder; his activity is thus not carried out in the context of a relationship of subordination, and so he is to be treated not as a 'worker' ... but as pursuing an activity as a self-employed person ... ' This completely ignores the legal personality of the company, or any of the duties imposed by company law on directors and shareholders (for example, to creditors), and so lifts the veil completely from the company. If this is a considered view of the Court to be applied to all such cases where art 48 might otherwise be invoked, it may have interesting repercussions, not least on its interaction with the EC company law directives.

52 that was to be applied, not article 48.[89] Next, the Court found that the fact that Asscher was a Dutch national was irrelevant. This reasoning relied on the decisions of the Court that allow a national of a state to claim rights under EC law against that state where the relationship is not purely internal. He was therefore to be treated as a Belgian national.

The third stage of the reasoning was to accept that, as a non-resident, he was being discriminated against in terms of disguised nationality. Here the Court could rely on its previous case law on covert discrimination. In other words, he could ignore his nationality to claim equal status with other non-residents. He could then, having been deemed to be a non-resident, claim that the adverse treatment against him as a non-resident was covert discrimination against him on grounds of assumed foreign nationality. Fourth, the Court found that there was actual discrimination here because of the different tax rates. In so doing, it noted that this was confirmed rather than removed by the terms of the relevant double tax convention.

The court then looked to find any justification for the discrimination. The Netherlands' attempt to defend its carefully integrated set of rates for social security and tax were set aside on the ground that they penalised the taxpayer for not paying Netherlands social security contributions when he was in fact paying Belgian contributions. An argument based on coherence of the fiscal system of the state was also dismissed. Further, the existence of Regulation 1408/71 precluded the Netherlands from using taxes to make up for any non-payment of contributions. There were therefore, in the view of the court, no sound reasons for the Dutch measures and the discrimination against Asscher could not be justified.

A clash of systems

The *Asscher* case brings to the fore the issues that must be resolved before a comprehensive set of answers can be given to the problems that are posed within the EU by mobile workers, but provide, it is suggested, unsatisfactory answers to most of the issues.

The first issue is the problem of recognising the interaction between tax and social security. Here, the framework of Community

---

[89.] See further, ch 7.

legislation is forcing apart systems which are gradually coalescing and which are going to have to coalesce further. The pressure on social security schemes caused by demographic shifts demands higher funding. If this is not to force up social contributions, then it will involve a transfer of costs to general taxes. Indeed, this has already started happening in several member states. The idea that the two are entirely separate systems is already artificial, and that artificiality will become increasingly obvious. It cannot be avoided, as the Advocate General purported to avoid it in *Asscher*, by saying that the two are different systems. In the Netherlands and several other member states they are not.

The second issue is the interaction of EC law and double tax conventions. Critics have pointed to the weakness of the Court when it tries to deal with these conventions. While the court is right in establishing the superiority of EC law over the conditions of a double tax convention in principle where the two are inconsistent, it seems far less happy in handling the conventions and deciding what they do and do not provide. Given that the conventions are a well-tried method of resolving bilateral problems between states that give rise to double taxation, they should not lightly be set aside. At least, they give a two-sided view to problems, unlike the one-sided analysis in the *Asscher* case, where the Court looked only at what had happened in the Netherlands, not in the EU as a while (ie in Belgium). Did Asscher pay, in total, more or less contributions and tax because he lived in Belgium than he would have done had he remained resident in the Netherlands? The answer is not clear from the case.

A third and, it is suggested basic, issue is more fundamental. It is about the nature of the systems in collision in these cases. On the one side we have the 'great freedom' of movement of workers. EC law requires that those workers should not suffer adverse consequences by moving from one state to another, because that would be unfair. States adopt the personal income tax and social security systems they do to achieve another kind of fairness – that of sharing a community's burdens fairly through that community. Fairness in income tax and social contributions require that all those who are part of the community should contribute their fair share. Fairness for free movers means that they should not be asked to pay more than that share.

The logic of decisions like *Asscher* does not achieve this fairness. They do not ask: is this person paying more tax within the

EU than someone who has not moved. They ask only: is this person paying more within this part of the EU? As a result, the free movers can, as I have argued elsewhere,[90] become free riders. They can, and therefore will, use freedom of movement to avoid paying tax or social security contributions. If this is so, then the Court's enthusiasm to support the free movers may, with hindsight, be seen to be misplaced. It will be helping those who are moving not to enjoy opportunities, but to avoid responsibilities.

[90]. D W Williams, 'Asscher: the European Court and the power to destroy', (1997) 6 EC Tax Review 4.

CHAPTER SEVEN

Taxing services and service suppliers

Once upon a time, a government that could tax goods effectively had an effective tax system. In an advanced economy it is not so simple. Traditionally, the economic wealth of a nation was created by producing goods. Much wealth is now in intangible form: intellectual property and knowhow; financial and professional services; telecommunications and information flows; and leisure and tourist activities. These changes have sidestepped the traditional ways of taxing. There can be no customs duties on cross-border flows of services or capital.

One traditional way of taxing services was by adding a fiscal element to the regulation of service activities. It used, for example, to be true for membership of the legal profession. This still happens with the high licence fees demanded of some service activities (for example, casinos and television stations). Beyond that relatively crude way of taxing services, and the implicit tax on the service element in the price of goods, services remained untaxed save for income and profits taxes.

Taxing services[1] and service suppliers[2] now presents the EU and its member states with a series of major fiscal challenges. The freedom of movement for services is one of the fundamental freedoms

---

[1.] 'Services' are defined in EC Treaty, art 60 as follows: 'Services shall be considered to be "services" within the meaning of this Treaty where they are normally provided for remuneration, in so far as they are not governed by the provisions relating to freedom of movement for goods, capital and persons. "Services" shall in particular include – (a) services of an industrial character; (b) services of a commercial character; (c) activities of craftsmen; (d) activities of the professions.' Separate provision is made in art 61 for transport services. This approach to the definition of services is also used for VAT. See note 14.

[2.] The term 'service suppliers' is taken from the General Agreement on Trade in Services, part of GATT 1994, discussed below.

of the Union, along with the free right of establishment. The traditional ring-fence approach to regulating and taxing suppliers of services cannot work in such a context. The challenge is accentuated because most forms of provision of services are highly mobile. It is easy to relocate the place where the services are provided, or the supplier, or both. Further, many of these services can readily be relocated outside the EU. It is far easier to enjoy the benefits of freedom of movement as a services supplier than is the case for individual workers. At the same time, the movements themselves cannot readily be traced and taxed, as can the movements of goods.

Modern telecommunications have almost reached the point whereby services can be provided remotely in a context where the 'source' or 'location' of the supply are increasingly meaningless as concepts. In a sense, there is nothing new in this. Mail order deliveries of goods, and remote provisions of services have long been a problem for state tax authorities in the USA. The additional challenge lies in the extensive nature and value of services that can now be provided remotely. Yet a balanced approach to taxing economic activity requires that services be taxed in the same way as goods.

States have attempted to rise to the challenges in a number of ways. Most important is the extension of the general turnover tax, VAT, to services. To that must be added the growing number of specific taxes on services. At the same time, income taxes (and, for the self-employed in some states, also social security taxes) capture a share of the profits. As we shall see, these taxes still present a series of challenges. First, can a VAT be imposed effectively on a national basis on services within a customs union? Second, can profits on services be taxed effectively without creating barriers to free movement. Third, there is a growing realisation that income tax and VAT overlap in taxing services. How can this overlap be handled? In this chapter, after noting briefly the relevance of general principles of EC law, we look at VAT on services. We then touch briefly on specific taxes, then income tax. We shall not consider the social taxes further, as the key issues were all dealt with when discussing taxation of workers.[3] Finally, we shall revisit the problems facing the EU.

---

3. Ch 6.

Free movement of services[4]

When examining the requirements within the EU for goods, we noted how important were the restrictions of article 95,[5] but that the limits against discrimination on the free movement of persons was more general.[6] Article 95 is of limited relevance to the provision of services. It may apply to the provision of services related to goods,[7] but that is all.

Instead, EC law provides for the free movement of services and of service suppliers by separate measures in articles 52 and 59 of the EC Treaty. Article 52 creates a right of establishment, including the right to take up and pursue activities as self-employed persons. Article 59 complements this by requiring freedom of movement for services.[8] Community legislation has given flesh to these provisions by requiring the removal of restrictions from both those moving to provide services and those moving to receive them.[9] There is no specific provision dealing with the movement of the services themselves, presumably because, as intangibles, there was no perceived reason for so providing, as there can be no equivalent to customs control over an international service.

The European Court has made it clear that it regards the provisions of articles 52 and 59 as directly effective, and has applied them to direct taxes in a series of cases that parallel the Court's decisions discussed in connection with article 48.[10] Indeed, in one recent case, the Court was asked a question put to it under article 48, and answered it under article 52. In so doing, the Court observed:

A comparison of articles 48 and 52 of the Treaty shows that they are based on the same principles both as regards entry into and

---

4. For points of specific relevance only to companies see ch 8.
5. See ch 5.
6. See ch 6.
7. Art 95 applies to taxes imposed indirectly on products. The European Court has ruled this to cover fees for tests on goods (*Simmental v Minister of Finance* Case 35/76, [1976] ECR 1861), and taxes on the use of goods (*Schottle v Finanzamt Freudenstadt*, Case 20/76, [1977] ECR 247.
8. For the definition of services see note 1.
9. Council Directive 73/148 on the abolition of restrictions on movement and residence within the Community for nationals of member states with regard to establishment and the provision of services (21 May 1973)(1973 OJ L 172/14). No express mention is made of taxation in this directive.
10. See ch 6.

residence in the territory of the member states by persons covered by Community law and as regards the prohibition of all discrimination against them on grounds of nationality.[11]

In the light of this ruling, the detailed analysis of the case law made in Chapter 6 is not repeated, as much of it applies here. There are, however, differences in terms of the relevant articles of the OECD Model Tax Convention, and in the operation of social security contributions. These and the cases are noted below. Before doing so, we must consider the difference between article 48 and article 52.

Employment and self-employment

In the *Asscher* case[12] the Court of Justice ruled that a company director running his own company was, for the purposes of Community law, self-employed. This confirms that the distinction between the status of an employee and that of the self-employed is a matter of Community law, as is the status of officers such as a company director.[13] Besides the distinction between articles 48 and 52, the division is also important for VAT purposes. A self-employed person is liable to register for VAT and collect VAT on payments for services. An employee is not liable to register.[14]

The thrust of both the Court's approach and that of rules for the various taxes is that a particular status or relationship attaches to an employee or worker. Someone who does not have that status, or that relationship with an 'employer', is self-employed, or (which is the same thing) is independently engaged in providing

11. *Asscher v Staatsecretaris van Financien* Case c-107/94, [1996] STC 1025 (discussed at length in ch 6, particularly at note 88).

12. Note 11 above and see ch 6 at note 88.

13. There is considerable law on the status of a 'worker' within art 48, although it is not defined in the EC Treaty. For a summary, see S Weatherill and P Beaumont, *EC Law* (Penguin, 2nd edition 1995), p 545.

14. The relevant provision is Sixth VAT Directive, art 4, imposing the duty to collect VAT on 'a taxable person acting as such' (art 2). A taxable person is a person 'who independently carries out in any place any economic activity . . . ' (art 4). This reflects the distinction in both common law and civil law between those who provide 'dependent services' and those who provide 'independent services' (the titles respectively of arts 15 and 14 of the OECD MTC, reflecting the French titles of those articles).

services. This raises the separate question as to the nature of a service. The VAT legislation, as we shall see, avoids defining the term. Article 52 does not make up for the deficiency, although article 60 offers a partial definition. Services are 'services' where they are normally provided for consideration, provided that they are not covered by the Treaty provisions relating to goods, capital or persons. They include, in particular, industrial services, commercial services, activities of craftsmen, and activities of the professions. In other words, this is the residual category of economic activity.

The precise status of an officer, such as a company director, or an individual appointed to public office, does not naturally fit within either status. Practice of states has varied on whether someone in Asscher's position might be regarded as an employee, as self-employed or – for some purposes – neither.[15]

Legal persons

EC law applies to legal persons as it does to individuals.[16] At present, there is no EC mechanism that of itself gives legal personality to an entity.[17] The status must therefore be derived from the laws of one of the member states.[18] This means that, for tax purposes, a legal person is based in at least one of the member states.

The only European form of entity recognised is that of the EEIG: the European Economic Interest Grouping.[19] This is a form of joint venture, but it is expressly provided that 'the profits or losses . . . shall be taxable only in the hands of its members'.[20] It was only because the EEIG is fiscally transparent that the entity

---

15. For example, by excluding such a person from the compulsory scope of a social security scheme.
16. EC Treaty, art 58 makes explicit provision for this in connection with arts 52 to 57. This covers companies and firms established by law, save for those that are non-profit making.
17. For an account of the harmonisation of company law between member states, and consideration of the establishment of a European Company, see Weatherill and Beaumont, op cit note 13, p 601. One of the reasons for the failure of this idea to make progress is the failure to agree the tax status of such a company.
18. Or of a third state recognised by those states.
19. Established by Council Regulation 2137/85/EEC on the European Economic Interest Grouping (31 July 1985) (1985 OJ L 199/1). See B Terra and P Wattel, *European Tax Law* (Kluwer, 1993), ch 12 for a full account.
20. Ibid, note 19, art 40.

was acceptable to all member states. As a result, there are no tax problems attached to the EEIG as such – in theory. In practice, the tax position 'is governed by many uncertainties',[21] and varies from state to state. This has limited the use of EEIGs for profit-making joint ventures. Nonetheless, they are most useful for non-profit ventures where the transparency for tax purposes is effective.

Branches and agencies

In international tax practice, an enterprise is taxed where it is resident – a direct analogy to the rules applying to individuals.[22] As we have already noted, nationality is not used as a basis for tax jurisdiction by European countries. The rules identifying the residence of individual entrepreneurs are the same as those for individual workers and others.[23] Where an entrepreneur is resident in the state, the state may claim tax on the worldwide business profits of the entrepreneur.

Separate rules apply to determine the residence of companies. State practices vary somewhat, and several EU states have alternative rules. For example, the UK regards a company as resident if either it is registered in the UK or it is resident in the UK as a matter of fact. Residence of a company is identified as the location of its central management and control.[24] In France and other civil law states, corporate residence is also determined by reference to the siege social (seat) of the company. Where a company has more than one residence, the OECD Model Tax Convention rule for dealing with the conflict is to prefer the claim for residence of the state where the centre of effective management of the company is located.[25] The state of residence of the company may tax the total worldwide profits of the company.

21. Terra and Wattel, op cit note 18, p 224. As they say, at present these uncertainties are answered by reference to the relevant national law. For example, although an EEIG is transparent, what is the effect of the activities of the EEIG in one state on the tax claims by that state to the profits of a member of the EEIG based in another state? Can the state claim tax, or must it ignore the position?
22. See ch 6.
23. These are discussed in ch 6.
24. For a summary of the rules, see Davies, *Principles of Tax Law*, (Sweet and Maxwell, 1996) ch 32.
25. OECD MTC, art 4, para 3.

Whether these rules actually base the claims to taxation on residence rather than nationality is not as clear as with individuals. This is because the agreed definition of the nationality of a company for tax purposes is the state from which the company derives its status as such.[26] The state of registration therefore gives a company its nationality. At the same time, under the tax laws of several EU states a company that is registered in the state is for that reason a tax resident of the state. In other words, the rules allocating nationality for tax purposes are in many states the same rules as those that allocate residence.

International tax practice recognises a second claim to the profits of a company. A state in which the company[27] has a branch or agency may tax the profits of that branch or agency. This is justified on the basis that the profits of the branch or agency are sourced in the state where it is located, not in the state where the company is resident.

A company that is resident in one state but that also has foreign branches or agencies is therefore potentially subject to double taxation on the profits of the foreign branches and agencies. The member states of the OECD (including all EU member states) have a standard model set of rules to deal with this problem. First, a common definition of a branch or agency is adopted. In international tax practice, the phrase used is 'permanent establishment', or PE.[28]

Article 7 of the OECD MTC provides that the state of residence of a business may tax the total profits of that business.[29] If the business has a PE (as defined in article 5) in another state, that other state may also tax the profits attributable to the PE. Rules are also laid down to determine how the profits of the PE are determined. If, as a result, the profits of the PE are liable to be taxed by both states, the state of residence must give double tax relief. It can do this either by exempting the profits of the PE from

---

[26]. OECD MTC, art 3.

[27]. Or other entrepreneur.

[28]. Strictly, PE is used for a branch or agency of a business (OECD MTC, art 5). A branch or agency of a professional person (usually an individual or partnership) is known as a 'fixed base' (OECD MTC, art 14). For most practical purposes, there is no distinction between a PE and a fixed base. See P Baker, *Double Tax Conventions and International Tax Law* (Sweet and Maxwell, 2nd edition, 1996), commentary on art 14.

[29]. Art 14 applies the same rule to the profits of a professional.

its taxes,[30] or by providing a credit for the PE state tax against its own tax.[31] The effect is to stop the double taxation of the PE's profits, and also to stop the state where the PE is from taxing the company's profits more generally.

The EC right of establishment

The right of establishment under EC law[32] means that a company[33] may move its activities to any other member state. It is therefore free to establish a branch or set up an agency in any other state. It may also move its centre of effective management to another state, and possibly its central management and control.[34] Whether this amounts to a change of residence for tax purposes depends on the tax laws of the states concerned.

A company which transfers its residence – if it can – will become a resident of the new state. A company transferring only part of its activities will have a PE in that state but will not be a resident. The company itself will be a non-resident. Does the non-resident have any rights with regard to the treatment of its PE? It does, both under the OECD MTC, and under EC law.

The OECD MTC[35] gives some protection against discrimination through the tax laws of the state where the PE is. The PE of an enterprise resident in another state where there is a DTC in operation 'shall not be less favourably levied' than a resident enterprise. This does not ensure identical taxation, but prevents it being, for example, at a higher rate of tax than if the PE were a local enterprise.

The European Court of Justice has confirmed that EC law also gives rights to a PE. In its first decision on direct taxes, often referred to as the *Avoir Fiscal* case,[36] the Court ruled that under

---

30. OECD MTC, art 23A.
31. OECD MTC, art 23B.
32. EC Treaty, art 52.
33. Or other entrepreneur, but not a non-profit body.
34. This depends on the laws of the states concerned. In *R v HM Treasury, ex p Daily Mail* Case 81/87, [1988] STC 787, the ECJ ruled that, in the present state of EC law, there was no Community right to move the central management and control of a company within the EC. However, the national rules (of the UK) that then stopped the company moving have since been repealed in part.
35. Art 24, para 4. See Baker, op cit note 28, commentary on art 24.
36. *EC Commission v France* Case 270/83, [1986] ECR 273. The avoir fiscal is a tax credit against the tax due on dividend income broadly similar to the UK tax credit for ACT (advance corporation tax).

EC law the French branch of a foreign company was entitled to the same advantages under the French tax law in question as a French company. The argument before the Court made play on the fact that the foreign company could have established itself in France either through a locally incorporated subsidiary or – as it did – through a branch. If a local subsidiary had been established, it would have received the tax credits in question, while the local branch did not. The Court accepted this. It did, however, note that discrimination on the grounds of residence might be justified in some cases.[37] This must be examined more generally.

Nondiscrimination and the provision of services

We have seen that the EC Treaty contains a formidable provision against discrimination between local and foreign products within the EU in the guise of article 95.[38] This may apply to some services linked with goods, but it does not apply to services generally. Nor is there any equivalent provision in the Treaty dealing with services. This is because the underlying international obligations were limited to products at the time the EC Treaty was drafted. This has changed since 1994 with the adoption of the General Agreement on Trade in Services (GATS) as part of GATT 1994.

The GATS extends to services the key obligations against discrimination from the GATT. GATT Article I, the most-favoured nation clause, is applied to services by GATS Article II. GATT Article III is echoed by GATS Article XVII: 'each member shall accord to services[39] and service suppliers of any other member . . . treatment no less favourable that that it accords to its own like services and service suppliers.' These bind member states either as part of the EU or as individual members of the WTO.[40]

---

37. For a full explanation and analysis, see Terra and Wattel, op cit note 19, p 22, where the underlying significance of the decision is also analysed.
38. See ch 6.
39. As elsewhere, 'services' are defined as a residual: 'services' includes any services except those which are part of governmental authority, that is, neither on a commercial basis nor in competition with service suppliers: GATS, art I, para 3.
40. Competence to sign GATT 1994 was divided between the EU and the member states following the ECJ's Opinion 1/94, 15.11.1994. See D McGoldrick, *International Relations Law of the European Union* (in this series, 1997), p 194, and authorities cited there.

As a result of concerns expressed during negotiation of GATS, there are important reservations applying to this agreement. It does not automatically apply to all services. There are also specific reservations dealing with direct taxes. A direct tax rule may discriminate despite Article II, provided that the discrimination is based on a DTC binding the state or some similar obligation in an international agreement.[41] Rules aimed at ensuring the equitable or effective imposition or collection of direct taxes[42] are also allowed to override article XVII. The result is that there are no new obligations (save in connection with state aids[43]) relating to direct taxes in the GATS. Nevertheless, there is a new provision that is the equivalent of GATT article III applying to indirect taxes on services and service suppliers. But it is not an express obligation of EC law.

One reason for the exclusion of direct taxes from the scope of GATS is the existence of the network of DTCs. In particular, negotiating states felt that issues of discrimination were best dealt with by the new traditional means of bilateral agreements. These will regulate taxes that might offend articles II and XVII. Article 24 of the OECD MTC and specific equivalents provide, in particular, for a state agreeing a DTC to offer the taxpayers that are nationals of the other state party the same treatment as received by its nationals. The same provision protects discrimination based only on residence. In effect, this provision will override the national laws of the parties to a DTC, and those national laws as overridden will themselves override the GATS provision.

This complex provides the current international backdrop to the EC legal requirements of nondiscrimination within the EU on services and service suppliers, as both the GATS provisions and the OECD MTC are relevant in considering the position of all member states.

Discrimination and direct taxes

The European Court has interpreted articles 52 and 59 as protecting companies and other service providers in some, but not all, dis-

---

41. GATS, art XIV, point (e).
42. Defined in detail as a note to art XIV, broadly including all taxes on income or capital, payroll taxes and taxes on capital appreciation.
43. These are discussed in ch 10.

criminatory situations. The analysis is in part the same as that applying to discrimination against employees, though other issues are also raised.

The most straightforward situation is that of the individual entrepreneur. That position was considered in some detail in the *Wielockx* case.[44] The case concerned a Belgian national, resident in Belgium, but deriving his income as a self-employed individual in the Netherlands. He wanted to claim a deduction against Dutch tax for a contribution to a voluntary pension reserve. It was refused because he was a non-resident. The Court echoed its judgment in the *Schumacker* case[45] in stating that differentiation on grounds of residence was not itself discrimination. However, discrimination existed in this case. It therefore had to be considered whether the discrimination was justified. The main justification was the argument for fiscal coherence, in the light of the *Bachmann* case.[46] However, in the view of the Court this argument could not succeed because there was a DTC between Belgium and the Netherlands dealing with the issue. The decision has since been criticised, in part because the Court misunderstood the DTC issues. It rested its argument on a provision relating to the taxation of pensions, when it was actually addressing an issue about taxing profits.[47] Nonetheless, taken together with the *Asscher* case,[48] and the clear common development of the significance of article 52 and article 48, the Court has established limits on the abilities of member states to discriminate against individual non-resident entrepreneurs. Only in the *Werner* case[49] did the Court decline to interfere at all. That case concerned an accusation of discrimination against Germany by a non-resident German national who worked as a dentist in Germany. It was held that EC law placed on limits on the German tax authorities in this situation.[50]

44. *Wielockx v Inspecteur der Directe Belastingen* Case C-80/94, [1995] STC 876.
45. *Finanzamt Köln-Alstadt v Schumacker* Case C-279/93, [1995] STC 306. See ch 6.
46. *Bachmann v Belgium* case C-204/90, [1994] STC 855, [1992] ECR 1-249. See ch 6.
47. See J F Avery Jones, 'Carry on discriminating' (1996) 36 European Taxation, no 2, p 46. The UK government felt that it was not necessary to take action following this decision for that reason.
48. See note 11 above and ch 6.
49. *Werner v Finanzamt Aachen-Innenstadt* Case C-112/91, [1996] STC 961, [1993] ECR I-429. The report is particularly interesting for the comprehensive review of relevant law in the submissions to the Court.
50. It is understood that the tax authorities have settled a challenge to their action being taken by Werner before the German Supreme Court in terms that suggested that their action might have been challenged successfully there.

The case law relating to companies is far less developed. Nonetheless, the approach adopted in the *Avoir Fiscal* case,[51] has been endorsed by several subsequent decisions. In the *Commerzbank* case,[52] article 52 was used together with article 58 as the basis for ruling that a refusal to pay interest on a repayment of overpaid tax to a non-resident company was discrimination.[53] The Court made short shrift of British attempts to justify the discrimination. A similar approach was evident in the *Halliburton* case.[54] The taxpayer was a wholly owned Netherlands subsidiary of an American parent company. It purchased from a German subsidiary in the same group the German company's PE in the Netherlands. Tax relief was refused, though it would have been granted if both companies had been Dutch. The Netherlands government defended the case in part because it was a Dutch company, not a German company, that was the taxpayer, and in part because it did not have all the relevant information to operate the rule for foreign companies. Both arguments justifying the discrimination were rejected. The Court pointed out that EC law provides means[55] by which the Netherlands tax authorities could gain the information they needed. The action was discrimination because the German company was placed in a less favourable position because it was selling a PE to the position had it incorporated its Dutch PE.

The Court's jurisprudence therefore suggests that it is prepared to intervene very readily in the application of corporate direct taxes between companies in different member states if any differences emerge. How extensively it is prepared to do this remains to be tested in a range of cases that are expected to come before the Court in the next few years. These look in particular at transactions between companies, including the payment of a dividend from one company to another, and when companies are regarded

---

51. See note 36.
52. *R v Inland Revenue Commissioners, ex p Commerzbank AG* Case C-330/91, [1993] STC 605.
53. The case followed an earlier case between the same two parties, in which the English court ruled that the Inland Revenue had misapplied a double tax convention to Commerzbank, and therefore overtaxed the bank: *Inland Revenue Commissioners v Commerzbank* [1990] STC 285.
54. *Halliburton Services BV v Staatssecretaris van Financien* Case C-1/93, [1994] STC 655.
55. It referred to mutual assistance directives, discussed at p 20.

for fiscal purposes as part of the same group.[56] It is possible that, if the Court continues on its present course, and if it finds that neither the OECD MTC nor article 73d of the EC Treaty[57] justify discrimination, then it will force several member states totally to redesign their corporation tax laws and the relevant DTCs.[58] It is far from clear that this would be possible,[59] let alone desirable; nor is it clear what the revenue costs of such developments might be. It is clear that such action is the province of the legislature, not the Court, and that the failure by the one to act should not be regarded as empowering the other to force such action. Happily, developments in indirect taxation, while not free from problems, are not as problematic.

VAT on services

We saw in Chapter 5 that VAT is imposed on supplies of goods and services. However, it was explained in that chapter that in practical terms the treatment of services was not the same as that of goods. We therefore discussed only the framework of VAT and how it applied to goods. How does it apply to services?

There is no definition of the term 'services' in the Sixth VAT Directive. Nor is there a clear line between 'goods' and 'services' or, rather, between supplies of goods and the provision of services.[60] What is a supply of services, or the provision of services? The framework of the Sixth VAT Directive makes the two kinds of supply mutually exclusive but jointly exhaustive of transactions made for payment.[61] The Directive makes it clear that the exploita-

---

56. See further ch 8.
57. See ch 10.
58. The relevant DTCs will include the DTCs with third states, such as the USA. The results of any such action will therefore not be confined to the EU. Detailing the issues would, unfortunately, take far too much space because of the need to explain the technical issues raised at some length to illustrate why this statement might be true. For a discussion of some of the issues, see *International Taxation of Dividends Reconsidered in Light of Corporate Tax Integration*, IFA Seminar Series, Vol 19a, 1995.
59. As was stated in the first paragraphs of this book, tax law cannot be changed without democratic assent. See further the general comments of L Hinnekens in 'The Monti Report: the uphill task of harmonsing direct tax systems of EC Member States' [1997] EC Tax Review, 31.
60. See ch 5, note 77 on the importance of this point.
61. Sixth VAT Directive, art 6, para 1, read with art 2, para 1.

tion of tangible property for the purpose of obtaining income on a continuing basis is an economic activity.[62] The precise line between a supply of goods and a supply related to goods but which is a service is in part left to member states. For example, the supply of goods under a hire purchase contract is to be regarded as a supply of goods.[63] But it is for member states to decide if a contract for work and materials involves a supply of goods.[64]

More generally, 'supply of services' is a wide term and embraces the provision and the use of intellectual property and similar rights,[65] most rights related to immovable property,[66] and the supply of staff (but not the supplies by those staff). It also includes any transaction which is, or which is closely connected with and necessary for, an exploitation of property and which is not a supply of goods.[67]

For the charge to VAT to apply, it must also be shown that the provision of services is a taxable provision, and not exempt. It must also be shown that the supply takes place in the territory of the state. Special rules apply where the service is an international service. Once these aspects of the provision are shown, the general rules about the need to identify the taxable person, and the valuation of a supply apply in the same way as for supplies of goods.[68]

Taxable provisions of services

As with supplies of goods, VAT applies to all supplies of services within the scope of the tax unless the supply of services is exempt. Unlike supplies of goods, the Sixth VAT Directive exempts many

---

62. Sixth VAT Directive, art 4, para 2.
63. Sixth VAT Directive, art 5, para 4(b).
64. Sixth VAT Directive, art 5, para 5(a).
65. Sixth VAT Directive, art 6, para 1 provides that a supply of service 'may' include assignments of intangible property. The structure of the Directive as a whole clearly assumes, however, that the 'may' (which was added to the draft at a later stage) is superfluous. This is a small example of the structural weaknesses of the EC VAT.
66. But see further ch 9.
67. *Rompelman v Minister van Financien* Case 268/83, [1985] ECR 655; *van Tiem v Staatsecretaris van Financien* Case C-186/89, [1993] STC 91.
68. See generally the outline in ch 5.

provisions of services from the tax.[69] These include:[70] financial, insurance and betting services;[71] medical, health, and welfare services; educational services and services for young people; sport and cultural services, and services provided by many non-profit bodies; non-commercial television and radio; postal services; supplies of the use of land and buildings.[72] These cumulative exemptions remove many forms of provision of services from the effective scope of VAT. A series of special exemptions remove others. The most important is that EC VAT law allows states to impose conditions restricting registration for small businesses. The UK has used this to exclude many small self-employed service suppliers.[73] The net result is that VAT is in effect a tax on supplies of selected services. Recent developments are likely to place the taxation of even these services under pressure when they are, or can be, supplied cross-border.

International services

International services present governments with a major problem in imposing VAT. Many taxable kinds of services can now be provided on an international basis. We have seen that many of the kinds of personal services such as those of doctors and teachers are exempted, as are many smaller suppliers of household services such as painters and plumbers. Many of the remaining kinds of

---

69. The Second VAT Directive took an even narrower approach, and only required that a list of ten kinds of provision of services be included within the scope of the tax. Extension of VAT to services generally was therefore not mandatory until 1977 when the Sixth Directive took effect. Even then, a number of the exceptions from the Second Directive have been allowed to be carried forward as (nominally) transitional exemptions: Sixth VAT Directive, art 28(3) and Annex F. These include services provided by lawyers and some other professions; telecommunications services; supplies connected with cremations and funerals; public supplies of water; and passenger transport. These transitional exemptions are still in use in several states, including the UK.
70. See Sixth VAT Directive, art 13A and 13B.
71. These are discussed in ch 9.
72. For land and buildings see further ch 9.
73. The requirement is that the taxable person has a turnover of taxable supplies of at least £48,000 (1997 level) in the last 12 months. In effect, this means a weekly turnover (excluding holidays) of £1,000. This is quite a high figure for a person providing only services, where there is little turnover in goods involved.

services can now be provided internationally: use of intellectual property, services of, or provided by the use of, telecommunications; or professional or expert advice.

VAT has proved to be an inefficient way of taxing either services or service suppliers on international transactions. This is because its strength lies in two aspects of the tax: it captures tax on all goods coming into a tax territory by a form of customs duty, and it captures transactions within that territory by reference to cross-checking of invoices for the transactions. In the case of services, the former is impossible. Cross-checking assumes that both the service supplier and the customer are within the jurisdiction and that both are registered for VAT. In an international transaction, the service supplier may be outside any state operating a VAT. Alternatively, the ease of modern communications may mean that the service is supplied from or to a location where neither the supplier nor the customer have a PE or other strong link. Indeed, in the extreme case, it may be practically impossible even for those involved in the transaction to trace from or to where it is made. For example, if the service is provided by way of data transfer to a holding computer indirectly from another computer, which states are the relevant ones for VAT?

Even before the problems of cyberservices,[74] the rules for granting jurisdiction over services were complex. The simple destination-based approach used for goods[75] does not work in most cases. This is because the services themselves cannot, in reality, be taxed. The only taxable elements are the suppliers and customers or goods or other tangible assets to which the services are related. The result is a range of second-best rules.[76] If land is involved, then the services are to be taxed where the land is. A similar rule applies to transport services, and to services related to tangible movable property. Artistic, cultural, educational, entertainment, scientific, sporting and similar services and their organisation, are to be taxed where they occur. All other activities[77] are taxed either

---

74. I do not apologise for making up this word. If I had not, someone else would have done – and probably has. It is an obvious and appropriate derivative from cybernetics, that is, the study of control and communications in complex systems.

75. See ch 5.

76. They are set out in the Sixth VAT Directive, art 9, unless indicated otherwise.

77. With a number of specific exceptions laid down in other articles of the Directive.

where the service supplier is based[78] or where the customer is based. The customer is to be taxed if registered for VAT in the EU[79] and if the services relate to: intellectual property and supplies of information; financial and insurance services; most forms of professional services; supplies of staff; equipment leasing and hiring; and advertising and agency services. In all other cases, the supply is taxed on an origin basis. If the state of origin does not impose VAT, then the supply is untaxed. The unfavourable comparison with locally-supplied services of a similar nature is obvious.

The problem that the current rules cause is shown by the recent decision of the EC Commission to encourage all member states to seek a derogation from the existing rules to deal with telephone call-back services. If you telephone between EU states, you can use a telephone service in either of the states. Alternatively, you could use a service based in a state without a VAT, such as the USA, or the Cayman Islands. If the call charges are the same, then you save the tax just by the way in which you make the call. The result is a major loss of revenue by European telecommunications companies due directly to the effect of VAT. It also means lost VAT, not to mention lost corporation tax. The rule is being replaced in all states by one that locates the telephone service where the call takes place. There are two problems with this. First, where does a telephone call take place? Second, it may cost more to monitor the call in order to ascertain how it is taxed than to make the call. A tax which imposes compliance costs that exceed 100 per cent of the value of the thing being taxed makes no sense. But what alternatives are there?

---

[78]. Identification of the 'base' may itself cause problems. See, for example, the dispute between the Danish and UK tax authorities in *Customs and Excise Commissioners v DFDS* Case C-280/95, [1997] STC 384, about whether tickets for the Danish ferry company's trips sold in England by a branch of the Danish company were to be taxed in the UK or Denmark. The analogy with discussions about PEs is unavoidable.

[79]. This is done by a 'reverse charge' – the customer is treated as making the supply as well as receiving it. If the customer is fully taxable, the only result is that the customer will pay the output tax but reclaim it as input tax. This neutralises both the tax liability and the credit in the same way as would occur had goods been imported.

CHAPTER EIGHT

Taxing multinational enterprises

Why is there a chapter specifically devoted to multinational business? Is it not the case that, in an effective single market, all businesses can be multinational? An analysis based on freedoms of movement must recognise that this is so. At the same time, such an analysis conceals the problems of a person that is itself multinational in a way that an individual never can be. In particular, freedoms of movement for a multinational enterprise (MNE) partly take place *within* the organisation of the MNE. This presents taxation problems that increase costs of, and distort activities and growth of, an MNE. These therefore create tax barriers to development of MNEs. A truly integrated market must allow for that development, and reserve the controls for competition law. In this chapter, we explore the tax barriers and the measures taken to abate their effects. Conversely, MNEs offer opportunities for tax avoidance that member states must guard against. These issues are also considered, but we must first consider the identity of an MNE.

Most larger commercial organisations consist of a group of legal entities[1] – usually companies – working together. In other words, an MNE has multiple legal personality, usually with a parent[2] company and a group of subsidiary companies. The parent, directly or indirectly, controls the subsidiaries. The separate com-

---

1. A complete survey of this topic should include a discussion of the different legal entities that exist, such as limited liability partnerships, unlimited companies, companies with no separate legal status, and so forth. This must remain beyond the scope of this book.
2. In many parts of the EU, these are referred to in the appropriate language as mother and daughter companies. For simplicity, this chapter ignores issues relating to consortiums and joint ventures, except where there is specific EC action.

panies will also be divided between active or trading companies, and passive or holding companies. A major enterprise may consist of many dozen such grouped companies. Each of these companies is a separate legal person. In economic reality, however, they are all part of the same entity, the MNE itself. The most fundamental question is therefore whether an MNE is recognised as a single economic entity, or as a series of legal entities.[3]

Internal relationships within an MNE

At the heart of an MNE must be the core company. In the absence of any progress with legislation of a European company,[4] that company must be based in one member state, and therefore taxed in that state.[5] It will then have subsidiary and other companies in that state and elsewhere. The group will probably also have a research and development unit, and finance and holding companies. It is likely that not all of these will be in the EU.[6] As an entity, the group's central management runs the group as one business, probably through divisions that reflect group products or functions rather than national boundaries. The MNE's accounts should also be consolidated.[7] How far do tax laws reflect this reality?

There is no current alternative in Europe[8] to the taxation of an MNE separately in each of its national parts. This means that all the flows of goods, services, capital and labour between the constituent parts of the MNE are liable to be regarded as if they

3. The separate issue of a local branch of a foreign enterprise is discussed in ch 7.
4. Commission proposal for a regulation for a Statute of a European Company (Societas Europa) (1991 OJ C 138/8). This proposal ignores the taxation issues that arise, partly in order to avoid the measure being subject to the fiscal veto. It is understood that it is currently making no progress towards adoption.
5. The precise rules for determining the fiscal residence of a company vary from state to state. However, the relevant double taxation conventions will normally locate a company for fiscal purposes where its centre of effective management is located: OECD Model DTC, art 4, para 2.
6. There are strong fiscal arguments for having at least part of the group in a tax haven. There are some tax havens, however, in the EU. See ch 10.
7. EC Seventh Company Law Directive, Dir 83/349 (1983 OJ L193/1).
8. Some states in the USA introduced the alternative of unitary taxation (or formula apportionment of international profits) in the 1980s. This was strongly opposed by the EC and its member states, including the UK. The states were not supported by the federal government and the approach has since been abandoned by most states. It is not used elsewhere in the world, although its adoption by the EC has been urged by some commentators.

occurred between separate national entities rather than within an entity.[9] Each of these issues causes separate problems. They may also arise within countries and also between them. Some states recognise groups of companies as single economic entities. This is what the Dutch call the principle of fiscal unity,[10] but several other EU states have no such approach.

In the absence of fiscal unity, each national company is taxed as though all transfers between a parent company and the subsidiaries are between non-related companies. The result is that tax accounts have to be drawn up separately by each subsidiary and the parent. These accounts may be on inconsistent bases, and may not reflect the same timing of transactions or views about individual items in the accounts. For example, there may be difficulties in sharing central management expenses, incurred by a parent company on behalf of the group, between the subsidiaries. A loss incurred by a subsidiary may not be transferable back to the parent although it is incurred for the benefit of the MNE as a whole. Alternatively, the expense may not be recognised as an expense of the subsidiary. Payments from subsidiary to parent by means of dividends and interest, and often also royalties and management fees, may be subject to withholding taxes and sometimes VAT. Transfers of assets between the companies may be liable to review for both income tax and VAT adjustments. All these difficulties will increase the compliance costs of an MNE, will reduce its internal cash flows as compared with a company operating as a fiscal unity, will increase the uncertainty of its ultimate tax liability, and will often leave it with unrelieved double taxation and input tax.

Fiscal unity in the EU

The Dutch principle of fiscal unity provides for consolidation for tax purposes of separate entities if a parent company has 99 per cent of the shares of a subsidiary. In such a case, the two companies are treated as if they are one. Some, but not all, other states allow tax consolidation, but the qualifying criteria for consolid-

9. In the absence of specific provisions, the assumed international tax approach is the arm's length approach. See OECD Model DTC, commentary to art 9 and other OECD reports cited there.
10. That is, the taxation of the group as one taxpayer.

ation and the effects of that consolidation vary.[11] Only three states extend this approach beyond national boundaries, and each does so only in a restrictive manner.[12]

The effective restriction of fiscal unity to local subsidiaries only might be argued to be discrimination against foreign companies. For example, the UK grouping rules allow tax consolidation for many purposes between a parent company and subsidiaries in which the parent has 75 per cent of the voting rights.[13] This only applies to subsidiaries resident in the UK. Does this constitute unlawful discrimination under EC law against subsidiaries in other member states?

The House of Lords recently referred this question to the European Court in the case of *ICI v Colmer*.[14] It did so on legislation that predated the UK membership of the EC because the language of the sections was ambiguous as to the scope of the operation of the corporate group provisions concerning subsidiaries of a UK company elsewhere in the EC, given the rights established for those companies by articles 52 and 58 of the EC Treaty.[15] There were arguments in the case that the point should not be referred to the European Court because it was not a practical problem. It may therefore be that the Court is not called on, or finds itself not called on, to answer this question. Nonetheless it will arise at some time.

The argument that discrimination exists is based upon the allegation that discrimination against non-resident companies based elsewhere in the EU is a disguised form of nationality discrimination. While this might be an ideal, there is no express and specific requirement that states move to that ideal in current EC legislation. Arguments against the European Court ruling that the UK tax authorities must take account of EU-resident companies as if they were UK-resident companies were not fully rehearsed in the House of Lords decision. They include arguments that this does not constitute discrimination and, if it does, it is excused by overriding considerations of fiscal coherence.[16] They may include an

---

11. For a summary (as at 1992) see Ruding Report, Table 3A.25, p 269.
12. They are listed in Ruding Report, p 58.
13. This is oversimplified, as the tests are elaborate and are subject to anti-avoidance safeguards. See Income and Corporation Taxes Act 1988, ss 468–468I.
14. [1996] STC 352. The point was not raised in any of the lower levels of appeal.
15. The House of Lords did not consider whether any other EC Treaty provisions might be relevant, for example art 73b and 73d.
16. See p 107.

argument that such a decision might create more discrimination than it removes. This could be argued because of the wide variation of the terms of national legislation, currently coordinated through relevant double taxation conventions. A requirement of tax consolidation in one state by judicial decision will involve no corresponding duty on any other state involved.

If, for example, the UK were to find itself giving the advantages of group tax consolidation to a subsidiary in another state, when that state afforded no reciprocal consolidation, major distortions in cross-border flows would result. If that occurred, neither the European Court nor any existing EC legislation can provide a solution. Indeed, the only solution might be the removal in the UK of tax consolidation. Both this and the alternative of a state tolerating non-reciprocal tax reliefs for subsidiaries might increase economic discrimination on MNEs and the cost to states with forms of tax consolidation.

At the time of writing, the nearest case decided by the European Court is the *Avoir Fiscal* case.[17] It is difficult to predict whether the European Court would be prepared to go as far as to find that the UK tax consolidation provisions offend against EC law. If the Court does so, it will render much of the following discussion – and some of the EC's few legislative provisions in the area – unnecessary. A European Court decision interpreting the requirements of the relevant articles of the EC Treaty as imposing EC fiscal unity will solve many specific problems discussed below. Unless that solution is available, problems must be solved by more specific measures removing the individual barriers emerging on particular kinds of transaction or tax measure.

Fiscal unity and VAT

The approach of fiscal unity is also important for liability to VAT. If a group of companies is regarded as a fiscal unity for VAT, then supplies made between members of the group are not subject to VAT. Essentially, the problem of defining a group for VAT purposes is the same as for corporate taxes. There is, however, one difference. Each company constituting part of a group for VAT

---

17. *EC Commission v France* Case 270/83, [1986] ECR 273. See p 126.

purposes must be economically active. Otherwise, the company cannot be a taxable person, and so cannot be absorbed into a taxable group of persons. The European Court has confirmed this approach. It has ruled that a company that had no activities but was merely a holding company could not be a taxable person.[18]

The Sixth VAT Directive allows, but does not require, member states to recognise fiscal unity within the state. It may be applied to persons who, while legally independent, are closely bound to one another by financial, economic and organisational links'.[19] Some, but not all, states make use of this approach. There is no provision relating to cross-border links.

The group structure of MNEs presents a differing series of challenges for VAT purposes than those that apply for tax purposes. In part, this is because an MNE may register for VAT in any state in which it is conducting taxable transactions. If it does so, it finds the key rules of the tax the same in each member state. The consistent use of the destination basis of VAT is also important because it protects the neutrality of taxation of imported goods and some services. Limited pressure exists for the same kinds of measures for VAT as we consider in this chapter for the direct taxes. For that reason, the topic is not further considered here. Nonetheless we will note in the next chapter that there can be an overlap between VAT on cross-border payments and withholding taxes on those same payments.

Harmonising national corporate taxes

National corporate taxes within the EU vary significantly in their rules for defining profits, the rates of tax applied to those profits, and the systems within which those profits are taxed. This has long been recognised within the EC, and various measures were proposed to remove the various differences. These started with the Neumark Committee's report[20] and the van den Tempel study.[21] Both assumed that there should be at least a common corporate

---

18. *Polysar Investments BV v Inspecteur der Invoerrechten en Accijnzen, Arnhem* Case C-60/90, [1993] STC 222, applying Sixth VAT Directive, art 4.
19. Sixth VAT Directive, art 4, para 4.
20. See EEC Reports on Tax Harmonization (1963).
21. A J van den Tempel, *Corporation Tax and Individual Income Tax in the EC* (EEC Commission 1970).

tax system, if not a harmonised tax. Specific proposals dealing with individual problems were first tabled in 1969. A proposed directive aimed at a common system was tabled in 1975, but made no progress.[22] Measures aimed at harmonising company tax rates and the corporate tax base did not get even this far.[23]

No progress was made in any of these areas until the pressures of the forthcoming single market made action imperative. Decisions were galvanised by Commission Guidelines on Company Taxation published in 1990.[24] This focused the need for action on the tax problems posed by cross-frontier cooperation for MNEs. It urged adoption of three draft directives already proposed by the Commission that it put forward as a package for early adoption: the mergers directive, the parent companies and subsidiaries directive, and the arbitration procedure directive.[25] It urged early adoption of two other measures: a draft losses directive, already proposed, and a proposed directive abolishing withholding taxes on interest and royalties. It also argued for rules on transfer pricing and the transparency of incentives. Finally, it pointed out that without other action, the relevant treaty measures would themselves apply to guarantee the principle of equality of treatment. Separately, it withdrew its 1975 proposals for a common corporate tax system, and announced the establishment of the Ruding Committee.

The package of the three directives had long been blocked by some member states unable to accept their current terms. Shortly after this report, the blockage was removed. With little detailed consideration, the merger and parent-subsidiary directives were adopted. The arbitration proposal was recast into a convention agreed within the Council, and adopted at the same time in that form. It has subsequently been ratified by all member states, including those who have since joined the EU. The detail of each of

---

22. Proposal for a Council Directive concerning the harmonisation of systems of company taxation and of withholding taxes on dividends (1975 OJ C 253/2).

23. For accounts of the various published reports and initiatives, see P Farmer and E Lyal *EC Tax Law* (OUP, 1994), ch 2. The preliminary draft proposal for a directive on the harmonisation of rules for determining the taxable profits of undertakings was never adopted by the Commission and therefore not published.

24. SEC (90)601 of 20 April 1990, reproduced as an annex to B Terra and P Wattel, *European Tax Law* (Kluwer, 1993), at p 326.

25. These informal short titles are those in the Guidelines. They now have even shorter informal titles (merger, parent-subsidiary, and arbitration).

these measures is important, and is still developing through both EU and national legislative and judicial action. The key points and problems are discussed below.

The Parent-Subsidiary Directive[26]

The main aim of the Directive is to eliminate the disadvantage suffered by companies in different member states within a parent-subsidiary relationship because of inconsistencies in treatment by national tax systems. In doing so, it supersedes relevant provisions in bilateral double tax conventions.[27] However, the scope of the Directive is limited in several ways. First, it applies only where the parent has a 25 per cent interest[28] in the subsidiary.[29] Second, it is subject to national safeguards to prevent fraud or abuse.[30] Third, it applies only to companies of a form listed in the Directive.[31] Fourth, each company must be resident for both national law purposes and double tax convention purposes within a member state.[32]

Where a dividend[33] is paid from a subsidiary to a parent, the Directive places limits on the taxing powers of both states involved. The state from which the dividend is sent must exempt the

---

26. Council Directive 90/435/EEC on the Common System of Taxation applicable in the case of Parent Companies and Subsidiaries of Different Member States (23 July 1990)(1990 OJ L225/6). The original proposal was published at 1969 OJ C 39 (22 March 1969).

27. These broadly follow the form of OECD Model DTC, art 10. This restricts the withholding tax that the source state may impose on a dividend paid by a subsidiary to a parent with a 25 per cent interest in it to 5 per cent. The article does not require relief for underlying tax, but does bar other, less direct, forms of double taxation.

28. This figure and some of the language are taken from the OECD Model DTC, art 10.

29. Strictly, this is not a parent-subsidiary link but rather an FDI link. The precise form of the link is left partly to national discretion: Parent-Subsidiary Directive, art 3.

30. The phrase in art 1, para 2 of the Directive. This phrase, which has no precise meaning in UK tax law, where there is no concept of tax 'abuse', is one of several in the Directive that have proved too imprecise to allow either direct effect or clear guidance to national authorities.

31. Directive, art 2. This list is now felt to be too restrictive, and amendments have been proposed (1993 OJ C 225/5).

32. Art 1.

33. It does not apply to other payments from a subsidiary, such as a payment on liquidation of the subsidiary.

dividend from withholding tax if the 25 per cent link exists.[34] In other words, the dividend must be received gross in the state of the parent company. That state must also observe restrictions. It may not itself impose a withholding on the dividend.[35] More important, it must either exempt the dividends from taxation or allow relief for the underlying tax[36] against any tax it levies. The effect is that the state where the subsidiary is resident is free to tax that company's profits. The dividend of those profits to the parent company may not be taxed as such by the state of the subsidiary. The state of the parent company may tax the dividend, but must recognise that this is derived from taxed profits. It must also allow relief[37] for the tax already paid on the profits funding the dividend.

The Merger Directive[38]

The key to this Directive lies in the definitions of 'merger', 'division', 'transfer of assets' and 'exchange of shares', as its provisions operate only when one of these events occurs. A merger occurs when one or more companies, on being dissolved without going into liquidation, transfers assets to another company. This cannot occur in the UK, because a company under UK company law is liquidated before it is dissolved.[39] A division is the reverse process to a merger.[40] The more usual commercial transactions are a transfer of assets in exchange for a transfer of securities representing the capital of the company receiving the assets, and an exchange of

---

34. This is not as far-reaching as it sounds. There are exceptions for Germany, Greece and Portugal in the Directive. Further, the Directive does not apply to imputation systems, and therefore does not apply to the ACT imposed on a distributing company in the UK, or the similar measures in other states with imputation systems. Further, most of the member states already have double tax conventions in place reducing their withholding taxes, in some cases more significantly than this Directive.

35. In practice, states did not do this anyway!

36. Underlying tax is the tax paid by the subsidiary on the profits it has earned in order to be able to fund the dividend.

37. Up to the level of any tax it would itself impose.

38. Council Directive 90/434/EEC on the Common System of Taxation applicable to Mergers, Divisions, Transfers of Assets and Exchanges of Shares concerning Companies in different Member States (23 July 1990) (1990 OJ L 225/1).

39. Directive, art 2(a). This reflects a difference between the UK style of company law and that in most other member states. The proposed EC Tenth Company Law Directive deals with this point. It has not been adopted by the EU and there are no current proposals to adopt it.

40. Art 2(b). The usual term in the UK is demerger. A division, in this sense, cannot occur in the UK for the same reason that a merger cannot occur.

shares by which one of the exchanging companies receives shares carrying a majority of the voting rights (and therefore control) of the other.

The purpose of the Directive is to remove tax barriers against cross-border linkages of companies. Under national tax laws, such transactions normally incur heavy tax costs if the transaction involves assets or value leaving the jurisdiction. This is because many member states impose a corporate level tax on any capital gains realised on a transfer or exchange of shares, or on the liquidation of a company. While some states allow this tax charge to be postponed if the capital is reinvested in another business, this does not usually apply if the new investment is outside the tax jurisdiction of the state. However, not all states impose these charges, and individual provisions and reliefs vary widely.[41] At the time the Directive was adopted these could occasionally take as taxes half the values transferred and in others none at all. Such provisions clearly rendered some transfers uneconomic, and the regime as a whole distortionary.

The main solution offered by the Directive is to remove the distortion by removing the tax charge. This is done by exempting the companies[42] involved from capital gains tax[43] on the values realised, if there is a locking-in or reinvestment of those values.[44] The Directive also protects against a tax charge on the cancellation of any shares involved or on the allotment of the new shares.[45]

Two other problems are also tackled. The first is the effect on the income tax liability of the company receiving the assets or shares. That company must be treated in the same way as the transferring company would have been treated. For example, valuations, reserves, gains and losses, and exemptions relating to the transferred assets should all be transferred across on a national treatment basis, subject to the valuations being consistent with those of the transferring company. The second is the position of a permanent establishment (PE).[46] If a PE in a third state is transferred from one company to another, then the transferring company's

---

41. See Ruding Committee Report, Table 3A.6, p 243 for a summary of the 1992 position.
42. This applies in both states.
43. Strictly, it is an exemption from the various taxes listed in art 3, most of which are corporation taxes, but which include charges to tax on capital gains.
44. Directive, arts 4, 9. A member state may tax any cash realised from a transaction: art 8, para 4.
45. Directive, arts 7, 8.
46. For discussion of the status of a PE, see ch 7.

state is required to renounce taxing rights, and the state of the PE is to apply the Directive together with the state of the receiving company.[47]

The Directive is subject to similar, but unfortunately not identical,[48] limits as those that operate for the Merger Directive.[49] Application to cases where the company receiving the shares obtains less than 25 per cent of the capital of the transferring company is not mandatory.

Both these Directives are now in effect, and some implementing legislation has been passed in member states. However, a detailed recent survey has shown that none of the states has carried out the measures fully. In addition, the European Court has decided the first of a number of cases referred to it alleging non-implementation. With the changes in national and bilateral provisions that have followed, the two measures have lowered two of the most important tax barriers confronting MNEs.

The Arbitration Convention[50]

A main concern of national governments, when taxing MNEs, is that the MNEs will avoid taxation through manipulation of their transfer pricing. Transfer pricing is the name given to the operation by which an MNE must attribute values to any goods, services or other assets or rights transferred across frontiers between member companies of the MNE.

For example, a parent company in one state supplies its subsidiary in another state with partly-finished goods. It also supplies the know-how to train staff to finish the goods, and with the necessary intellectual property licences to sell the goods. It will probably impose a price, charge or royalty on the subsidiary to

---

47. Directive, art 10.
48. Partly for this reason, amendments have been proposed which would bring the Directive more in line with the Parent-Subsidiary Directive: 1993 OJ C 225/3.
49. The anti-avoidance provision refers (in English) to 'tax evasion or tax avoidance': art 11. Evasion is assumed to be a mistranslation from the French, as the French term 'evasion' is broadly the same as the English term 'avoidance'. The uncertainty of the meaning in the Merger Directive (note 38) is thereby compounded by the different wording of this Directive.
50. Convention on the elimination of double taxation in connection with the adjustment of profits of associated enterprises (23 July 1990)(published at 1990 OJ C 225/10), based on a proposal for a directive originally published at 1976 OJ C 301/4.

pay for those assets and rights. The sums paid will count as a deduction against the profits of the subsidiary and as part of the profits of the parent. The amount chosen as the price is therefore of direct concern to both tax authorities. If the price is high, then the profits of the parent are raised and those of the subsidiary depressed. If the parent has tax losses, or the tax rate in the subsidiary's state is higher than that in the parent state, the tax authorities of the subsidiary state might suspect tax avoidance to be a reason behind the precise prices used.

What may then happen is that the tax authorities of the subsidiary may refuse to accept the prices used by the MNE, and may insist that a lower price be used for the assets supplied. They will disallow the claim for a deduction above that amount. However, the tax authority of the parent may not agree, and may insist on calculating the profits on the assumption that the price was fully received. If this happens, the MNE is being taxed excessively, because the parent is being taxed on a sum that the subsidiary is not allowed fully to treat as an expense.

Under the OECD Model double tax convention, two rules apply in a case such as this. The first is that the tax authorities are entitled to review any transfer price if it is not an arm's length price.[51] The second is that where one tax authority adjusts a price under this provision, the other tax authority should make an appropriate adjustment (called a secondary adjustment) to its own assessment in recognition of the other recalculation.[52] However, there is nothing in the OECD Model to compel a secondary adjustment. Further, not all EU member states accept the second rule. Nor is there any other mechanism available in a double tax convention to impose a solution on the national tax authorities in a situation like that in the example. The Arbitration Convention operates to apply a remedy where double taxation results from transfer pricing adjustments. The convention accepts – indeed repeats – the first of the two associated enterprise rules.[53] It also repeats a rule dealing with the sharing of profits between a permanent establishment and the company of which it is a PE.[54]

---

51. OECD Model DTC, art 9, para 1.
52. OECD Model DTC, art 9, para 2.
53. Convention, art 4, para 1.
54. OECD Model DTC, art 7, para 2, repeated in Convention, art 4, para 2.

In both cases, the Convention provides a mechanism to ensure that a secondary adjustment is made in any case where one of the tax authorities involved finds it appropriate to adjust profits. Where a taxpayer's profits have been adjusted by a tax authority, and the taxpayer believes that this is not in accordance with the principles for adjustment, it may refer the matter to the two tax authorities involved. If the tax authorities fail to resolve the issue, the matter must be referred to an advisory commission. This advisory commission is charged with the task of recommending a way of eliminating the double taxation. The commission's opinion must be considered by the two states. They may decide to adopt the opinion, or another method of resolving the problem. 'If they fail to reach agreement, they shall be obliged to act in accordance with that opinion.'[55] Although the procedure is hedged around by safeguards, and includes lengthy time limits on the states, the resulting arbitration is mandatory, as is a resolution of any problem it identifies.

Because the Convention required formal ratification, it was a little time before all the member states formally accepted the Convention. They have, however, now done so. It is also understood that the first cases have now started going through the arbitral procedure, although they will receive no formal publicity. Because the Convention is not part of EC law, the European Court has no role in interpreting it. Nor do general EC legal principles apply to it. It would, it is suggested, in any event be inappropriate for a body like the European Court to be charged with offering an opinion in this kind of case.

Nonetheless, the Convention applies a compulsory remedy where none was available before. It is a significant advance on the approaches available under general international tax law.[56] It will be combined in practice with recent OECD clarification of the principles on which transfer pricing adjustments should occur.[57] Cautious though it seems, this Convention may be an important precedent for increasing certainty and reducing excessive taxation in this important and sensitive area.

[55.] Convention, art 12, para 1.
[56.] There is no international tax court, nor general arbitral body for tax matters. Prior to this Convention, only a few cautious bilateral agreements for arbitration had been reached (for example between the USA and Germany), but they were not compulsory.
[57.] Transfer Pricing Guidelines (OECD, 1996).

The Ruding Committee

The Ruding Committee[58] was formed when the package of the two Directives and Convention were being adopted. Its remit was much wider. It considered in detail how related companies within a group might be prejudiced by tax barriers. Its particular concern was the extent to which such barriers created relative incentives for businesses directly investing in a subsidiary[59] abroad rather than at home. Its findings suggested a bias in most systems against both inward and outward foreign direct investment. In its view, the tax systems of all member states provided higher effective tax rates on both inward and outward FDI to an extent that constituted discrimination.

Problems with intra-group dividends were identified as the single most important cause of tax discrimination against cross-border direct investment in a single market. The Ruding Committee[60] concluded on the basis both of its own and other research that 'as regards the causes of [investment] discrimination within the Community, it would appear . . . that withholding taxes levied by source countries on cross-border dividend payments between related companies are the main reason'. In the Committee's view, discrimination also resulted from the different ways in which member states handled double taxation of other cross-border income flows. Yet it found that withholding taxes imposed on interest payments were unimportant. Differences in corporation tax rates also caused significant distortions. However, differences in the corporation tax systems of the member states were not significant, save for the effect of unrelieved advance corporation tax.[61] The Committee also concluded that these differences had little effect on the relative costs between states of local investments. Calculation of profits, and the differing national tax rates, did cause differences.

---

58. See Ruding Committee, Report (1992). The Committee was set up under the chairmanship of Mr Ruding in 1990 to consider and make recommendations on distortions caused to businesses within a single market by the taxation of business. The Committee report contains valuable primary evidence on these distortions as well as a full analysis and bibliography.
59. The report examines this rather than branches because most such investment takes place through subsidiaries: Report, p 73.
60. Report, p 78.
61. This was a reference to an exclusively British problem, now partly dealt with by changes to the British ACT system. See Report, p 78.

The Committee's report was produced at impressive speed. Yet it argued its case thoroughly both from empirical evidence and from legal principle. It offered a three-phase programme for achieving the target it was set – identifying specific measures necessary to remove or mitigate distortions in the internal market caused by differences in taxation. The three phases were to be completed as full economic and monetary union was completed.

In Phase I, the Committee urged the adoption of the arbitration convention and transfer pricing guidelines to go with it. It also urged adoption of a draft directive on losses, a draft directive on withholding taxes on interest and royalties, and common action on the member states' double tax conventions. More controversial was a proposal for a minimum corporation tax rate of 30 per cent. Phase II included the adoption of a uniform 30 per cent withholding tax on dividends, subject to waiver; the adoption of a maximum corporation tax rate of 40 per cent; and common rules allowing unincorporated businesses to be taxed as companies. Phase III would see a common form of corporation tax, and a full extension of the reliefs behind the various directives to most kinds of businesses.

The Ruding Report received a cautious welcome from the Commission. Viewed five years on, neither the Commission nor the member states have moved far. The only recommendation fully realised is the adoption of the Arbitration Convention. Some of the measures are still under consideration, as noted below. Some have seen some progress at national level, but not EU level. The fiscal veto remains as important as ever. Because of this, other measures such as the withholding tax on interest and the moves to a common corporation tax system and rate structure have seen no progress. Nor are they likely to do so. Meanwhile, as we have seen, the challenge put to Ruding has been taken up by the European Court. Perhaps for political reasons, there is little in the Ruding Report about the principles of EC law and the possible role of the Court. Yet, lacking a legislative response to the challenges placed not only by the Ruding Committee but by the evidence it assembled, it is only the Court that can move.

The draft interest and royalties directive[62]

The OECD Model double tax convention recommends that source states levy a withholding tax of 10 per cent on interest payments,[63] but refrain from levying a withholding tax on royalties paid for intellectual property and similar rights.[64] Despite this, national practice within the EU varies quite widely. Several states impose both kinds of withholding tax. Only the Netherlands never does so. The Commission therefore proposed the abolition of withholding taxes within corporate groups in the same way as has been achieved by the Parent-Subsidiary Directive. The 1990 proposal, as amended, is, like that Directive, a simple text applying to the same categories of taxpayer and subject to broadly similar limits. It is understood that the current version of the text has developed some way from this simple approach to a more elaborate and careful document. It is still under active consideration, and there is some hope that it will, in modified form, be adopted as current tax plans evolve.

The draft losses directive[65] and other proposals

The Commission published a draft losses directive at the same time as the draft interest and royalties directive, but it has received a less positive response. The proposal is designed to allow losses from foreign permanent establishments and subsidiaries against the profits of the parent in the parent's state. Some states currently allow the transfer of losses of foreign PEs, at least where they impose worldwide taxation on a company and therefore also tax the PE's profits.[66] There is little enthusiasm for allowing losses of subsidiaries even where this is offset by the taxation of future profits. The draft is therefore making little progress.

---

62. Proposal for a Council Directive on a Common System of Taxation applicable to Interest and Royalty Payments made between Parent Companies and Subsidiaries in different Member States (6 December 1990)(1991 OJ C 53/26, amended 1993 OJ C 178/18).
63. OECD Model DTC, art 11.
64. OECD Model DTC, art 12.
65. Proposal for a Council Directive concerning Arrangements for the Taking into Account by Enterprises of the Losses of their Permanent Establishments and Subsidiaries situated in other Member States (6 December 1990)(1991 OJ C 53/5).
66. This applies in the UK.

There is no other action taking place at the time of writing on formal proposals to help MNEs. Although Monti, the current Commissioner responsible for taxation, has encouraged practical suggestions for forward movement, the pace has again slowed. Attention is currently concentrated on two ways of making progress. The first is the jurisprudence of the Court, and reactions to it. The second is a detailed study of the individual provisions in the double taxation conventions of the member states. This will identify more systematically than previous studies the precise extent of the common ground and the differences between the member states.

Both these moves will aid tax competition rather than coordination unless there is a change of political will. The European Court cannot impose positive measures – it can only criticise. The double tax conventions can coordinate, but only by reducing existing barriers rather than replacing them with something more positive. Yet in the end, do we need more than that? The MNEs think so. They are still pressing for common rules for determining taxable profits and in particular for removing the ever-present threat of transfer pricing disputes. They and others also look towards the achievement of a multilateral tax convention, or at least an EU Model that incorporates EC law and also international tax law. The chief beneficiaries of all such changes will be the MNEs. Until those objectives are achieved, it is the MNEs that must bear the compliance costs of meeting multiple and conflicting requirements. They will also seek to reduce their exposure by appropriate tax planning. This we will turn to in the final chapter.

CHAPTER NINE

Taxing cross-border savings and investment

To date, the EU has signally failed to achieve any lasting coordinated positive action on the taxation of savings or investment. This is also true of taxation on the ownership of assets in one state by a person resident in another. The only legislative achievement has been an amendment to the EC Treaty defensive of national interests.

This failure does not signal that the matter is one of little importance. On the contrary, it is the perceived importance to individual member states of the right to keep national taxation practices in this area that has caused the problems. While there has been little EU action, there has sometimes been significant action at national level. That action has often been negative – that of repealing or reducing existing taxes – rather than national tax increases. This has caused the effective repeal of the only positive measure in this area that was adopted in the earlier years of the EEC, the capital duty. There is still prolonged debate about some other proposed EU measures.

Free movement of capital and payments

Behind the uncertainty and disagreement on tax questions lies the achievement of significant freedom of movement for capital within the EU. The key treaty provisions were recast from 1994 by the Treaty of European Union.[1] They now require freedom of movement of capital throughout the EU together with freedom of

---

1. EEC Treaty, arts 67–73 were replaced by arts 73a–73g with effect from 1 January 1994.

movement between member states and third countries.[2] Freedom of movement of payments is also imposed.[3]

These freedoms, although stated absolutely, are subject to both permanent and transitional limitations. One deals expressly with taxation: article 73d. Freedom of movement is to be without prejudice to rights of member states 'to apply the relevant provisions of their tax law which distinguish between taxpayers who are not in the same situation with regard to their place of residence[4] or with regard to the place where their capital is invested'.[5] The article also excepts from requirement of free movement any measures designed to prevent infringement of national tax laws.[6]

Broader than the free movement of capital is the freedom to own assets in another state. This is not, as such, one of the four freedoms, but it is a consequence of them, taken together with the prohibition on economic discrimination on grounds of nationality. Until capital could be moved freely from one state to another, residents in one state might not have been able to pay for capital assets of any significance in another state. This was because, until the freedom was granted, exchange controls stopped sufficient capital moving to other states to allow asset purchases. No particular concerns arise with ownership of tangible, movable property (which themselves can be moved by way of import). Few tax problems arise for income from land owned in another state, but taxing income from intellectual property or similar intangibles owned or used in another state can cause problems.

There is a general prohibition in the EC Treaty against doing anything to prejudice national rules of property ownership.[7] This, taken together with the fact that free movement of immovable property is an oxymoron, has meant that both the EU and the international trading community have paid little attention to the tax-

---

2. EC Treaty, art 73b, para 1.
3. EC Treaty, art 73b, para 2. This echoes a requirement of the GATT that free movement of goods be paralleled by free movement of the means of payment for the goods. In practice, this has caused little problem in the field of taxation, although exchange control rules do impose limits in many cases.
4. This wording is an echo of the terminology used in the OECD Model DTC art 24 barring discrimination against non-nationals 'in the same circumstances, in particular with respect to residence': art 24, para 1.
5. EC Treaty, art 73d, para 1(a).
6. EC Treaty, art 73d, para 1(b).
7. EC Treaty, art 222.

ation of land. It is for this reason that, apart from a brief comment later in this chapter, the subject is ignored in this book.

Taxation of intellectual property and similar rights (IP for short) presents a more significant problem. IP can be subject to both indirect and direct taxes. The EU has taken significant measures to ensure protection of IP throughout the EU.[8] More recently, GATT 1994, through the adoption of TRIPS,[9] has made it easier to transfer the benefits of IP from one state to another. Therefore it is also easier for owners to enjoy income from foreign use of their IP. We will examine this topic after dealing with movements of capital.

To complete the picture, we must also note that some states tax the ownership of capital by means of a wealth tax or capital tax. Provided that the tax is applied in a non-discriminatory way, this is not likely to give rise to positive distortions within the EU. By contrast, it is likely to place the state imposing the tax at a disadvantage if capital and assets can be moved freely elsewhere.

Tax barriers on cross-border capital movements

Realisation of the freedom of movement of both capital and payments has been assisted by significant secondary legislation in the fields of banking, investment and insurance. On present plans, it will be facilitated further from 1999 by the adoption of a single currency. The measures taken to date have ensured that capital is now highly mobile within the EU. It can also move freely into and out of the EU.

Competition, combined with the coordination measures for banks and similar institutions, has forced down the fees imposed for handling financial transactions. In practice, the only other two costs of a financial transaction are the foreign exchange costs and risks and the differential effects of taxation. Adoption of a single currency will remove both currency costs and risks. Differences in national taxation will then be exposed as the only significant variable between states affecting the allocation of capital.

8. For a summary see S Weatherill and P Beaumont, *EC Law,* (Penguin, 2nd edition, 1995) ch 26.
9. TRIPS is the standard abbreviation for the agreement on rights in intellectual property adopted as a part of GATT 1994.

The resulting pressure on national tax systems is already intense, but member states are still of two minds about how to handle this. They are divided between those arguing for a harmonised approach to the taxation of passive income,[10] and those content with individual national initiatives. The fiscal veto has ensured no substantive communal action. The result has been a downward pressure on individual taxes in the member states.

Although distortions have abated, they still exist. As a result, neutrality does not yet exist for capital movements within the EU. Investors look for two kinds of neutrality for capital, capital export neutrality (CEN) and capital import neutrality (CIN). CEN requires that there is no distortion between the returns made on outbound investments as compared with investments made in the home economy. CIN requires that the state receiving the investment treats inward investment neutrally with local investment.[11]

In international direct tax practice, investment is categorised into two kinds for this form of analysis: foreign direct investment (FDI), and portfolio investment. FDI means foreign active investment in the local economy, for example by starting a local manufacturing business. Portfolio investment is investment for passive income. Tax practice often treats FDI more favourably than portfolio investment. In particular, states usuallly make more effort at neutrality for FDI than for passive income being remitted out of the jurisdiction.

A failure to achieve neutrality may arise for a variety of reasons. Both direct taxes and indirect taxes can apply to cross-border flows of capital and payments. The source state of a payment of interest may levy a withholding tax on it, while the state of residence of the investor also imposes income tax liability. For this reason, abolition of the practice of imposing withholding taxes has been identified as a major way in which CIN could be achieved. This is because it removes a major discrimination in favour of locally provided capital.[12] At the same time, transaction taxes and

---

10. In US tax law a distinction is drawn between active income (earnings, profits, etc) and passive income. Within the UK this term is not used widely, reference being made instead to unearned income or investment income. Capital income is also a relevant international English term. The US phraseology neatly describes the important differences relevant to discussing the subject in the EU context, and is therefore used from time to time.

11. For a discussion of the significance of these concepts in the EU, see Ruding Report (1992), pp 34–7.

12. Ruding Report (1992) ch 4, especially p 78, and references there cited.

turnover taxes may also be imposed on the loan, or the document evidencing the loan, or on the payment of interest on the loan.[13] The potential for cumulation and for non-neutral effects, even if no discrimination is intended, is significant.

This chapter reviews what has happened with regard to the removal of tax-based distortions for differing kinds of investment[14] and savings and explores possible future action on the topic.

Indirect taxes on investment and investment income

Neither customs duties nor article 95 apply to movements of capital. Despite the fashion for calling savings methods 'financial products', they are not products in this sense of the word.[15] Conversely, article 95 can be used to prevent taxes being used to adjust the taxation of goods to reflect problems relating to currency costs.[16]

VAT also does not apply to movements of capital or of payments. The passive holding of investments is not an 'economic activity', and VAT does not therefore apply to the holder.[17] The European Court has also confirmed that the payment of a dividend on a share is not a payment of consideration for the investment within the scope of VAT.[18] A loan is a supply of a service, as is the provision of other financial services. The EC VAT nonetheless exempts all primary financial services from VAT.[19] As a result,

---

13. The Ruding Committee did not consider VAT as it was outside the Committee's terms of reference.
14. The chapter does not cover FDI by multinational enterprises or the treatment of dividends, as these are discussed in ch 8.
15. *Van Eycke v ASPA* Case 267/86, [1988] ECR 4769. The Court confirmed that the relevant provisions for savings schemes were the provisions on freedom of establishment and freedom of movement of capital, not art 95.
16. *Commission v Ireland* Case 55/79, [1980] ECR 481.
17. *Polysar Investment BV v Inspecteur der invoerrechten an Accijnzen, Arnhem* Case C-60/90, [1993] STC 222.This also applies to passive holders of bonds or other similar investments.
18. *Sofitam SA v Ministre charge du Budget* Case C-333/91, reported belatedly at [1997] STC 226.
19. Sixth VAT Directive, art 13B(d). The exemption reflects a failure to agree at the conceptual level on how a VAT form of tax can be applied to the intermediation charges imposed by banks on the costs of finance. The exemption has been review by the Commission but it is understood no clear way forward has been found.

there is no VAT on payments of interest, premiums or other similar payments for, or returns on, capital. The exemption also applies to charges for credit cards and other payment cards.[20] The cumulative effect of the legislative and judicial decisions is that movements of capital and payments are not subject to VAT. Some member states were not happy with this blanket approach. As a concession, the Sixth VAT Directive allows an option to tax financial services.[21] Only a few member states have chosen to use this option, and only with limited effect.[22] Insurance services are also exempt from VAT,[23] as are betting and gambling services,[24] without an option to tax.

The absence of a general VAT charge leaves the way open to impose individual excise or transaction taxes on financial services.[25] There are an increasing number of these. Wide use is made of insurance premium taxes, usually levied as a percentage of the amount of premium payable on an insurance policy. Betting taxes are also common. More traditionally, stamp duties[26] are levied on the documents by which investments are recorded, such as the registration certificate for, or transfer record of, a share in a company.[27] One attempt was made by the EEC to harmonise taxes in this area, by creating a company capital duty.

---

20. The Commission proposed a draft nineteenth VAT directive to remove this exemption, but the measure has made no progress.
21. Sixth VAT Directive, art 13C.
22. It is used in Germany, but on a single transaction approach, not a blanket approach. It is understood that the option to tax is used only on the largest transactions where it is in the interests of the customer to do so (because the customer can reclaim the total VAT imposed as input tax, thereby reducing the effective cost of the loan).
23. Sixth VAT Directive, art 13B(a).
24. Sixth VAT Directive, art 13B(f). This is mentioned because some kinds of share and commodity transactions are open to classification under national laws as betting transactions rather than investments. This is particularly relevant to secondary investments such as some forms of derivative financial instrument.
25. This is expressly recognised by the Sixth VAT Directive, art 33.
26. The practice dates from the mid-seventeenth century in Holland.
27. Document taxes are currently suffering from obsolescence as records are transferred to electronic data bases and do not exist in documentary form. This can be handled by supplementing the document tax with a backup tax. The UK has done this in reinforcing its stamp duty on the transfer documents for shares with a stamp duty reserve tax on share transfers where no document is produced.

The capital duty[28]

A description of capital duty should start at the end.[29] It was repealed in 1988 in the UK when it became under EC law, in effect, a voluntary measure.[30] It is not likely to be replaced by any similar measure. The measure will therefore be noted in outline only, and in the past tense.[31] Capital duty was imposed from 1972 on the creation or increase of capital in a capital company.[32] 'Capital company' was given a precise definition for the original member states of the EC, but as membership expanded the definition became less certain. The scope potentially covered 'any . . . company, firm, association or legal person operating for profit', but a member state could decide to restrict the definition if it wished.[33] 'Capital' was not directly defined, but both direct and indirect contributions to capital were covered, including contributions of assets in exchange for rights similar to those of shareholders, and the transfer of the effective centre of management[34] of a company.[35]

Capital duty had common rates and provision for exemptions that were at first largely common between the member states – or so it might seem to the casual reader. In reality there was considerable variation between states. A maximum rate of 1 per cent was laid down. Yet it should be remembered that 1 per cent of capital is a significant imposition, as it is related not to profit but to

28. Capital duty was assumed by the EC in 1969 to be an indirect tax and therefore within the scope of the obligation of harmonisation imposed by EC Treaty, art 99. In the UK stamp duty has been regarded as a direct tax (in which case it would not fall within art 99). While not a direct reason for its repeal, the repeal solved a longstanding uncertainty about the legislative basis for this measure.

29. Those who do not wish to start at the end should see B Terra and P Wattel, *European Tax Law* (Kluwer, 1993), ch 8 and E Brood 'Capital Contribution Tax in the EEC', (1993) EC Tax Review 96.

30. This was achieved by Directive 85/303, which gave member states the right either to exempt all transactions or to charge them at a rate of not more than 1 per cent.

31. It is still in effect elsewhere, for example the Netherlands.

32. Council Directive 69/335/EEC concerning indirect taxes on the raising of capital (17 July 1969)(1969 OJ Special Edn vol II p 412). It was amended by Directive 73/79/EEC (18 April 1973)(1973 OJ L 03/13), and Directive 85/303/EEC (15 June 1985)(1985 OJ L 156/23).

33. Directive 69/335, art 3.

34. National jurisdiction to impose capital duty was defined with primary reference to the state in whose territory the effective centre of management of the company was situated at the time of the transaction to be taxed: Directive 69/335, art 2.

35. Directive 69/335, art 4.

creation or movement of capital. States therefore sought to reduce the imposition to avoid the adverse effects of the duty. The uncertainties of the duty also led both to significant case law and significant criticism. It is therefore not surprising to find Terra and Wattell concluding their review of the duty in 1993: 'it seems to us that the tax should be either unified, or, even better, be abolished altogether.'[36]

Even when the duty was effective, it did not preclude duties on transfers of securities, or of the underlying assets, fees or dues for registration, or VAT. States used that latitude to tax other aspects of company capital, and capital duty did not therefore entirely remove the problem of multiple taxation.[37]

Direct taxes on investment

International tax law recognises the right of states to use income taxes to tax passive income by reference to both its source and its recipient. Typically, a payment of interest can be subject to a withholding tax in the state from which the payment is made. It can also be assessed to tax in the state where the person entitled to the interest is resident. National practice shows considerable variation in the use of these claims to tax. Luxembourg has for a long time refused to impose a withholding tax on interest paid to non-residents. This was not a problem while exchange controls prevented capital being moved to Luxembourg. Since the achievement of free movement of capital, Luxembourg has attracted significant savings and investments from neighbouring states.[38] Other states have sought to retain withholding taxes and even to impose them where none exist.[39] The competition is intense.

The main route for resolving problems with withholding taxes has been the use of double tax conventions (DTCs). Behind DTCs,

---

36. Terra and Wattel, op cit note 29, p 173.
37. Directive 69/335, art 10 did, however, prevent states imposing another form of tax on capital alongside the capital duty.
38. Particularly, it is widely understood, Belgium.
39. Germany, which does not impose a withholding tax on interest, has been particularly keen to do so. It tried to do so unilaterally in 1990 but this proved a dismal failure, and caused a major shift of investment from Germany to Switzerland and other states. The tax had to be revoked within six weeks of imposition. Since then, Germany has been keen to press for coordinated action in this area.

states have often sought to retain significant unilateral withholding rates[40] on foreign investment as well as local investment. Under a DTC, these rates will often be reduced sharply[41] or may disappear.[42] Most EU states have concluded DTCs with each other, but the result is still a patchwork containing distortions between member states. In addition, recent bilateral agreements between member states have tended to impose tighter conditions on entitlement to the reduced (or nil) withholding taxes on interest. This is because of fears about avoidance. They result from the combined pressures on the typical treaty article dealing with interest from both treaty shopping[43] and thin capitalisation.[44]

Taxing interest in the EU

The EU has been caught between the two rival views of its member states about withholding taxes on interest payments. The Commission rightly anticipated that when freedom of capital movements became possible[45] pressure would mount to avoid withholding

---

40. For example, the national rate of withholding on interest was (in 1996) 24 per cent in the UK, 30 per cent in Germany, and 35 per cent in France.
41. OECD Model DTC, art 11 provides for a recommended withholding rate on interest paid from one party to a beneficial owner in the other party of 10 per cent.
42. For example, the rates between France, Germany and the UK are all zero in both directions.
43. Treaty shopping is the name given to the process of selecting a structure for a transaction so as to use the best available treaties. A transaction may therefore be routed between two states because of advantageous terms in their treaties, rather than direct between one of the states and a third state. The OECD Model DTC allows a state to withdraw entitlement to a treaty benefit under an interest article if the recipient is not the beneficial owner of the interest. This is, however, only a limited comfort; OECD Model DTC art 11 and Commentary.
44. Thin capitalisation is the name given to corporate capital structure where the share or equity capital is kept low (thin) as compared with the debt or loan capital. The result is that most of the payments by the company to its providers of capital take the form of interest rather than dividends. Most major states now have national tax legislation in place to allow recharacterisation of excessive loan capital into equity capital. Where this happens the revenue authorities will treat the excessive payment of interest as dividends and demand taxation accordingly. Recent DTCs also contain measures allowing this national tax legislation to take effect. In terms of the OECD Model DTC, this will transfer the 'interest' payments from art 11 to art 10. It also permits the state from which the payment is made to refuse a deduction against profits for the excess interest payments.
45. By reason of Directive 88/361/EEC on the liberalisation of movements of capital (8.7.1988)(1988 OJ L178/5).

taxes on interest. It therefore proposed in 1989 that there should be a common withholding tax on interest throughout the EC of 15 per cent.[46] This was seen as a fallback position where no lower rate was in operation between member states by reason of a DTC. It was also subject to a number of other exemptions and limitations. There was little evidence of the possibility of unanimous support for this proposal. After the setback suffered by Germany in its attempt to impose a withholding tax in 1990, little further serious discussion has taken place about the adoption of this proposal (as against its general desirability in the view of some).

Taking the opposite tack, the Commission published in 1990 its proposal for the abolition of withholding taxes on interest and royalties between parent and subsidiary companies.[47] While member states are concerned lest this measure prove to be as problematic as the Parent-Subsidiary Directive,[48] it is still making quiet progress. There is seen to be a good chance that this will be adopted in due course. With neither measure yet adopted, the position remains that most of the relationships between member states are dealt with under the relevant DTC.

Personal savings in the EU

A separate dimension to the question of EU barriers comes when personal savings are considered. While traditional deposit accounts remain a major method of saving, the development of savings intermediaries has complicated things considerably. In addition to traditional direct savings in deposit accounts, and direct investment in shares, attention must also be paid to savings intermediaries such as unit trusts. We must also take account of designated savings schemes such as retirement and disability pension schemes and life assurance arrangements. Both social and economic pressures have caused states to offer considerable incentives for savings schemes, particularly for pensions. The result can be a complex picture of different forms of savings vehicle and method, each with its own tax regime.

[46]. See 1989 OJ C 141/5 (7 June 1989) and COM (89) 90–2 final.
[47]. This is discussed in the context of multinational enterprises in ch 8.
[48]. See ch 8.

The free movement of both individuals and their savings imposes considerable pressures on inconsistent regimes. This is by reason both of incompatibility with the freedoms of movement, and of tax competition between states and schemes. We discussed the problems caused by differential treatments of pension schemes when examining the free movement of the EU's citizens.[49] To that complex and largely unresolved problem we must now add a further layer of analysis. The problem can be illustrated by the first of the savings and investment vehicles to benefit from freedom of movement of capital, the unit trust.

Unit trusts

A unit trust[50] is a means whereby an investor can spread a limited investment into a wide variety of investments. The investor, with others, pays money into a trust. The trustees then invest the total funds into such investments as the trust deed allows. For example, the unit trust could be a general fund investing in all EU companies, or it could concentrate on perhaps small companies or companies involved in the leisure industry. Wider unit trusts also allow investment in bonds and securities. The individual investor gets the advantage of a spread of investments and of expert advice on those investments, in exchange for a charge levied on the fund.

In 1985, the EC passed the UCITS Directive.[51] This opened the way for investment in unit trusts elsewhere in the EC. Prior to the adoption of the UCITS Directive, unit trusts were mainly based in London and Luxembourg. The UK taxed unit trusts as companies subject to the corporation tax rate, while Luxembourg regarded unit trusts as mere intermediaries to be taxed on a transparency basis to the personal income tax. Both were justified approaches viewed in the contexts of their national tax systems.

The arrival of the UCITS Directive meant that for the first time funds going through London could also go through Luxembourg, or the reverse. The two jurisdictions were providing similar

49. In ch 6.
50. The UK terminology. In the USA they are referred to as mutual funds. We shall see that the European English version is UCITS.
51. Council Directive 85/611/EEC on the coordination of laws, regulations and administrative provisions relating to Undertakings for Collective Investment in Transferable Securities (20 December 1985) (1985 OJ L 375/3).

vehicles through which to invest in similar ranges of securities at similar rates of charge. Consequently, the key factor in competition between London and Luxembourg was tax. The terms were heavily in Luxembourg's favour. Its 'see-through' approach combined with a lower rate of personal income tax compared with the UK rate, meant it was significantly better for UK investors to invest through Luxembourg, than the reverse. This was so even if there was later worldwide taxation in the UK of parts of the income and capital gains of an investment.

The result, perhaps inevitably, was that the UK was forced to change its system for taxing unit trusts. They are still taxed as corporations, but at the basic individual rate of income tax.[52] This removed the tax advantage of Luxembourg and stopped the anticipated major transfers of funds there, at a cost to British tax revenues.

Article 73d

This process of levelling down, rather than levelling up, the differences between investments and savings schemes was set to continue. If it were also to be combined with a need to give tax benefits under pension and similar schemes to all EU nationals, the potential cost to national tax revenues could prove most expensive. There was considerable concern among member governments at the additional effect that non-discrimination rules might have on taxation in this area. They therefore used the opportunity of the Treaty of European Union to pass the measure set out above[53] to remove a need to extend the scope of nondiscrimination into measures relating to free movement of capital in the same way as it had started to extend in other fields.

Article 73d appears to reinforce the limits already present in most double taxation conventions.[54] In other words, non-nationals can claim advantageous treatment for a national tax system for their capital income or savings only if they are also resident in the

---

52. This means a current tax rate (1997) of 23 per cent rather than 33 per cent. See Income and Corporation Taxes Act 1988 ss 468–468I as amended in 1990 (and further amended in 1994). The French and Irish governments proposed similar changes to their tax systems.
53. See note 5.
54. In OECD Model DTC, art 24.

country. A non-resident is not in the same situation as a resident, so cannot claim discrimination preventing free movement of capital on that ground alone. The arguments used elsewhere that discrimination on this basis is invalid because it is disguised nationality discrimination will therefore not succeed. That is, it would seem, the argument of those who secured the EC Treaty amendment. Some commentators do not think the measure achieves its objective. In their view, the article is too limited to have the general effect of protecting states from all claims of discrimination on grounds of nationality, direct or covert. It will be for the Court to determine this.[55]

Taxation of rent from land

The state with primary taxing rights over land and income from land is the state where the land is situated. The rule applies regardless of whether the person receiving the income is a resident of that state or not. This rule, which accords with the general conflicts of law principles for immovable property, applies both to income tax[56] and to VAT.[57] Although many states have property taxes, including in particular local property taxes, it has not been argued until recently that differences in these taxes present a concern to the freedoms of movement within a single market. It may be noted that the significant differences in the extents to which member states rely on property taxes will cause differences in their other taxes. As a result, there will be some differences in the overall operation of taxes within the EU. However, compared with other more central problems in EU taxation, it is suggested that there is little for concern here either conceptually or in practice.

---

55. It is understood that cases are being taken on this point.
56. It is the basic rule in OECD Model DTC, art 6 (income from land), art 13, para 1 (capital gains from land), and art 20 (taxation of capital in the form of land).
57. Sales of land are regarded as sales of goods. Services related to land (including tenancies) are regarded as taking place where the land is: Sixth VAT Directive, art 9, para 2(a).

Taxation of royalties[58]

The taxation of royalties presents almost the opposite problem to that of taxation of land. It is a growing problem, and forms of IP on which royalties are paid are ever more mobile. There are conflicting view in the appropriate direct tax treatment, and also a potential conflict between direct tax and indirect tax.

The international income tax treatment of royalties on IP is broadly governed by article 12 of the OECD Model DTC. This recommends that royalties and similar payments should be taxed in the state of residence of the recipient only. On that basis, there should be no withholding in the state of source. In practice, there often is such a withholding, as the Model's recommendation is far short of unanimous.[59] Within the EU it is only the Netherlands that traditionally adopts the view that there should be no withholding.[60] Consequently, in many cases there is a claim to tax by the source state and often a claim by the state of residence as well. The source state claim is usually based on the gross amount of the royalty paid.

The situation is further complicated by VAT. Permission to use IP is regarded as a supply of services for VAT purposes. The EC rule is that a cross-border supply of IP occurs for VAT purposes where the customer's place of business is, if the customer is registered for VAT there, but otherwise where the supplier carries on business. This appears to mirror the uncertainties of direct tax as to the national authority to tax. More to the point, VAT and a withholding for income tax have the appearance of being much the same tax, as both are based on the gross amount of the royalty. Consider the following example.

---

[58]. The comment here is only on royalties payable in respect of IP. Royalties, for example, for the use of movable property such as those related to leasing arrangements are considered in ch 7.

[59]. Several states have reserved their positions on this point in the Commentary to the Model.

[60]. Most other states are prepared to forego the national non-treaty withholding tax rate in some of their DTCs, but none has been prepared to do in all their DTCs. In the absence of a DTC the rates can be high. For example, Greece would levy a 20 per cent withholding on royalties paid to Ireland in 1996, while the Irish rate on the reverse flow would be 27 per cent.

Example

Pat is the owner of a patent. She lives in Euland, a EU member state. She agrees to license use of the patent in Otherland, also an EU member state, to Roy in exchange for a royalty based on the number of items made under the patent licence. How will the agreement, and the royalties payable under it, be taxed?

Let us say that this year Roy has to pay $1,000 to Pat. Under the double tax convention between Euland and Otherland, the permissible withholding tax rate is 10 per cent. The VAT rate in both states is 15 per cent. When paying the royalty to Pat, Roy will be required to deduct 10 per cent, remitting only $900. Otherland receives the $100. Pat will be taxed in Euland on the $1,000 subject to double tax relief. If the relevant rate of tax on her income is, say, 30 per cent, she will have to pay a further $200 to Euland.

In addition, the royalty is subject to VAT. Under the rules, the VAT will be due in Otherland if Roy is registered for VAT, and in Euland if he is not. Assume that he is not so registered, and that Pat imposes the VAT. In this case, Pat will invoice Roy for $1,000 plus $150 VAT. Roy will have to pay $1,050 ($900 plus $150). Euland therefore receives the $150 VAT and the $200 income tax, while Otherland receives the $100 withholding tax.

Taking an overall view, the example shows income tax withholding and VAT operating much in the same way as taxes but in conflicting directions. Consider further what would happen if some other variants (within existing EU practice) applied. What if the withholding tax were 30 per cent, or zero? What if the VAT were accounted for not in the state of the supplier but in the state of the customer (perhaps by a reverse charge)?

Considering the two taxes together, and the different principles on which their charge may be based, it can be seen that the revenue from the royalty can shift from being a 40 per cent receipt by one state,[61] to a 40 per cent receipt by the other state to intermediate positions where that amount is shared more evenly between the states, and other positions where the net tax revenue

---

61. This assumes that the same state receives both a 30 per cent withholding tax, or a 30 per cent tax charge with no withholding levied by the other state, and also the 15 per cent VAT. Strictly, this is not 45 per cent because the total payment is $1,150, not $1,000. The amount received is $450, which is approximately 40 per cent of the gross.

received is significantly less than that total. All those variants can occur on existing EU law and national practice, not least because of the effective complete overlap in the way both income tax and VAT charge the same tax base in what may appear the same way. The one variant assumed here, for simplicity, is that the income tax withholding is taken as a percentage of the $1,000, leaving the balance to be paid net, while the VAT will be grossed on to the $1,000. Is that assumption always valid?

Taxing capital

Most EU states impose a personal tax on individuals when they die and when they make significant gifts. While these taxes can pose international problems, they are not seen as having an EU dimension. This is not further discussed in this book.

Some states also impose annual net wealth taxes, although the UK has never done this. Again, these have not been the subject of EU action. Nor is there any immediate reason why either competition or the four freedoms should require alignment of these taxes.

CHAPTER TEN

Tax, competition and tax competition

Most of the discussion in this book has been based on the unstated assumption that taxes apply evenly throughout the territory of a state. This was done to simplify the presentation. Unfortunately, it is not a valid assumption. Another unstated assumption is that transactions involve only the member states. The relationships between member states, it has been assumed, must be examined within the EU context, with the global context only as a background. This is also an oversimplification. It was adopted because the focus of much of the analysis and explanation has been on the way taxes affect free movement. We must now remove the oversimplification in order to examine the interaction between taxation and 'the principle of an open market economy with free competition'.[1]

In the unsimplified world, competition is important to tax systems in a range of ways. EU national tax systems make considerable use of special zones and regimes of a variety of kinds as incentives to taxpayers. Some are used to attract particular kinds of taxpayer or investment. Another approach is to emphasise features of the national tax system that are favourable to taxpayers but do not involve the state in changing its tax laws. States adopt these approaches in the knowledge that other governments are also adopting special zones and special incentives.

Further, EU taxpayers now have free access to the so-called tax havens[2] or low tax territories where tax systems are specifically designed to be favourable. The EU's customs union can operate as a self-contained entity, with a tariff wall and a consistent internal

---

1. EC Treaty, art 3a.
2. The term 'tax haven' is not a term of art, but a generic term for jurisdictions which offer preferential tax treatment as compared with some other jurisdiction.

regime because it is isolated to an extent by that tariff wall from the full rigours of outside competition. This is most effective for agricultural production, with its special regime of levies. It is, however, of limited significance for multinational enterprises operating both within and outwith the EU. Similarly, the income and social taxes applying to workers operate, to some extent, in a self-contained way, though there is increasing competition here also.[3] Further, the tax systems of the EU states do not, and cannot, exist in isolation from the rest of the world when dealing with services and capital. In these areas, tax systems themselves are part of the international competition.

EU special tax regimes

A few examples illustrate the nature of this process, and the diverse forms it can take. Within the EC, there are both favourable tax systems and favourable tax zones. Among the favourable regimes are:

- the refusal of Luxembourg to levy a withholding tax on interest paid for money deposited by foreigners in Luxembourg bank accounts;
- the participation exemption in the Netherlands by which the Netherlands tax authorities do not tax income remitted to a Dutch parent company from a foreign subsidiary, which therefore allows funds to flow through the Netherlands without Dutch tax on the dividend;
- the special regime available in Belgium for regional coordination centres for multinational enterprises, under which the centre is taxed only on its own activities, not on the funds flowing through it;
- the absence of a tax charge in the UK on capital gains realised by non-residents even where the assets are in the UK, so that sales of financial assets through the London market are untaxed in the UK;

---

3. In 1997, several major Swedish companies threatened that they would move out of Sweden if taxes were not reduced – the taxes in question being the income and social taxes on their staff not the (relatively low) corporation tax rate: 'Disappearing Taxes', *The Economist*, 31 May 1997, p 19.

- the Dublin Docks zone in Ireland where approved companies established in a defined part of the old Docks pay only 10 per cent corporate income tax rather than the much higher rate usually paid in Ireland;
- the Shannon Airport free zone, where factories may operate with both tax privileges and in an area outside the customs territory of Ireland, so that no duty is payable on goods brought into the zone and then reexported without formally entering Ireland (and similar zones in most other states);
- the offshore centre at Trieste in Italy where banks can process loans for central and eastern Europe under a favourable tax regime;
- the similar zone in Madeira offering favourable access to Portuguese banks;
- exemptions and reductions of taxes for companies operating from the Special Canary Islands Zone in Spain;
- regional tax incentives for productive investment in Greece outside the Athens-Piraeus area;
- tax credits for new commercial or industrial activity established in certain parts of France.[4]

Associated territories in Europe

In addition, attention must be paid to the tax regimes of areas associated with or under the control of EU members. For example, the UK is associated with the separately administered territories of the Channel Isles, the Isle of Man, Gibraltar, and the sovereign base area of Cyprus within Europe. The Isle of Man and Gibraltar have their own tax regimes, as do Jersey and Guernsey. Compared with the typically high tax rates of the UK, these territories have been viewed as havens.

The customs territory of the EU includes both the Isle of Man and the Channel Isles,[5] but not Gibraltar[6] or the British sovereign

---

4. For details of all these systems, see the Price Waterhouse series of booklets, *Doing business in* . . . , for each of these countries. For a brief account in one volume see the annual *Coopers & Lybrand International Tax Summaries*.
5. EC Treaty, art 227, para 5, authorises their partial inclusion in the EU.
6. Community Customs Code, art 3. Gibraltar is not part of the UK for EU purposes, although sensitivities leave it unnamed expressly: EC Treaty, art 227.

base area in Cyprus.[7] This, in effect, guarantees free movement of goods into and out of those territories. The Isle of Man also has a VAT aligned to that of the UK and therefore the EU.[8] Similarly, its social security contributions and benefits system works in close parallel to the UK system, and is linked by a reciprocal agreement with it. By contrast, its company tax rates are lower than the UK equivalents. The Isle of Man has a double tax convention with the UK but no other states.[9] Thus, for direct tax purposes, basing a company in the Isle can secure tax advantages, while for other tax purposes the benefits of the EU can be enjoyed at the same time.

Gibraltar is, by contrast, in an anomalous position, reflecting the continuing disputes between the UK and Spain. It can also be an advantageous place to establish a company. While a local company pays corporation tax at rates similar to those in Britain and Spain, an exempt company pays only a flat fee of a few hundred pounds a year. Such a company cannot trade within Gibraltar. Other forms of privileged companies pay at rates of tax agreed with the local authorities as low as 1 per cent.[10]

Similar territories are associated with several other member states. France has its overseas territories, and is also closely linked with Monaco, as Italy is with San Marino. Spain and Portugal also have their offshore islands, as do Denmark, Finland and Germany. Within the EEA, Liechtenstein has long had a secretive and favourable tax regime, while Andorra, between France and Spain, is also on the itinerary of tax planners if not many others. These are variously inside or outside the customs union or the (different) area covered by the VAT regime, and may or may not be governed by the EU's social security laws. They are often excluded from the EU's direct tax regimes and those of the member states. The boundaries for customs and tax purposes between the EU and the oldest tax haven of them all – Switzerland – are at times far from clear.[11]

---

7. EC Treaty, art 227 para 5.
8. Sixth VAT Directive, art 3(4) treats transactions relating to the Isle of Man as if they relate to the UK for VAT purposes. For the formal legislative link from the UK see the VAT (Isle of Man) Orders 1982, SI 1982 Nos 1067 and 1068.
9. It can be included within a UK double taxation convention if the other party agrees.
10. For a summary of the tax position in all the territories mentioned, see Coopers & Lybrand, *International Tax Summaries*, published annually.
11. For customs and VAT purposes, parts of Germany and Italy are treated as being in Switzerland: Community Customs Code, art 3; Sixth VAT Directive, art 3.

To that must be added another layer of complexity with the special tax regimes of candidates for membership of the EU. Cyprus has an established special tax regime used to channel funds in a tax-efficient way between western and eastern Europe, and Malta also has an offshore regime. More recently the newly emerged economies such as Hungary have discovered the advantage of 'friendly' tax systems for inward investments and flowthroughs of funds, while the states of central and eastern European have been in open competition with special incentives to attract foreign direct investment. In truth, for tax purposes the map of Europe is something of a patchwork quilt.

Overseas associated territories

Elsewhere, the British dependent territories include the Cayman islands, the British Virgin Islands, and Bermuda (among others). Bermuda, a dependent territory that has recently voted to stay dependent on the UK, has no income tax on corporations, no income tax on individuals, no income tax on non-residents, no natural resources taxes, no sales taxes, and minimal payroll and social taxes. It is therefore seen by some as an ideal place in which to establish an offshore company.[12] This may be used as a tax-efficient way of routing funds between other states, or as away of holding funds out of reach of other, higher, tax authorities. Capital can move freely to and from Bermuda and the EU, although Bermuda is not in any sense part of the EU.

Again, there are similar issues with the overseas dependent territories of France and other states – most famously the tax havens of the Netherlands Antilles and other territories associated with the Netherlands. Several of these are classic tax havens, like Bermuda, in the sense that they have legal systems designed to host foreign funds in secure but secretive regimes. Some – the Cayman Islands is perhaps the best known – have no income tax, nor do they need one for local budgetary purposes.

These sets of examples show the wide range of the preferential tax systems that exist within the EU, around it and associated with it. Without attempting any form of analysis, it may be noted that

---

12. An offshore company is a company established in a territory but engaged only in activities outside the territory.

these regimes can apply to all kinds of tax: customs duty, VAT, and income taxes. They also shows the potential that such systems have for distorting the patterns of activity in international trading and more specifically within the EU. This confronts the EU with one of its most important challenges.

The EU's dilemma

Competition is something much encouraged by the EC Treaty for business, but not for government. While business is to progress by competition within a market economy, the assumption behind much of the EU structure is that governments will cooperate. This ensures common standards for all citizens. The essential objective is that those common standards will rise, and continue to rise.[13] It is for this reason, for example, that there should be no competition between states in setting their social laws. Differences that exist should exist for other reasons, not as distortions of the single market. It is also the assumption behind the development of the social chapter – competition between states should be based on a high minimum standard for all those taking part.

Taxation laws present a special case that tests the conflict between competition in the private sector and cooperation in the public sector. Taxes are, at the same time, a major overhead to any business, and the necessary funding for any government. A business in competition wishes to drive down its taxes, while a government wishing to deliver increasing common standards to its citizens needs at least to maintain its taxes.

Current fiscal pressures demand more than maintenance of funds in western Europe. The pressures of the aging population[14] combined with the pressures of fast economic growth in several areas of the EU[15] mean that tax revenues have to grow in real terms. Indeed, there has been a steady pressure on the EU member states throughout the life of the EU to keep taxes high. This pressure has been strongest in states like Spain that have matured to fully developed states within the EU context.

13. The second preamble to the EC Treaty affirms 'as the essential objective of their efforts the constant improvement of the living and working conditions of their peoples'.
14. Discussed in ch 2.
15. Most notably the German lander that were formerly part of the German Democratic Republic.

The challenge to an individual state is therefore to adopt a tax system that helps keep its businesses competitive while also helping keep its citizens satisfied. There are a number of possible strategies that operate towards this goal. One is to adopt a tax system that favours inward investment by foreigners and local investment by local business. Is that legitimate practice within the EU?

Tax systems and fair competition

Article 92 of the EC Treaty provides that 'any aid granted by a member states or through state resources in any form whatsoever which distorts or threatens to distort competition shall, in so far as it affects trade between member states, be incompatible with the common market'. The article goes on to provide for a number of exceptions to this proscription. These exceptions are subject to review by the Commission, as is the general rule against state aids. Further, a member state is required to notify the Commission of any proposed state aid. It is the duty of the Commission, on receiving notification, to decide if the aid is or is not compatible with the common market. If the aid is found not to be compatible, the commission may make a formal decision requiring the state concerned to abolish or alter the aid.[16]

As with other trade rules, this concern reflects a more general concern addressed in the GATT. Article XVI does not go so far as to ban state aids, but it does provide a transparency rule. It also provides for negotiations where injury occurs.[17] While aimed primarily at direct aids to exports, it has been held that a direct tax system may constitute a subsidy of a kind requiring notification under this article.[18] However, this is a strictly limited rule compared with the EU regime.

[16.] See for a general account, S Weatherill and P Beaumont, *EC Law,* (Penguin, 2nd edition, 1995) ch 27; N Green, T C Hartley and J Usher, *The Legal Foundations of the Single European Market* OUP, 1991, ch 21.

[17.] A GATT member state should notify all other members of any subsidy that may increase exports or decrease imports. Any other member state that finds or anticipates serious prejudice from such a subsidy may seek its limitation.

[18.] See GATT, 23rd Supplement, Panel rulings on the DISC complaints 1973 (complaints about the US income tax rules on domestic international sales corporations, and complaints by the US against France, Belgium and the Netherlands relating to aspects of their direct tax systems).

It has been clear for some years that features of tax systems may amount to state aids that require review under article 92.[19] This means that state tax systems need to comply with the obligations of article 92 in addition to other treaty obligations. In particular, this obligation operates cumulatively with article 95, so that a state aid that might find approval under article 92 must still comply with the non-discrimination provisions of article 95, and vice versa.[20]

Now that the single market has removed many of the barriers to free movement, the importance of this requirement that tax systems are not used as subsidies is increasing. This is because, in the absence of other fiscal barriers, states see the need to ensure that their tax systems are viewed as attractive for both business and investment. The key issues are when a feature of a tax system becomes a state aid, and when such a state aid becomes incompatible with the common market.

Taxes as state aids

Almost any taxing or charging regime may potentially amount to a state aid if it has the effect of distorting trade between member states, whatever form it may take. At one extreme, this could apply to taxes imposed on motor tyres to pay for their disposal. This is an aid because all tyres sold in a state bear the tax, while the funds collected are paid out only to those in the state who dispose of the tyres (not those in other states doing so).[21] At the other extreme are the special tax zones such as that of Dublin Docks or Trieste.

The Irish special schemes allow support to both finance companies and manufacturing companies.[22] In the case of finance companies, they must be established within the International Finance Service Centre in the Customs House area of Dublin. If they meet the conditions for establishment, they are taxed at 10 per cent

---

19. For an early decision of the European Court confirming the relevance of art 92 to tax systems see *Italy v Commission* Case 173/73, [1974] ECR 709.
20. *Essevi* and *Salengo* Cases 142–143/80, [1981] ECR 1413.
21. See Commission Decision N 684/93 (31 December 1994) (1994 OJ C 390/15), approving such a scheme in Denmark.
22. Full details are available in C Haccius, *Ireland in International Tax Planning* (IBFD Publications BV, 1995).

rather than up to 40 per cent. They also receive special tax deductions and relief from local property taxes.[23] Is this a state aid? It would seem that it undoubtedly is. It is understood that the Commission has reviewed the matter under article 92, and has found that it is not incompatible with the common market in the short term.[24]

The Commission's thinking has been made much clearer in connection with its recent conditional approval of the offshore banking centre established by the Italian government in Trieste. This centre, in the Italian former free port close to the Slovenian border, was established as a consequence of the break-up of the former Yugoslavia, and the sharp loss of trade from the area with that country and, more generally, central Europe. However, the centre allowed offshore companies to use Trieste as a convenient staging post for onward investment and trade into Italy as well as neighbouring countries on advantageous terms. The Commission received no formal objections from other states, but approved the centre only on conditions. It therefore approved the Trieste scheme for a limited time, within a limited tax cost to Italy, and for limited purposes.[25]

Competition or cooperation?

The decisions about Dublin Docks and Trieste may seem perverse to those who expect the EU to be a seamless single market without distortions – and they are right at one level. A truly single market without frontiers and without distortions should not have exceptional tax regimes. But this is the EU's dilemma. Like it or not, the EU itself is in competition with other territories. Money going through Trieste might otherwise go through Cyprus or some non-European tax territory. Operations run from Dublin Docks might instead be run from an Asian low tax territory such as Singapore.[26]

---

23. These schemes have proved highly successful: 'Ireland: Europe's Tiger Economy', *The Economist* 17 May 1997, p 25.

24. The benefits are time-limited to 2005 for certain purposes and 2010 for others. The author is not aware of any published source in which the Commission's view on these schemes is directly recorded, nor the conditions made plain, but it is understood that the time limits are derived from the need to satisfy the conditions of art 92.

25. Commission Decision 95/452/EC (12.4.95)(1995 OJ L 264/30)

26. Singapore has a preferential tax regime with a 10 per cent rate (the same rate as Ireland and available under somewhat similar conditions).

Further, the EU is an expensive place to trade, not least because of its high labour taxes and costs. A factory in the emerging economies of south east Europe can produce almost as much as a factory in the EU from the same number of employees – but it pays them for two weeks' work what in the EU is earned in a day. Further, the factory will probably be given a generous tax incentive for its inward investments and local profits. How should the EU react to this? This is the second level of dilemma in the Trieste decision – the funding is still European funding. Does not this decision reflect the historic importance of the ending of the division of the European continent and the need to create firm bases for the construction of the future Europe?[27]

Throughout its existence, the EEC, then EC, then EU has been confronted with tax problems. The problems of 50 years ago – of markets divided by customs tariffs – have been solved. To that extent, this book describes a signal achievement. The EEC then tried to solve the problems of distortions caused by internal sales taxes. It has been quite successful in this endeavour also, through adoption of the VAT. It also tried, but with less success, to find common solutions to the problems of taxing businesses. Answers to those problems are perhaps now developing. But as each problem is tackled, others emerge. Currently, member states are caught between remonstrating against tax competition by others, and joining in the competition themselves. The Commission has been focusing on the problems caused by the differential funding of social security systems between states, and the high element of social and general taxation in labour costs. The Court has been dealing with cases that confront it with the clash between complete removal of discrimination between taxpayers and the integrity of national tax systems. Each is faced with the problem of balancing competition with cooperation.

There are no easy answers to any of these issues. Furthermore, it is now obvious that most of these problems have to be answered in a global context. It is no longer enough to solve the problems between the member states alone. At the same time, the problems reflect the fact that tax is a means to an end, and therefore the intended objectives are also involved. Unsolved behind these problems are others. One is the problem of financing the EU itself – the

---

27. The words are those of the second recital of the TEU.

challenge of federation or confederation. Another is the never-ending problem of ensuring that taxpayers pay their taxes throughout the EU. Always, there is a need to seek solutions by a consensus which reflects the diverse representative democracies of the member states. For taxation and representation are inseparable.

Bibliography

1 Key studies

There is limited good UK literature on EC tax law, although rather more English language material. Three detailed monographs in English, and one in French, are of particular value, and one in French.

A Easson, *Taxation in the European Community*, (Athlone Press, 1993) is an update on Easson's pioneering *Tax Law and Policy in the EC* (Sweet & Maxwell, 1980), the first English language specialist study of the topic. Easson's study is policy-based, and includes good historical material. The present edition went to press just as the single market was opening for business. Professor Easson is a tax lawyer based in Canada, and the discussion reflects his international tax expertise and common law background.

B Terra and P Wattel, *European Tax Law* (Kluwer, 1993) is based on a tax practice course taught in the Netherlands, and is strongly legislation-based, with selected cases. It is comprehensive, but is focused on EC law rather than its context. Its authors are leading Dutch academics (Terra is one of the world's leading experts on the European form of VAT).

P Farmer and R Lyal, *EC Tax Law*, (Oxford University Press, 1994) is by contrast written by EC lawyers, one of whom is based at the European Court of Justice. It is strong on the case law experience of the European Court, and in placing the Court's decisions in their context in the general jurisprudence of the Court, but contains less of a practical or contextual flavour.

D Berlin's *Droit Fiscal Communautaire* (Presses Universitaires de France, 1988) is the best French full length study of the topic.

Although now dated, it has a strong theoretical framework that has influenced subsequent studies (including this one). It is a definitive study of the law as at its publication.

The bibliography includes works referred to in the text, and other relevant readings and reports. No attempt is made in this selective bibliography to draw attention to all relevant publications, in particular all the papers and articles in the specialist periodicals. Readers should consult the following periodicals in particular for further reading:

E C Tax Journal, periodical specialist journal – required reading for a full coverage of this topic (Kluwer, Deventer).

European Taxation, monthly specialist journal – also required reading for full coverage (including a bibliography of relevant publications) (IBFD, Amsterdam).

Intertax, monthly international tax journal with stress on EU material (Kluwer, Deventer).

Tax Notes International, weekly US-based updating service with worldwide coverage, but monitoring all EU developments (Tax Analysts, New York).

2 Other books and reports

H J Ault, ed, *Comparative Income Taxation* (Kluwer, 1997).

P Baker, *Double Taxation Conventions and International Tax Law* (Sweet & Maxwell, 2nd edition, 1994).

S Cnossen, *Tax Coordination in the EC* (Kluwer, 1987).

Coopers & Lybrand, *International Tax Summaries* (Coopers & Lybrand, published annually).

F de Hossen, *Direct Tax Initiatives of the European Community* (Kluwer, 1990).

EC Commission, *A Community strategy to limit carbon dioxide emissions and to improve energy efficiency* (SEC(91)1744, 1991).

EC Commission, *Community Public Finance* (Commission of the EC, 1991).

EC Commission, *Environmental Taxes and Charges in the Single Market*, COM(97)9.

EC Commission, *Report of the Committee of Independent Experts on Company Taxation* (The Ruding Report) (Commission of the EC, 1992).

EEC Commission, *Corporation Tax and Individual Income Tax in the EEC* (EEC Commission, 1970).

BIBLIOGRAPHY

EEC Commission, *The EEC Reports on Tax Harmonisation* (IBFD Publications BV, 1963).

M Edwardes-Ker, *International Tax Treaty Service* (In-depth Publishing, Dublin, updated looseleaf).

N Green, T C Hartley and J Usher, *The Legal Foundations of the Common Market* (Oxford University Press, 1991).

B Greve, ed, *Comparative Welfare Systems* (Macmillan, 1996).

C Haccius, *Ireland in International Tax Planning* (IBFD Publications BV, 1995).

IBFD, *Guides to European Taxation:*
   Volume I The Taxation of Patent Royalties, Dividends, Interest in Europe
   Volume II The Taxation of Companies in Europe
   Volume III Taxation of Private Investment Income
   Volume IV Value Added Tax in Europe
   Volume V Taxation and Investment in Central and Eastern European Countries
   Volume VI Taxation of Individuals in Europe
   (IBFD Publications BV, various dates, looseleaf).

IFA Seminar Series, vol 12, *Taxation and Human Rights* (Kluwer, 1988).

J Kay and M King, *The British Tax System* (Oxford UP, 1991).

C Lee, M Pearson and S Smith, *Fiscal Harmonisation: An Analysis of the European Commission's Proposals*, IFS Report Series No 28 (Institute for Fiscal Studies, 1988).

Loyens Lefebvre Radler, *The Parent-Subsidiary Directive and International Tax Planning* (IBFD Publications BV, 1992).

Loyens Lefebvre Radler, *The Merger Directive – Practical Tax Issues* (IBFD Publications BV, 1993).

K Messere, *Tax Policy in OECD Countries: Choices and Conflicts* (IBFD Publications BV, 1997).

G Morse, D Williams and D Salter, *Davies, Principles of Tax Law* (Sweet & Maxwell, 1996).

D Newbury and N Stern, *The Theory of Taxation in Developing Countries* (Oxford University Press, 1987).

OECD, *Environmental Taxes in OECD Countries* (OECD, 1995).

OECD, *Model Tax Convention on Income and on Capital* (OECD, updated looseleaf; condensed version, 1996).

OECD, *Revenue Statistics* (OECD, annual editions).

OECD, *Taxing Consumption* (OECD, 1988).

A Ogus and E Barendt, *The Law of Social Security* (Butterworths, 4th edition, 1995).

M Pearson and S Smith, *The European Carbon Tax: an assessment of the European Commission's proposals* (Institute for Fiscal Studies, 1991).

BIBLIOGRAPHY

C Shoup, *Fiscal Harmonization in Common Markets* (Columbia University Press, 1967).

F G Snyder, *The Law of the Common Agricultural Policy* (Sweet & Maxwell, 1985).

C Stanbrook and P Bentley, *Dumping and Subsidies* (Kluwer, 3rd edition, 1996).

D Strasser, *The Finances of Europe* (EC Commission, 7th edition, 1992).

D Swann, *The Economics of the Common Market* (Penguin, 8th edition, 1995).

G Teixeira, ed. *Business Taxation in the European Union* (Wiley Chancery, updated looseleaf).

B J M Terra and J Kajus, *A Guide to the Sixth VAT Directive* (IBFD Publications BV, 1991).

B J M Terra and J Kajus, *A Guide to the European VAT Directives* (IBFD Publications BV, updated looseleaf).

O Thommes and R Betten, *EC Corporate Tax Law* (IBFD Publications BV, updated looseleaf).

S Tindale and G Holtham, *Green Tax Reform* (Institute for Public Policy Research, 1996).

P Watson, *Social Security Law in the EEC* (Croom Helm, 1979).

S Weatherill and P Beaumont, *EC Law* (Penguin, 2nd edition, 1995).

D Williams, *The National Insurance Contributions Handbook* (FT Law & Tax, updated looseleaf).

D Williams, *Taxation Principles and Policy* (Teach Yourself series, Hodder & Stoughton, 1992).

D Williams, *Trends in International Taxation* (IBFD Publications BV, 1991).

World Bank, *The Old Age Crisis* (International Bank for Reconstruction and Development, 1994).

D Wyatt and A Dashwood, *The Law of the European Communities* (Sweet & Maxwell, 1993).

Index

active income 156
agency 124–6
agricultural levies 30–1, 46–7
alcoholic drinks 75–6, 78, 93
Andorra 172
anti-dumping
  code 58
  duties 56–8, 65
appeals 105
approximation 35–6
Arbitration Convention 146–8
arms length principle 138, 147

Belgium 76, 107–8, 115–6, 129–30,
  160, 170
branch 114–6
British dependent territories 173

Canada 70
capital duty 159–60
capital export neutrality 156
capital import neutrality 156
capital gains taxation 145
capital taxes 168
cars, taxation of 78, 93
cascading taxes 80
Channel Isles 59, 171
charges of equivalent effect 60–1, 74
commercial defence instruments 8,
  58
common commercial policy 37
Community Customs Code 62–7
company groups 136–40
company residence 124, 137
company taxation 141–50, 149

competition 32–4, 175–6
  of tax systems 3, 162, 164, 169,
  174
countervailing duties 56–8
cross-border shopping 94
customs duties
  Abolition in EU 59–60
  administration 67
  capital 157
  EC Treaty 29–30
  effects 55
  history 53
  Internal taxes as 61,69–70
  international laws on 58
  origin 63–4
  own resources 47–8
  preferential tariffs 65
  protective duties 57–8
  reductions in 56
  valuation 64
  VAT as 84
Cyprus 66, 171–2, 173, 177

Denmark 78, 91, 108, 172
diplomats 103
direct taxation 8
discriminatory taxes 71–7
dividend taxation 149, 157
  see also withholding tax
double tax conventions 12–15, 108, 152
  183 day rule in 102
  and national law 17
  EC law 17, 117
  GATS 128
  land 165
  migrant workers 102–103

transfer pricing 147
withholding taxes 160–1
Dublin docks zone 171, 176–7
duty-free shops 93

EC law
and double tax conventions 117
ECSC 28–9, 50
EC tax convention 17–19
EC Treaty and tax 29–40
economic activity 89
EFTA 65
employment and self-employment
    115, 122–3
EMU 36–7
environmental taxes 38, 92
establishment, right of 121, 126–7
EU
    and GATT 71–3
    as taxpayer 51
    budget 42–6
    competition 175–7
    customs territory 59
    customs union 59–62
    foreign relations 39
    income tax 50
    international tax commitments
        9–10
    regulations 112
    special tax regimes 170–1
    taxing powers 2–5
Euratom 40
Europe Agreements 66, 73
Euro-Med Agreements 66
European company 137
European Court 8, 106
European Economic Area 65, 73, 113
European Economic Interest
        Grouping 123–4
evasion 146
exchange controls 154
exchange of information 85
excise duties 92–5

federal taxation 70
fiscal coherence 107, 139
fiscal discrimination 75–7
fiscal protection 77–9
fiscal unity 138, 140–1
fiscal veto 5, 156
foreign direct investment 156
foreign workers 100–102

France 78, 80, 171, 172
free movement 3, 5, 31–2
    and MNEs 136–8
    of capital 153–5, 161–2
    of citizens 98–100
    of payments 154
    of services 119–22
    of workers 98–9
free trade areas 65
frontier workers 97, 113–14

GATS 127–8
GATT 9–10, 56, 71–3, 175
Germany 104, 107–108, 109–11,
        129, 158, 160, 162
Gibraltar 171–2
goods
    cross-border acquisition 86
    freely circulating 69–74
    VAT on 87–8
    See also products
Greece 83, 171

harmonisation 35–6
human rights 19–20
Hungary 173

income tax 100–103
    and social security 112, 116–17
    and VAT 167
    personal allowances 109–11
indirect taxation 8
individual taxation in EEC 97
intellectual property 132, 155, 166–8
interest taxation 151, 158, 160–2
    See also withholding tax
intergovernmental cooperation 20–21
internal taxation 74
international tax law 12, 15–17
Ireland 171
Isle of Man 59, 171–2
Italy 171, 172

land, taxation of 155, 165
Liechtenstein 172
losses 151
Luxembourg 104, 160, 163–4, 70

Malta 66, 173

Merger Directive 144–6
migrant workers 100–111, 113–14
mineral oils 93
MNEs
    taxation of 137–8
most favoured nations 71, 127
Monaco 59
mutual assistance 83

Netherlands 114–16, 129, 130, 166,
    170, 173
non-discrimination 5, 71–7, 154,
    164
Norway 65–6

OECD 10–11
    Model Tax Convention 11–15
own resources 42–51

Parent-Subsidiary directive 143–4
passive income 156, 160
pension contributions 101, 106–109,
    129–30, 163
permanent establishment 125, 145–6
Poland 66, 73
portfolio investment 156
Portugal 171, 172
products 74–9, 157

rent 165
residence 16
    of individuals 101
royalties 166–8
see also withholding tax
Ruding Committee 142, 149–50
Russia 73

San Marino 59
savings 162–5
services 86, 119, 123, 127, 131–2
    international services 133–5
similar products 75
Singapore 66, 177
smuggling 54
social contributions and taxes 8, 19,
    23, 26
social security 27–8, 96–8, 112–14
Spain 171, 172
stamp duties 92, 158, 159
state aids 175–7

see also subsidies
subsidiarity 63
subsidies 57
supply 86
Sweden 169
Switzerland 4, 65, 70, 73, 160, 172

tax havens 169
tax policy 23–6, 96–7, 177–9
taxation and representation 1, 6, 179
thin capitalisation 161
tobacco 93
transfer pricing 146–8
transport policy 32
treaty shopping 161
Trieste 171, 176–7
Turkey 59
turnover taxes 91

UCITS Directive 163
unit trusts 163–4
United Kingdom 130, 133, 139, 158,
    163, 168, 170, 173
United States of America 1, 3, 70, 156

value-added tax 79
value added tax 8, 19, 79–92, 131–5
    charge to 85
    consideration 88–9
    destination-based 84
    exempt supplies 87, 132–3
    financial services 157–8
    goods 87–8
    harmonisation 82–5
    input tax 91
    introduction 80
    land 86
    MNEs, on 141
    origin-based 84
    output tax 91
    own resources 48–9
    rates 87
    services 120, 131–5, 166
    taxable amount 87
    taxable person 88–9
wealth tax 155, 168
withholding taxes 104, 156–7, 162
    on dividends 12, 149–50
    on interest 12, 149, 151, 160–2
    on royalties 151, 166
worker 115
WTO 9–10